The Redeemer Reborn

THE REDEEMER REBORN

Parsifal as the Fifth Opera of Wagner's *Ring*

Paul Schofield

AMADEUS
PRESS

AN IMPRINT OF HAL LEONARD CORPORATION

NEW YORK

Library
University of Texas
at San Antonio

Published in 2007 by Amadeus Press
An Imprint of Hal Leonard Corporation
19 West 21st Street, New York, NY 10010

Printed in the United States of America

Book design by Mark Lerner

Owing to limitations of space, acknowledgments of permission to quote from previously published and unpublished material will be found following the Index.

Library of Congress Cataloging-in-Publication Data is available upon request.

ISBN-10: 1-57467-161-8
ISBN-13: 978-1-57467-161-2

www.amadeuspress.com

For my master, the late Reverend Master Jiyu-Kennett, founder of Shasta Abbey and the Order of Buddhist Contemplatives

When the vines have withered,
  the trees have fallen
    and the mountains have crumbled away,
The valley stream, in cascades,
  will gush beyond its banks
    and the very rock will pour forth fire.

Zen Master Keizan, *The Denkoroku*, fourteenth century, Japan

Contents

Acknowledgments   ix

Introduction: The Journey Begins   1

1. *Die Sieger*: The Forerunner of *Parsifal*   5
   Schopenhauer and Buddhism   6
   Wagner, Schopenhauer, and Buddhism   13

2. The *Ring* and *Parsifal* as One Work   35
   Alberich-Klingsor   38
   Wotan-Amfortas   40
   Brünnhilde-Kundry   41
   Siegfried-Parsifal   44

3. Tragedy as Mysticism   47

4. Wagner and the Grail   77
   The Fisher King   88
   The Tavatimsa Heaven   94
   The World of the Grail   98
   The Christianization of the Grail   112
   The Bloodline of the Grail   121

5. *Parzival*   125
   Parzival and Wagner   149
   Lohengrin   184

6. The Separation and Reunion of the Spear and Grail   187

    Wagner's Sources for the *Ring*   197

    The Sins of the Fathers   205

    Siegfried   223

    Parsifal   249

    The Final Redemption   279

Epilogue   289

Notes   291

Bibliography   301

Index   305

Acknowledgments

I would like to thank the late Reverend Master Daizui MacPhillamy, who at the time he read my manuscript was the head of the Order of Buddhist Contemplatives. Rev. Master Daizui checked all the passages I had written about Buddhism and offered both corrections and suggestions. In every case I accepted the changes he suggested I make.

I would also like to thank Steve Sokolow, president of the Wagner Society of Northern California; Mark R. Wheeler, associate professor of philosophy at San Diego State University; and the late William O. Cord, himself an author of several books on Wagner. Steve, Mark, and Bill all read early drafts of this book, offering many helpful suggestions.

Thanks also to Robert Fisher, editor of *Leitmotive*, the scholarly journal published by the Wagner Society of Northern California. Parts of this book have previously appeared over the years as articles in *Leitmotive*.

Finally I would like to thank my agent, James Fitzgerald, and my editors, Carol Flannery, Jessica Burr, and Barbara Norton, for believing in this project.

The Journey Begins

In the summer of 1990, when I was in San Francisco for the revival of the Nikolaus Lehnhoff production of *Der Ring des Nibelungen*, I had the chance to talk with a particular opera conductor, and I asked him what he thought of *Parsifal*. He replied, "*Parsifal* is the one I don't have a handle on."

Parsifal is, and always has been, the one many people "don't have a handle on." It is the most thematically complex, intriguing, perplexing, and mystifying of any single opera ever written. It remains mysterious, however, only when we continue to view it as a separate opera, standing by itself unconnected to any previous Wagnerian work. When we view it in its proper context, it emerges from the shadows of mystery into its true light: the fifth opera of the *Ring*.

The idea of *Parsifal* being the fifth opera of the *Ring* is not new. In 1950, for example, the composer and teacher Leon Stein wrote in his book *The Racial Thinking of Richard Wagner*, "As for *Parsifal*, we shall see that, far from being a consistent Christian expression it is actually rooted in Paganism, and is in truth *the fifth opera of the Ring*."[1] This statement comes from the chapter "Wagner and Christianity" and is made in the context of Wagner's rejection of organized Christianity and subsequent embracing of Teutonic myth and German culture. Stein believes that *Parsifal* continues in the Germanic pagan tradition of the *Ring* and is thus its fifth opera. Stein does not develop the connection between the *Ring* and *Parsifal* beyond this particular context.

Bernard Förster, Robert Gutman, and Franz Winkler are other authors who have connected *Parsifal* to the *Ring*. But no one has yet understood the full connection of these great works, or what it is at the deepest levels that makes *Parsifal* the actual closing opera of the cycle. *Parsifal* is indeed the fifth opera of the *Ring*, but for reasons that go much deeper than those put forth by Leon Stein. The link between the *Ring* and *Parsifal* is far more profound than just a tradition of Paganism versus Christianity. What Stein has left out is the all-important subject of Buddhism, Wagner's acceptance of its central teachings, and his incorporation of those teachings into the *Ring* and *Parsifal*.

Much has been written over these past two decades concerning Wagner and Buddhism, but I have yet to read any article or book that truly shows an understanding of the extent to which Wagner both understood Buddhism and incorporated that understanding into his later music dramas. In the course of this book I would like to use my experience of nine years as a Buddhist monk to explain and illuminate just how profound the connection between the *Ring* and *Parsifal* really is.

Wagner read as many books on Buddhism as were available to him in European translations during his lifetime. He believed very seriously in reincarnation, which he himself termed metempsychosis and which Buddhism most often terms rebirth. Wagner also had an intuitive understanding of the moral and spiritual purpose of rebirth: that what we do and learn in one lifetime carries over into the next. In the following chapters I will show that the true connection between the *Ring* and *Parsifal* lies in what Buddhism understands as the process of karma and rebirth, and that the four main characters of the *Ring* are reborn in *Parsifal*, completing in *Parsifal* the spiritual journey actually begun in the *Ring*. I will explain how a connection between the *Ring* and *Parsifal* was in fact embryonic in Wagner's own ideas going all the way back to his *Wibelungen* essay of February 1849. I will also show that the idea of characters from one opera being reborn as characters in another for the purpose of spiritual progress and eventual enlightenment comes directly from Wagner himself.

Although Wagner never planned a production of the *Ring* and *Parsifal* as one work, he fully intended to have *Parsifal* serve a religious purpose in his time, just as the *Passions* of Bach and the tragedies of the ancient Greeks had done in their times. He termed the *Ring* a *Bühnenfestspiel,* or "stage festival play," and *Parsifal* a *Bühnenweihfestspiel,* or "stage consecration festival play." Therefore, in putting the *Ring* and *Parsifal* together as one work I do not mean to violate any conscious intention of Wagner, but rather to expand on what I believe to *be* that intention, bringing out from the inexhaustible richness of these five music dramas a view and scope that have been there all along but that until now have never been fully understood or elucidated.

It will be my thesis in this book that the *Ring* and *Parsifal* taken together constitute one, unified, five-opera cycle and ideally should be performed as such. I believe that Wagner had an intuitive sense of this connection all along, even though he himself never specified such an interpretation. By examining his letters, prose works, conversations with his second wife, Cosima, and of course the texts of the operas themselves, I will show the extent to which this concept was inherent in his own ideas. I will also expand on those ideas, explaining in detail how and why the four main characters of the *Ring* are reborn into the opera *Parsifal,* there to strive for the redemption that is not, in fact, attained at the end of the *Ring.* I will elucidate the Buddhist teaching of karma and rebirth and show how this process is what connects the *Ring* and *Parsifal* at the deepest levels. I will explain how and why Alberich is reborn as Klingsor, Brünnhilde is reborn as Kundry, Wotan is reborn as Amfortas, and Siegfried is reborn as Parsifal. I believe that with the *Ring* and *Parsifal* as one work, Wagner achieved the greatest of all artistic feats: the portrayal in symbolic form of the entire panorama of existence, from the original Fall to final enlightenment and salvation. This journey begins when Wotan breaks

the branch of the World Ash-tree and Alberich steals the gold
of the Rhine, thus separating Spear and Grail. (Wagner's association of the Rhinegold with the Holy Grail will be explained
fully in chapter 6.) The journey culminates in the reunification
of the Spear and Grail in the Grail Castle of Monsalvat, the
Mount of Salvation.

CHAPTER 1

Die Sieger:
The Forerunner of Parsifal

In order to have a full understanding of *Parsifal* as the fifth opera of the *Ring*, it is necessary to appreciate the importance of Wagner's 1856 sketch for the specifically Buddhist opera *Die Sieger* (The Victors). It has been my experience over the years that very few people, even those who consider themselves ardent Wagnerites, know very much about this planned opera, and yet it is essential to Wagner's own progression and development from the pre-Schopenhauer years through the later operas of *Tristan und Isolde*, *Die Meistersinger von Nürnberg*, the *Ring*, and *Parsifal*. For it is in the story of *Die Sieger* that Wagner first shows his understanding of karma and rebirth.

Wagner first read Arthur Schopenhauer's *The World as Will and Representation* over the last few months of 1854. He had finished the four-opera poem of the *Ring* late in 1852 and he began the composition of *Das Rheingold* that same year, completing it in May of 1854. By the fall of 1854 he was already well into the composition of *Die Walküre*, and he finished Schopenhauer's book before the year was out. Upon finishing, Wagner immediately professed himself a disciple. He was to reread it multiple times throughout the remainder of his life.

The World as Will and Representation was a revelation to Wagner. It not only gave him a philosophical context for many of the ideas he had already intuitively incorporated in his earlier operas, it also opened up for him the world of Buddhism and its teachings.

Because this is so important a chapter in Wagner's life and in the development of his ideas, I am going to take a few pages to explain, briefly and as simply as possible, the basic ideas of Schopenhauer's philosophy and how Wagner eventually went beyond that philosophy with the *Ring* and *Parsifal* as one work. As we will see, it was *Die Sieger* that marked the beginning of Wagner's transcendence of Schopenhauer, opening the door into the final light of *Parsifal*.

Schopenhauer and Buddhism

> What is that which eternally is, which has no origin?
> And what is that which arises and passes away, but in
> truth never is?
>
> Plato, *Timaeus*, 27 D

The epigraph asks the question from which all philosophy starts, and which it tries to answer. We can rephrase this question by asking, "What is it that is eternal, but which to ordinary minds is unseen and unknown, and what is it that seems to be real, but which in fact is illusory and ephemeral?" We will see how Schopenhauer answered this question in his great philosophical work *Die Welt als Wille und Vorstellung*.

"That which eternally is, which has no origin," Schopenhauer called the "thing-in-itself." This is a phrase he borrowed from Kant, and it refers to what philosophy often terms the "noumenon." "That which arises and passes away, but in truth never is," Schopenhauer called the "phenomenon." Schopenhauer believed the noumenon to be one, undifferentiated, without origin, and outside of time, space, and causality. The phenomenon is the manifestation of the noumenon in time, space, and causality. It could be said that what we think of as all creation is phenomenon. All objects that exist in time and space constitute phenomenon, and here the plural, phenomena, can also be used. All objects of our perception constitute this phenomenon, and Schopenhauer called this phenomenon "representation." But there must be a force through which the noumenon manifests as phenomenon, which holds the universe together in time and space, and which continues to operate within time and space as long as physical creation exists. Schopenhauer called this force "will." He then went further and identified the noumenon and will as one and the same, and thus Schopenhauer's title can also be read as *The World as Noumenon and Phenomenon*.

Concurring with both Hinduism and Buddhism, Schopenhauer believed that the outward world of phenomena can be known to us only through our perceptions. We cannot know the sun from the inside, only from the outside. We can see it with our eyes and feel its heat on our bodies, but what we know as the sun is just a representation of it, not the thing-in-itself. What we experience is a mental picture of an object, not the essence of the object itself. We know the object only in relation to our own perception. Schopenhauer then takes the next step and states that all outward phenomena have no substantial existence apart from mental perception. Thus the outward universe is maya, from the Hindu word for "illusion." It is a phantasmagoria, a dream, that which arises and passes away, but in truth never is.

Schopenhauer did not claim that this insight was original. He acknowledged that Berkeley and Kant had understood it, and that it had been a basic understanding and teaching of both Hinduism and Buddhism for thousands of years. Schopenhauer was very insightful in his understanding of "representation." He did not, however, fully understand all the aspects of the force he called "will," and it was Wagner's intuitive perception of this that led him to go beyond Schopenhauer with *Die Sieger*, the *Ring*, and *Parsifal*.

For Schopenhauer, the idea of "will" goes far beyond volitional action alone. This has been a point of confusion for many people. The German word for "free will" is *willkür*—not the *wille* of Schopenhauer's title. Thus there is not the same opportunity for confusion in German as there is in English translation. However, volitional action on the part of sentient beings is still *part* of Schopenhauer's overall concept of "will," and we shall see that in the end he put too much under the heading of "will," causing him to misidentify a very crucial aspect of existence. This misidentification, along with a misunderstanding of Buddhist teaching concerning Nirvana, caused Schopenhauer to arrive at a final conclusion that is not consistent with Buddhism. An understanding of what Schopenhauer's "will" comprised will lead us into the world of the *Ring* and *Parsifal*.

Schopenhauer's "will" is both conscious and unconscious. It is the driving force of the universe, the universal will-to-life that brings creation into existence, that causes the plants to grow and the stars and planets to revolve in their orbits. It is the force in sentient beings that causes them to strive for survival, to reproduce, and to seek the objects of their desire. It appears in both the impersonal forces of nature *and* in the volitional conduct of human beings. Because it is the force that causes us to seek the objects of our desire, it is, in Schopenhauer's mind, the force that binds us to the wheel of birth and death. But Schopenhauer's understanding of this force is not completely the same as Buddhism's.

Schopenhauer incorporated a number of Buddhist teachings into his philosophical system. He specifically quotes the Four Noble Truths, which he calls the "four fundamental truths":

> All improvement, conversion, and salvation to be hoped for from this world of suffering, from this Samsara, proceed from knowledge of the four fundamental truths: (1) *dolor* [suffering], (2) *doloris ortus* [the origin, or cause, of suffering], (3) *doloris interitus* [the cessation of suffering], (4) *octopartita via ad doloris sedationem* [the eightfold way to the cessation of suffering].[1]

The Buddha taught (1) that suffering exists and is a fundamental aspect of all life; (2) that the cause of suffering is craving, or desire; (3) that because suffering has a cause, it also has an end; and (4) that the way to the end of suffering is the Noble Eightfold

Path: Right Understanding, Right Thought, Right Speech, Right Action, Right Livelihood, Right Effort, Right Mindfulness, and Right Concentration (or Meditation).

Schopenhauer had great insight into the first three truths. He saw a world that contained much more suffering than joy. He also understood the true nature of desire—that it can never be fully or permanently satisfied. As soon as one desire is fulfilled, another appears, and the continual striving to satisfy desire can never bring lasting peace: "Thus the subject of willing is constantly lying on the revolving wheel of Ixion, is always drawing water in the sieve of the Danaids, and is the eternally thirsting Tantalus."[2]

Also in keeping with Buddhism, Schopenhauer held that because there is a fundamental unity of noumenon and phenomenon, all things come from the same source. This means that humans, too, all come from the same source and are therefore inherently one with each other. Thus to harm another is to harm oneself, and the suffering of another becomes the suffering of oneself. This idea led directly to Wagner's theme of fellow-suffering that is so prominent in *Parsifal*. Schopenhauer further understood that because the outward world of phenomena is ultimately illusion, it is temporary and subject to cessation. Buddhism teaches that everything subject to causation is impermanent. His understanding of the third Noble Truth accorded with Buddhism: that because suffering has a cause—craving—it has an end. What he did not understand completely was the fourth Noble Truth: he understood that there was a way to the cessation of suffering, but he did not understand what that way actually involved.

His incomplete understanding of the fourth Noble Truth stemmed from two sources: he put too much under the heading of "will," thus misidentifying what it is that binds us to the world of birth and death, and he did not understand the true nature of Nirvana. This led him to misunderstand what Buddhism means when it says that "Nirvana is extinction."

The Sanskrit word *Nirvana* comes from two words, *nir* and *vana*. *Nir* means "not" or "no," and *vana* means "craving," or

"desire." Thus *Nirvana*, literally translated, means "no craving,"
or "no desire." Schopenhauer understood this etymologically.
But he did not understand the true nature of the state attained
by having no desire. It is not, as Schopenhauer thought, a final
nothing or state of oblivion, nor is it the extinction of being or
consciousness. When Buddhism says that "Nirvana is extinction," it means that Nirvana is the extinction of the illusion of
a separate self. It is the extinction of the flames of greed, hate,
and delusion. It is emancipation from the wheel of birth and
death, what Christianity calls eternal life. It is eternal meditation forever at one with the great Dharmakaya, the great eternally shining light. The Buddha specifically said, "Nirvana is
the highest bliss."[3] It is not an eternal sleep.

Here is Schopenhauer's passage that discusses Nirvana and
extinction:

> As a rule, the death of every good person is peaceful and gen-
> tle; but to die willingly, to die gladly, to die cheerfully, is the
> prerogative of the resigned, of him who gives up and denies
> the will-to-live. For he alone wishes to die *actually* and not
> merely *apparently*, and consequently needs and desires no
> continuance of his person. He willingly gives up the existence
> that we know; what comes to him instead of it is in our eyes
> *nothing*, because our existence in reference to that one is *noth-
> ing*. The Buddhist faith calls that existence *Nirvana*, that is to
> say, extinction.[4]

Misunderstanding the true nature of Nirvana led Schopenhauer to a view of what it is that binds us to birth and death, and
thus what it is that needs to be renounced, that differs funda-
mentally from Buddhist teaching. He insightfully perceived that
what he called the "Saints and Mystics" practiced a discipline that
involved renunciation. He knew that their practice was aimed at
release from suffering. He knew that "willing" on our part led to
suffering, for the reasons described above, and that the way to
end suffering thus involved the cessation of willing. But because

he had tied "willing" to the "will," it was not only willing that had to be renounced. It was the will itself.

What Schopenhauer arrived at was what he called "the denial of the will-to-live":

> Thus it may be that the inner nature of holiness, of self-renunciation, of mortification of one's own will, of asceticism, is here for the first time expressed in abstract terms and free from everything mythical, as *denial of the will-to-live*, which appears after the complete knowledge of its own inner being has become for it the quieter of all willing.[5]

By denying the will-to-live, the saints and mystics, in his view, put an end to willing and thus to life itself, and from there, the whole world:

> Finally, the universal forms of this phenomenon, time and space, and also the last fundamental form of these, subject and object; all these are abolished with the will. No will: no representation, no world.[6]

These ideas are not consistent with Buddhist teaching. This fundamental difference between Schopenhauer and Buddhism is also a fundamental difference between Schopenhauer and Wagner. Exploring this divergence will lead us directly to the way in which Wagner went beyond him, and to the way in which the *Ring* and *Parsifal* are to be seen as one work.

I mentioned at the start of this book that Wagner not only believed in rebirth, he also had an understanding of the moral and spiritual purpose for rebirth, that what we do in this life affects our future lives. This is something Schopenhauer did not fully comprehend. The subject of rebirth in Schopenhauer is complex, for at times he writes as though he has accepted it into his philosophy. In the end, however, he says that it is the will itself that continues to take repeated rebirths, finally gaining enough knowledge to abolish itself. This is not what Buddhism teaches.

Buddhism teaches that we have all inherited past karma from our own karmic stream. This karmic stream contains karma, both meritorious and non-meritorious, accumulated from many lives in many realms. Beings will continue to be born from this stream until all the karma in that particular stream is converted and cleansed. Karma in this context refers to the consequence of action, for all actions, words, and thoughts have consequences. Thus the Law of Karma, according to Buddhism, is the law in the universe that governs the consequence of action. Upon cleansing all the karma in one's own stream, one attains Nirvana, the state of enlightenment free from all rebirth. This has been explained by the famous Buddhist monk Narada Thera in the following passage (Narada uses the Pali forms of Kamma for Karma and Nibbana for Nirvana):

> As long as one is bound up by craving or attachment, one accumulates fresh Kammic activities which must materialize in one form or other in the eternal cycle of birth and death. When all forms of craving are eradicated, reproductive Kammic forces cease to operate, and one attains Nibbana, escaping the cycle of birth and death.[7]

Thus it is not the "will" in the full Schopenhauerian sense that binds us to birth and death. It is craving for the objects of our desire and the repeated pursuit of those objects and desires. It is our own uncleansed karma that binds us to rebirth. As long as there is uncleansed reproductive karma in our stream at the time of our death, that reproductive karma will condition a new birth somewhere in the realm of impermanence. And this will continue, over and over again, until all of the karma in our own particular stream is finally cleansed. Thus what the "Saints and Mystics" renounce is not the will-to-live, or the will itself, but the pursuit of karmic desire, both mental and physical. Spiritual training is itself a great *act* of will and therefore cannot be a renunciation of the individual will. And a human being couldn't put to rest the Universal Will even if he or she wanted to. Spiritual practitioners do not silence or deny the will. Through great and long effort, they let go of craving and the pursuit of worldly desire. This leads to the eternally shining light of Nirvana, not to the oblivion of a final nothing. "When all forms of craving are eradicated, reproductive Kammic forces cease to operate, and one attains Nibbana, escaping the cycle of birth and death." This is what Schopenhauer was trying to explain with his denial of the will-to-live, but he did not understand this idea well enough to identify it properly or to use the right terms to describe it. To fully understand Wagner's *Ring* and *Parsifal* as a single work, we must turn not to Schopenhauer, but to Buddhism.

Wagner, Schopenhauer, and Buddhism

On the intellectual and philosophic levels, Wagner accepted Schopenhauer's ideas—with two major exceptions. The first concerned suicide. Schopenhauer had said that suicide was not a way to deny the will-to-live, because committing suicide was, in Schopenhauer's mind, an act of will. When one committed suicide, one was not denying the will-to-live, only rejecting one's unhappy conditions. The will itself had not been put to rest. Nor had desire been put to rest. Wagner thought that there was an exception: the suicide of two lovers who were not rejecting unhappy conditions, but rather were seeking eternal union in the noumenon. This is, admittedly, more artistically symbolic than directly philosophic, but it needs to be mentioned, because I will be discussing *Tristan und Isolde* and the *Ring* shortly.

The second issue concerned romantic love being a way to put an end to willing, a way of denying the will-to-live, which Wagner thought it could be. Schopenhauer had not allowed this; he believed that romantic love was a manifestation of what he called the *affirmation* of the will-to-live, not a *denial* of the will-to-live, especially because romantic love led to procreation. Wagner, however (as he details in a long letter to Mathilde Wesendonck dated December 1, 1858), believed that romantic love could be a way of pacifying the will, and thus a way to find eternal release

from the world of impermanence and suffering. Wagner considered Schopenhauer to have made a mistake in omitting this and
even contemplated writing to Schopenhauer to inform him of
his oversight. Schopenhauer had indeed said that in the act of
romantic love two people could come very close to knowing the
true nature of the noumenon, for the act of love can be a way,
at least momentarily, of transcending the self. But this is very
different from saying that romantic love in general is a way of
denying the will-to-live. With the exception of these two points,
however, Wagner accepted Schopenhauer's ideas as a kind of
gospel.

This acceptance included the idea of renunciation and denial
of the will-to-live as the way to salvation and escape from the
seemingly endless rounds of existence and suffering. Wagner
also, like Schopenhauer, thought that release from this world of
suffering brought annihilation and oblivion. Wagner came to
see his earlier operas in a Schopenhauerian light, even though
he had composed them prior to reading Schopenhauer. Wagner
wrote to August Röckel in 1856:

> The period during which I worked in obedience to the dictates
> of my inner intuitions began with the flying Dutchman; Tan-
> nhäuser and Lohengrin followed, and if there is any single poetic
> feature underlying these works, it is the high tragedy of renun-
> ciation, the well-motivated, ultimately inevitable and uniquely
> redeeming denial of the will.[8]

In spite of this statement, and others like it, Wagner actually went far beyond Schopenhauer when it came to the operas
themselves. What we will see here is that on the intellectual and
philosophical levels, Wagner professed discipleship. On the intuitive and artistic levels, however, Wagner rejected Schopenhauer and struck out on his own to forge a path that ultimately
led him to Buddhism.

The years 1854–57 were among the most creatively intense
and fruitful of Wagner's whole career. During this time he not

only continued on the composition of the *Ring*, finishing *Die Walküre* and starting on *Siegfried*; he also conceived *Tristan und Isolde, Die Sieger,* and *Parsifal.* Wagner began sketching *Tristan* at the end of 1854, and he wrote the sketch for *Die Sieger* in May 1856 and the first sketch for *Parsifal* in 1857. Even though this last sketch has been lost, we know that he was working simultaneously on all of these projects. It is very important to understand the import of the *Ring, Tristan, Die Sieger,* and *Parsifal* all developing in his mind at the same time. It is with *Die Sieger* that Wagner made his first great break with Schopenhauer.

In *The World as Will and Representation,* Schopenhauer had listed the books on Hinduism and Buddhism that he had read and that had influenced his philosophy. Thus Wagner knew where to go for his own reading in this area. By 1856 Wagner had read enough about Buddhism to know that the Buddha had ordained women, and that his chief attendant, Ananda, had been instrumental in convincing the Buddha to found the order of female monks, called *bhikkhunis* in Pali. (*Bhikkhu* is the Pali word for a male monk.) *Die Sieger* means "The Victors," and the term "victor" is used here in the specific Buddhist context to refer to those who have been victorious in their quest for enlightenment. Wagner knew the history of the founding of the order of *bhikkhunis,* but for dramatic purposes he created a fictional character named Prakriti who becomes the first *bhikkhuni.* I will summarize Wagner's sketch in my own words. The verbatim translation can be found in the works of William Ashton Ellis.

Prakriti is a maiden born into the clan of Chandalas, who at the time of the Buddha had a very low status in Indian society. The Buddha and Ananda visit Prakriti's city, and Prakriti falls in love with Ananda. Knowing that he is a celibate monk and therefore unavailable for marriage, Prakriti goes to the Buddha to ask him what she can do. The Buddha tells her that in her previous life she was the daughter of an arrogant Brahmin. The Chandala king of that time, remembering a previous life of his own where he had been a Brahmin, asked the arrogant Brahmin for his daughter's hand in marriage, for the king's son had fallen in love with the girl. She, however, haughtily refused, cruelly mocking the sorrow of the son. The Buddha tells Prakriti that because she behaved this way in her former life, she was now born Chandala herself, feeling the pangs of unrequited love so as to know the pain she had caused and mocked before. The Buddha then tells her that she can expiate her former actions and find full redemption by entering his monastic order. Because she has asked him for union with Ananda, the Buddha offers it to her in the context of monastic training. He tells her that she must share the monks' vow of chastity. At first she "sinks down horrified and sobbing" when she realizes what it is she has to renounce, but in the end she says yes to the Buddha and is admitted into the order of monks. Ananda welcomes her as a sister, and the order of *bhikkhunis* is founded.

Even though Wagner never completed the full opera of *Die Sieger*, we can see that he, unlike Schopenhauer, had understood the karmic connection between previous and future lives. This leads us to the next all-important step that Wagner took beyond Schopenhauer, a step that can be illuminated by putting *Die Sieger* and *Tristan* side by side.

Tristan und Isolde is sometimes considered the most overtly Schopenhauerian of all Wagner's music dramas. But even with *Tristan* we see Wagner wanting to break past the bounds of Schopenhauer's philosophy and surge into a wide-open world beyond it. At first glance the story of *Tristan* seems to be a perfect representation of salvation through the denial of the will-to-live, and the end of suffering attained through the oblivion of death. The two lovers shun the world of day and light, which here symbolizes the outward world of phenomena and of ordinary life, the world of representation. They seek the shelter of the night and its darkness, symbolizing the inner world of the noumenon and withdrawal from life. In the outward world of phenomena, the two lovers, separated in body and by individual existence, long to shed their phenomenal forms and become united in the undifferentiated noumenon, where the phenomenal world can never intrude or burst in on them and keep them from their eternal union. Thus they become united forever in death, all suffering abolished.

The music, too, is overtly Schopenhauerian—the most ingeniously composed music of yearning ever written. Throughout the whole opera, until the very end, we are rarely given orthodox resolutions of dissonances. Through the use of suspensions and strident diminished and augmented chords, the sense of yearning and rising desire is maintained throughout the whole work until the "Liebestod," where at the end the resolution into major triads brings a sense of relief and release, the final end of all desire and yearning in the eternal night of death.

Romantically, there is no greater opera ever written. But as a representation of Schopenhauer's philosophy it has several key problems. This brings us to an important point, namely that Wagner's artistic and spiritual intuition went beyond his intellectual and philosophical concepts.

We have already seen that Wagner disagreed with Schopenhauer on the subjects of suicide and of romantic love not being a way to deny the will-to-live. In addition, Tristan and Isolde cannot find unity with each other in the noumenon, symbolized by death, because by definition the noumenon is undifferentiated, and thus no individual existence is possible in the noumenon. Nor is consciousness of individual existence possible, at least not in the way that Schopenhauer conceived of individual consciousness. Besides, according to Schopenhauer, individual consciousness ends at death, so lovers cannot unite in death in a way in which they would be conscious of their unity. To be unified in the noumenon means to be unified with all things; the two lovers are not unified just with each other. It is here that we see how *Die Sieger* goes further, philosophically and spiritually speaking, than *Tristan*. Union in the noumenon between individuals cannot come through romantic love, but only through the mystical union of enlightenment, in which one is unified with all that is. Here one finds true "love" in the spiritual sense, not in the romantic sense, and this is exactly what happens in *Die Sieger*. Prakriti can never

have love with Ananda in romance, but she can find a much
greater love in enlightenment and thus be unified with Ananda
much more profoundly. The most important aspect of Buddhism to understand here is that enlightenment and Nirvana
are not extinction and non-being, but rather emancipation and
"highest bliss." Rather than oblivion in eternal night, Prakriti
and Ananda have found eternal life in everlasting light. This
is the true salvation, and the true union of individuals in the
noumenon. *Die Sieger* was never developed because its most
important ideas found final expression in *Parsifal*, and I will
discuss *Parsifal* shortly. But what is important to understand
now is the way in which *Die Sieger* goes beyond *Tristan*, for we
see Wagner already dissatisfied with Schopenhauer and intuitively leaving him behind.

We can now move on to the *Ring* and *Parsifal* and see how
these works, also, cannot be seen as true representations of
Schopenhauer's philosophy. I will begin with Brünnhilde's immolation from the point of view of Schopenhauer's renunciation
of the will and show that although Wagner on the level of his
conscious conceptions saw this scene as Schopenhauerian, on
the intuitive level it is not.

Wagner's first version of the poem of the *Ring*, written in
1848, was the libretto for the opera at that time called *Siegfrieds
Tod* (Siegfried's Death). In this original version, the gods do
not perish. Siegfried, carried to Valhalla by Brünnhilde, has
redeemed the gods through his death. The ring is returned to
the Rhine, the enslaved Nibelungs are freed, and Wotan is "appointed" supreme ruler of the gods and of the world. Brünnhilde sings:

Hear then, ye mighty gods,
your wrongdoing is annulled;
thank him, the hero who took your guilt upon him.

Only one shall rule:
All-Father! Glorious one!

Rejoice in the freest of heroes!
Siegfried I bear to thee:
Give him greeting sweet,
The warrant of endless might.

The chorus then adds:

Wotan! Wotan! Ruler of gods!
Bless thou the flames!
Burn hero and bride,
burn too the faithful horse;
so that, wound-healed and pure,
All-Father's free consorts
may gladly greet Valhalla,
joined in endless bliss![9]

Here we certainly see a utopian political interpretation, with the revolutionary hero Siegfried redeeming government and society. It is interesting, though, that the old order is not destroyed and replaced, as Wagner's own revolutionary tracts of that period had promised. The old order is redeemed and corrected, and given a second chance. Wotan here can be seen, after redemption by Siegfried, as the utopian "enlightened ruler," an idea Wagner had put forth in his *Vaterlandsverein* speech of 1848, where he suggested a republic ruled by one enlightened monarch.

We also see a connection to *Parsifal* in the words "wound-healed and pure." Even as early as 1848 the concept of wound-healing was linked in Wagner's mind to redemption and salvation.

However, this version of the ending of *Siegfrieds Tod* was not to last. The first correction was a minor one, where Brünnhilde's lines are changed to:

Blessed atonement I perceived for the lofty,
holy, eternal, sole gods!
Rejoice in the freest of heroes!

To the brother-greeting of the gods
his bride leads him.[10]

The second change was a major one, for now the gods do not
continue to rule, but rather pass away, their guilt redeemed. This
change came in 1851, after the Revolution of 1848–49, but before
Wagner had read Schopenhauer. Brünnhilde now sang:

Powerless depart,
you whose guilt is forgone.
From your guilt sprang the joyfullest hero,
whose free deed has redeemed it:
you are spared the anxious conflict
about your ending might;
pass away in joy before the human deed,
before the hero whom you begat!
I proclaim to you blessed death-redemption
from your anxious fear.[11]

The redemption in death seen here is another example of how
many of Schopenhauer's ideas were latent in Wagner all along,
needing only the actual reading of *The World as Will and Representation* to come into conscious view.

But this was not the final version either. Wagner finished his
four-opera libretto in 1852, and it was privately published in 1853
so that he could send copies to his friends and supporters. *Siegfrieds Tod* had now become *Götterdämmerung*, and Brünnhilde
had a long passage addressed to the chorus after the lines, "I cast
now the flame / at Walhall's glorious height."

You, race who remain
in blossoming life,
this rede I give you—
heed it well!
When you see, in the glittering fire,
Siegfried and Brünnhilde consumed;

when you see the river-daughters
bear the Ring away in the deep:
northward then
look through the night!

When the heaven there gleams
with a holy glow,
then know you all
that Valhalla's end you behold.
Though gone like breath
be the godly race,
though I leave behind
a world without a ruler,
my holiest wisdom's wealth
to the world I now reveal:
Not goods nor gold
not godly splendor,
not house or hall, nor lordly pomp,
not guileful bargains'
treacherous bonds,
nor feigning custom's
harsh decrees—
blessing in weal and woe
Love alone can bestow![12]

This is the first time we see love playing a part in the redemption. Brünnhilde's last words of wisdom to the world
are that humankind's machinations in the quest for wealth
and power can never produce a happy, just world; only love
can bestow the blessing that the world needs. This passage
is referred to as the Feuerbach ending (though Brünnhilde
has twenty-three more lines addressed to her horse, Grane)
because of the influence that Ludwig Andreas Feuerbach's
philosophy had on Wagner during these years, and as we
have seen, the idea of love as being able to redeem never left
Wagner completely. But it was not to be his main theme after

reading Schopenhauer. It was not redemption through love, but redemption through renunciation, that imbued all his later music dramas.

It did not take Wagner long after reading Schopenhauer to alter the ending of *Götterdämmerung* again. In 1856, while *Tristan* and *Die Sieger* were taking shape, Wagner replaced the Feuerbach passage with:

> Mourning joy's
> deepest compassion
> opens its portal to me:
> who values life above all,
> let him turn his eyes away from me!
> Who through compassion
> watches me as I depart,
> on him there glimmers from afar
> the deliverance that I yearn for.
> So, with greeting,
> I take my leave of you, world.[13]

These lines are virtually pure Schopenhauer, not only in the references to compassion, but also in the renunciation of value in life and in the world, for example, "who values life above all, / let him turn his eyes away from me!" However, Wagner was still not satisfied. He replaced this passage with what is now known as the Schopenhauer ending:

> If I fare no more
> to Valhalla's fortress,
> do you know whither I go?
> From the land of desire [*Wunschheim*] I depart,
> the land of illusion [*Wahnheim*] I flee for ever;
> the open gates
> of eternal becoming
> I close behind me:
> to the desire-free, illusion-free

holiest chosen land,
the goal of world-wandering,
released from rebirth
she who understands now departs.
The blessed end
of all things eternal,
do you know how I attained it?
Deepest suffering
of grieving love
opened my eyes:
I saw the world end.[14]

Notice the lines "released from rebirth / she who understands now departs." Barry Millington translates lines 9–13 of Brünnhilde's passage as follows:

to the holiest chosen land,
free from desire and delusion,
the goal of world-wandering,
redeemed from rebirth,
the enlightened one now goes.[15]

We certainly see a reference here to Buddhism, not just to Schopenhauer. The "enlightened one," released from rebirth, desire, and illusion, enters Parinirvana, the state of eternal Nirvana one enters after physical death on earth. The world is seen in this passage not as a place of value or knowledge, but as a land of desire, illusion, and suffering. We again have pure Schopenhauer put into a few poetic lines. However, although Wagner presented a draft setting of the Feuerbach passage to King Ludwig II for his private enjoyment in 1876, he never published a musical setting of any of the passages I have just quoted. The setting we have now, which is considered the "definitive" or "final" version as well as the currently performed version, leaves out both the Feuerbach passage and the Schopenhauer passage, as well as the earlier ones, and goes straight from

I cast now the flame
at Walhall's glorious height.

to

Grane, my horse!
I greet my friend!
Can you tell, my friend,
to where I must lead you?
In fiery glory
blazes your lord,
Siegfried, my hero and love.
To follow your master,
Oh! Are you neighing?
Lured by the fire,
the light and its laughter?
I too am yearning
to join him there;
glorious radiance
has seized on my heart.
I shall embrace him,
united with him,
in sacred yearning,
with him ever one!
Hiayoho! Grane!
Ride to your master!
Siegfried! Siegfried! See!
Brünnhilde greets you as wife![16]

However, Wagner did include the Feuerbach and Schopen-
hauer passages with the 1872 published annotated libretto to the
Ring. After Brünnhilde flings the torch onto the funeral pyre,
Wagner presents the Feuerbach passage with a note:

Before the musical execution of the poem, at this point there
were the following stanzas for Brünnhilde as she turned around

once again. In these stanzas the poet had endeavored, in a sententious way, to anticipate the musical effect of the drama; but in the course of the long interruptions that kept him from the musical execution, he was impelled toward another version of the farewell stanzas which expressed his idea better.

Wagner then presents the Schopenhauer passage, adding:

Since the sense of these stanzas is fully expressed by the agency of the musical drama, the composer finally decided to omit them.[17]

Wagner himself said to let the music make the final meaning clear. What, then, do we have at the end of *Götterdämmerung*?

Textually, we seem to have *Tristan* all over again. Wotan has willed his own end, and in the process has put an end to his own willing. We have the perfect Schopenhauerian denial of the will-to-live. Brünnhilde has closed with the lines "Siegfried! Siegfried! See! / Brünnhilde greets you as wife!" Just as in *Tristan*, the male hero has died, and the woman sings a final *liebestod* before joining him in death. Brünnhilde, too, renounces life and seeks redemption in death. Wagner seems to have represented the philosophy of Schopenhauer perfectly.

But we are not left with text alone. We are left with music, a long musical recitation for orchestra that is certainly one of the greatest passages for orchestra we have ever had, or ever will have. The music, with the exception of Hagen's single line "Give back the ring!," tells us what is happening. Siegfried's funeral pyre ignites the Gibichung hall, the Rhine overflows its banks before subsiding into calm, the Rhinemaidens celebrate the return of the ring, and Valhalla catches fire and burns, with all the gods assembled in the great hall. We hear a final grand and glorious interweaving of themes throughout the whole orchestra, followed by a brief moment of rest, and out of this rest comes the last theme we are left with, the theme we take with us from the theater. I will give as simplified an explanation of these various themes as I can, for Wagner truly has let the music have the final say.

Brünnhilde had told the Rhinemaidens to retrieve the ring from her ashes. In a great flood the Rhine overflows its banks and washes over the funeral pyre. Swimming on the crest of these waves, the Rhinemaidens recover the ring, and seeing this, Hagen madly rushes into the flood with the words, "Give back the ring!": "Woglinde and Wellgunde twine their arms around his neck and draw him with them into the depths as they swim away. Flosshilde, swimming in front of the others toward the back, joyously holds up on high the regained ring."[18]

As Hagen is pulled to his death, the "curse" motif breaks amidst great agitation in the orchestra. The curse is now dissolved, and the ring is returned to its rightful place. As the Rhine overflowed its banks, the chromatic "fire" motifs were combined with and then replaced by diatonic arpeggios, the flood quenching the flames; and now, with Hagen's death, the agitation quiets to a soft lull. Out of this comes the original Rhinemaidens' theme played on the woodwinds as Flosshilde holds the ring aloft. After the statement of the Rhinemaidens' theme, the horns take up the "Valhalla" theme, and at the end of this the flutes once again play the Rhinemaidens' motif, but now with a stunning difference. Soaring above this motif, played on the violins, is the theme now known as the "redemption through love" theme. This theme was first heard in *Die Walküre*, when Sieglinde sang it to Brünnhilde after she learned that Brünnhilde had given the name Siegfried to the child in her womb. As these two themes end together, the brass again take up the "Valhalla" theme, and then we again hear the Rhinemaidens' motif in the woodwinds with the "redemption" theme above it in the strings. The brass then embark on a grand recitation of the "Valhalla" theme with new orchestration and extended development. For the first time this theme is no longer pompous and hollow, but truly profound and tragic. The gods at this point are visible in Valhalla encompassed by fire, and one can say from the quality of the music that in death they attain a grandeur they could never achieve in life. At the end of this development we hear the first half of Siegfried's theme, and as the horns hold their final note we hear the "twilight of the gods" theme, which is the inverse of the original ascending "nature" motif with which *Das Rheingold* began. The descending "twilight" theme finally settles, and the note held by the horns fades into silence. Out of a brief rest comes one last statement of the "redemption" theme, and from here the orchestra resolves into the final chords of benediction and peace.

After reading Schopenhauer, Wagner came to see the ascending E-flat-major "nature" motif from *Das Rheingold* as an expression of the will-to-live bringing the world into existence, and the descending "twilight" theme as an expression of its opposite, the denial of the will-to-live. Looked at this way, the *Ring* ends with both Wotan and Brünnhilde renouncing the will-to-live and voluntarily entering death, and with Siegfried's theme giving way to the "twilight" theme, which represents the final abnegation of the will-to-live and the dissolution of the phenomenal world, the world of representation. Thus we seem to have a final nothing, a final oblivion.

However, we are not left with the "twilight" theme. We are left with the "redemption through love" theme.

This name is a misnomer for at least two reasons. First, love does not redeem in the *Ring*, though it makes a great heroic effort. As mentioned above, after reading Schopenhauer, Wagner's primary idea was not redemption through love, but rather redemption through renunciation. Secondly, Wagner himself never called this theme the "redemption through love" theme. The theme we hear is that to which Sieglinde, in Act III of *Die Walküre*, had sung the words "O hehrstes Wunder!" (O radiant wonder!). Stricken with grief at the death of Siegmund, Sieglinde had been asking Brünnhilde to kill her:

> O warrior maid,
> who asked you to save me?
> I might have died
> in the field with him;
> for perhaps the weapon
> that dealt his death,

that killed my Siegmund,
had pierced me too.
Far from Siegmund,
Siegmund, from you!
Now only death
can unite us!
So I shall curse
this care that has saved me
if you refuse my grievous entreaty:
strike with your sword in my heart!

Brünnhilde then replies:

Live still, O maid;
know that love commands you!
Rescue the son
who will grow from your love:
A Wälsung lives in your womb!

Sieglinde, upon hearing this, is transformed, and she immediately pleads for her life:

Rescue me, brave one!
Rescue my child!
Save me, you maidens,
and shelter my son!

The Valkyries and Brünnhilde, knowing that Wotan and a great storm are approaching, frantically try to find a direction for Sieglinde to flee where she will be safe from the wrath of Wotan. Sieglinde cries out, "Rescue me, maid! Rescue a mother!" Finally they decide on the east, in the forest where Fafner the giant turned himself into a dragon and lies guarding the Nibelung hoard, for Wotan fears that forest and will not go there. As Wotan approaches, Brünnhilde sings to Sieglinde:

Fly him swiftly,
away to the east!
Bold in defiance,
endure every ill,
hunger and thirst,
thorns and the stones;
laugh at the pain
and grief that will come!
But one thing know,
and guard it ever:
the noblest hero of all,
he shall be born,
O maid, from your womb!

Brünnhilde then gives Sieglinde the broken pieces of Notung:

For him you must guard
these broken pieces
of the sword his father
let fall when it failed him;
for he shall forge
the sword once more.
His name, now learn it from me:
Siegfried—victorious and free!

Sieglinde then sings:

O radiant wonder!
Glorious maid!
Your words have brought me
comfort and calm!
This son of Siegmund,
Oh! We shall save him:
may my son return
to thank you himself!

Fare you well!
Be blessed by Sieglinde's woe!

Wagner twice named this theme. On July 23, 1872, he had said
to Cosima, "I am glad that I kept back Sieglinde's theme of praise
for Brünnhilde, to become as it were a hymn to heroes."[19] In an
unpublished letter to the chemist Edmund von Lippmann dated
September 6, 1875, Cosima wrote, "Unable to answer you personally, my husband asks me to tell you that the motive which
Sieglinde sings to Brünnhilde is the glorification of Brünnhilde, which at the end of the work is taken up, as it were, by the
entirety."[20]

Nowhere is there any mention of "redemption through love."
Naming this theme, however, is not the most important aspect
of understanding its place in the drama. Ultimately, it does not
matter what we call it. What matters is the emotional effect it
has on us and our reaction to the drama as a whole. On January
25–26, 1854, Wagner wrote a long letter to Röckel, answering,
among many other things, Röckel's question: why, if the ring
was returned to the Rhine, did the gods have to perish? Wagner
replied:

> It must be said, however, that the gods' downfall is not the result
> of points in a contract which can of course be interpreted and
> twisted and turned at will—for which one would need only the
> services of a legally qualified politician acting as a lawyer; no, the
> necessity of this downfall arises from our innermost feelings—
> just as it arises from Wodan's feelings. Thus it was important to
> justify this sense of necessity *emotionally*.[21]

This is where and how Wagner goes beyond Schopenhauer,
not consciously or philosophically, but emotionally and intuitively. The theme that Sieglinde sings—and if it needs a name, we
can call it the "O radiant wonder" theme—is a theme of joy, of renewed life in the face of imminent death, of renewed hope in the
midst of despair and suffering, and of a willingness to continue

on when just a moment ago she had been asking only for death. It is a celebration of the will-to-live in the face of the indescribable odds and sufferings that Sieglinde knows are ahead, a will-to-live redeemed from the desire for death by the knowledge of a child in her womb. In addition, we hear Sieglinde's theme *twice* combined with the Rhinemaidens' theme. Flosshilde is triumphantly holding the ring aloft, returned and redeemed, and the Rhinemaidens are again frolicking happily in the water, just as they were at the start of *Rheingold*. Their theme is one of celebration in the joy of life, which we not only see onstage but hear in the orchestra. We are certainly aware of the great tragedy that has just taken place, but emotionally, when we leave the theater, it is with thoughts of hope, renewal, and faith in the fundamental goodness of life. Nothing could be more anti-Schopenhauerian.

Wagner wanted the music to have the last word, and indeed it does. He wanted us to understand the events of the *Ring* emotionally, not just intellectually, and indeed we do. We leave the theater with the memory of the "O radiant wonder" theme in our heads. Nothing in the *Ring* itself *guarantees* that a new, better order will spring from the ashes of the old, but we instinctively feel that this is what will happen, or at least that it can happen. Emotionally, if not philosophically, we feel uplifted. In all the many performances of the *Ring* that I have attended over the years, I have never once left the theater thinking about Schopenhauer. I have never once sat in my seat during the Immolation Scene and the following orchestral passage analyzing the denial of the will-to-live. It just doesn't work. Those who like the idea of redemption through love can make a point from one particular angle: that Brünnhilde's great love for Siegfried is what *allows* her to make the selfless renunciation that accomplishes the final redemption. Fine. If we do see the work from this point of view, though, we again reject Schopenhauer, for intuitively and instinctively we could never believe that such a great love and sacrifice will lead to nothing more than oblivion and nonbeing. Such an idea stands too strongly against everything we feel and intuit in the music.

Wagner placed a great deal of importance on his artistic instincts. When we listen to the *Ring*, we follow our instincts and our intuitions, not a complex system of philosophical ideas. It is not Schopenhauer we take from the theater, nor even Wagner's interpretation of Schopenhauer. It is something else, and this is where Wagner has transcended Schopenhauer, subconsciously if not consciously. Wagner, in his music, sees the path to salvation as involving not cessation, abnegation, and denial, but regeneration, renewal, and spiritual rebirth. And this is precisely what the Grail symbolizes in *Parsifal*.

I mentioned before that *Tristan* is sometimes called the most Schopenhauerian of Wagner's operas, but the same can also be said of *Parsifal*, on one level. We certainly see compassion and fellow-suffering as being at the center of Parsifal's ability and authority to be the redeemer. We also see Parsifal as one who has renounced the will-to-live. In this context, the wound of Amfortas is the wound of willing, the wound caused by the affirmation, not the denial, of the will-to-live. This is symbolized by the lust to which Amfortas succumbed when he was tempted by Kundry, whereby he lost the spear and betrayed his position as keeper and guardian of the Grail. The consequence is a wound which will not heal, and which cannot be healed until cured by a redeemer who has renounced all willing. When Parsifal is kissed by Kundry, he feels the same welling up of sexual desire that Amfortas felt, and he recognizes this passion, and in a wider sense this insatiable willing, as the core and origin of Amfortas's suffering. He then takes the next step and recognizes it as the origin of all human suffering. In this context, sexual desire is a symbol for all willing. It is not sexual desire alone that is the core of suffering, but willing itself.

Therefore, when Parsifal rejects Kundry's advances, he is renouncing willing. Because he masters willing, he is able to renounce the pursuit of willing and the pursuit of any objects of the will. Thus he has attained the Schopenhauerian salvation, the denial of the will-to-live.

This works to some extent as long as we are willing to ignore the central symbol of the whole opera: the Grail.

Wagner was very knowledgeable about the traditional versions of the Grail story, as I will discuss in detail in chapter 4, and he knew exactly what the symbols in these stories meant. He incorporated all of the major symbols found in the traditional legends into *Parsifal*: the Waste Land, the Bleeding Spear, the Loathly Damsel, the Grail Castle, the Castle of Maidens, the wound that could not be healed except by the redeemer, the Dolorous Stroke, the Sacred Meal, the Grail Guardian and his aged father, and of course the Grail itself. In virtually every traditional version of the story, the Grail, despite the many outward forms it takes—such as magic stone, platter, dish, cauldron, chalice, or heavenly vision—has the specific properties of providing food to the assembled guests and renewal of life to the aged. The most important symbol of all is enlightenment itself. The quest of the Holy Grail is the quest for enlightenment, and the attainment of the quest of the Grail is the attainment of enlightenment and salvation. Everything about the Grail symbolizes renewal, regeneration, and both physical and spiritual life.

Just as at the end of the *Ring* the intellectual concept of oblivion and nonbeing does not reconcile with the grand musical theme of hope and renewal, so in *Parsifal* that same intellectual concept of denial, abnegation, and cessation cannot be reconciled with the central symbol of the opera, the Grail and its accompanying ceremony. The Grail ceremony, and the Grail itself, both symbolize, on the largest of scales, renewal, regeneration, and continuing life. The whole *point* of the Grail ceremony is to give regeneration and renewed life, both physical and spiritual, to the knights and the Order of the Grail. It is this very ceremony that Parsifal, as both redeemer and new Grail Guardian, performs. We cannot watch, contemplate, and comprehend a sacred religious ceremony symbolizing renewed life and spiritual regeneration while at the same time interpreting the opera as a representation of a philosophy of denial and extinction. Wagner has again transcended Schopenhauer, even without consciously intending to do so. Parsifal's performance of the Grail ceremony is of course an act of will and therefore cannot be a symbol of the denial of the will. What Parsifal has renounced is not the will, but the pursuit of desire and illusion. Having resisted the temptation of Kundry, he breaks the chains that bind us to birth and death. This allows him to recapture the Spear and to destroy Klingsor's castle of illusion. This is Parsifal's enlightenment. That enlightenment still needs testing and maturing before Parsifal can accomplish the full mission of redemption, and thus he wanders for many years before returning to Monsalvat. When he does, he is ready to redeem Amfortas's suffering and to perform the ceremony of the Grail. The performance of this ceremony gives new life and strength to the Grail knights and is the symbol of the manifestation of enlightenment in creation. The Grail is a symbol of eternal life, not eternal oblivion. Once again we see the impossibility of a Schopenhauerian interpretation holding up to what actually happens in the opera itself.

Having disassociated the *Ring* and *Parsifal* from Schopen-hauer, we are now free to explore the avenue Wagner opened up with *Die Sieger*. This avenue leads directly to the interpretation of the *Ring* and *Parsifal* as one unified cycle.

CHAPTER 2

The *Ring* and *Parsifal* as One Work

In the following chapters I will be discussing all the aspects of an interpretation of the *Ring* and *Parsifal* as one five-opera cycle. Right now I want to lay the groundwork that will set up the later discussions. I will base it on the Buddhist understanding of karma and rebirth and show how this is the link between the *Ring* and *Parsifal*.

There is a great "karmic cleansing" at the end of the *Ring*, with both water and fire, the two biblical symbols of baptism. One of the meanings of the word "baptize" is to cleanse, or purify. John baptized with water, and Jesus with fire. The "fiery baptism of the spirit" in Christianity has a parallel in Buddhism in the symbol of fire as a cleansing of karma. When in the Buddhist scriptures one encounters a vision of a Bodhisattva "surrounded by fire," the fire symbolizes the burning, and thus the cleansing, of karma. We can also recall the prophet Elijah being taken up into heaven in a "chariot of fire."

But not all of the karma of the *Ring* is cleansed at the end, and thus further rebirth is needed in order to carry this out. Buddhism teaches that not all of one's karma that needs rebirth is necessarily negative. Meritorious karma, what is called *kusala* karma, also conditions rebirth along with the negative or *akusala* karma. The merit of positive deeds influences one's rebirth just as much as the negative deeds. Thus, even though there is uncleansed karma left over when one dies, each successive rebirth can work toward enlightenment because of the merit gained in each lifetime from spiritual training, genuine contrition for one's negative deeds, and/or wisdom gained at the end of one's life.

This is what happens in the *Ring* and *Parsifal*. The four main characters of the *Ring* are reborn in the opera *Parsifal*. Alberich is reborn as Klingsor, Wotan as Amfortas, Brünnhilde as Kundry, and Siegfried as Parsifal. On a subtle level, Siegmund and Sieglinde are reborn as Gamuret and Herzeleide, though the latter do not actually appear in the drama.

The idea of characters from one opera reincarnating in another actually originated with Wagner himself. In a letter to Mathilde Wesendonck of August 1860 Wagner wrote:

> Only a profound acceptance of the doctrine of metempsychosis has been able to console me by revealing the point at which all things finally converge at the same level of redemption, after the various individual existences—which run alongside each other in time—have come together in a meaningful way outside time. According to the beautiful Buddhist doctrine, the spotless purity of Lohengrin is easily explicable in terms of his being the continuation of Parzifal—who was the first to strive towards purity. Elsa, similarly, would reach the level of Lohengrin through being reborn. Thus my plan for the "Victors" struck me as being the concluding section of Lohengrin. Here "Savitri" (Elsa) entirely reaches the level of "Ananda." In this way, all the terrible tragedy of life would be attributable to our dislocation in time and space: but since time and space are merely *our* way of perceiving things, but otherwise have no reality, even the greatest tragic pain must be explicable to those who are truly clear-sighted as no more than an individual error: I believe it is so! And, in all truth, it is a question simply of what is pure and noble, something which, in itself, is painless.[1]

Although Lohengrin cannot be the literal reincarnation of Parsifal, because Parsifal is Lohengrin's father, Wagner very clearly sees Savitri as a rebirth of Elsa. (Wagner is here not worried about the chronological problem of a character from the Middle Ages being reborn as a character in the Buddha's time. He is thinking spiritually. He had, by this time, renamed Prakriti Savitri.) Additionally, Wagner had not originally conceived *Die Sieger* as a conclusion to *Lohengrin*, but after a number of years came to see this as a genuine possibility. A character from one opera is reborn as a character in another for the purpose of finding salvation, the error of action in the first opera being expiated in the action of the second. Although Wagner never completed *Die Sieger*, the idea he put forth in this letter to Mathilde *did* come to fruition, and on a much larger scale, in the *Ring* and *Parsifal*.

Wagner also shows a remarkable insight into one of the basic teachings of Buddhism. The idea of our "dislocation in time and space" leading to error, and the essentially illusionary nature of our existence in time and space being redeemable through enlightened sight and understanding, is parallel to the Buddhist teaching of maya and karma. We create karma by acting from the illusion of self, and by seeing the ultimate nonreality of self we can reverse the error and act instead from an enlightened point of view, thus cleansing the karma we have made and living our lives in a way that creates no new karma. Our actions are then expressions of enlightenment, not delusion. This is at least part of what is meant, for example, by saying that Jesus's actions were without sin.

According to the Buddhist idea of karma and rebirth, there is no inherently individual, unchanging entity or "soul" that simply transmigrates from one life to the next, maintaining its individual identity from one existence to another. This is what Buddhism terms *anatta*, or "no separate soul." Rather, the uncleansed reproductive karma left over at the end of one life will condition rebirth in another life, in whatever form and circumstance offer the best opportunity for the cleansing of that karma. What continues from one life to the next is not an individual personality, but rather what Narada Thera has called "a continuity of a particular life-flux."[2] Among the aspects of this "life-flux" can be particular karmic tendencies, habitual patterns of thought and behavior, which can continue from one life to the next until the karma associated with them is cleansed. Zen Buddhism sometimes uses the term *koan* to describe these patterns. The term *koan* is complex and can be used in different ways in Zen, but I will use it here in relation to the characters of the *Ring* and *Parsifal* in regard to their habitual thoughts and actions, thoughts and actions that carry over from the *Ring* into *Parsifal*. One's own "personal koan" can be described not only as a manifestation of these karmic tendencies, but also as the core spiritual question that motivates a person's search in this lifetime, the distilled essence of what has yet to be worked through and taken care of.[3]

When karma conditions rebirth in human form, the new person is not completely the same as the previous person, nor is this new person completely different. The new person has inherited karma from the previous person, but it is very important to realize that the new person is not the same as the old one in all aspects. This is particularly true if a good deal of merit was gained in the previous life. The new person will also inherit this merit, not just the uncleansed karma. The new person has the opportunity to correct the errors of the past, thus cleansing the old karma. If this is not done, the new person runs the risk of falling back into the old tendencies and habits, thus perpetuating and compounding the old karma rather than cleansing it. If old karma is compounded, its cleansing often becomes more difficult and painful in the future.

With this in mind we can look at the rebirths of the characters mentioned above. The basic explanations given here will be expanded in the following chapters.

Alberich-Klingsor

Alberich's personal koan is greed. At the start of *Das Rheingold* that greed takes the form of sexual lust. Alberich lusts for the Rhinemaidens and is spurned by them. Frustrated in his pursuit of sexual satisfaction, he learns that if he renounces love he can acquire the gold of the Rhine, which will give him power over the world. His greed for sex then turns into greed for wealth and power, and he forswears love in return for the Rhinegold.

Alberich, like all the other characters of the *Ring*, gains insight and wisdom in the course of the events of the *Ring* and the final conflagration. In *Parsifal*, then, he is reborn as Klingsor. Klingsor has inherited the koan of greed, for this koan was not resolved or converted by any action that Alberich took. But because of the insight gained by Alberich, Klingsor has enough spiritual inclination to ask for admittance into the Order of the Grail. Celibacy is a requirement for entrance into the Brotherhood, and because Klingsor has not yet learned to control sexual desire, he fails in his attempt to become a Grail knight. He retires from Monsalvat to a valley where he tries to overcome this desire and attachment, but he is unable to do so. He then castrates himself, hoping that this will gain him entrance into the Order, but Titurel, at that time the Grail King, scorns Klingsor and his hideous act and refuses to admit him. Klingsor is furious with rage at the refusal and vows to capture the Grail by force. He uses his castration to gain magic arts, and with these arts he creates a castle and pleasure garden where he ensnares the knights of the Grail through the very temptation he himself was unable to overcome: lust.

We have here a mirror of Alberich. Alberich too had been rebuffed and in return renounced love for power and wealth. Klingsor is rebuffed, and his self-castration is another form of renouncing love. Attempting to capture the Grail through the use of magic power mirrors Alberich's attempt to gain power over the world through the Rhinegold. Klingsor has made a genuine attempt to convert his karma, but through weakness and anger he gives up too soon, reverting back to the actions of his previous life and thus continuing and compounding the error rather than converting and cleansing it. Because of this he does not achieve salvation in this lifetime. Klingsor will have to be born again, achieving in some future life the emancipation the others attain at the end of *Parsifal*.

Wotan-Amfortas

Wotan's personal koan is ambition fired by hubris, excessive pride that leads to error in judgment and error in action. (I will expand upon this in the next chapter when we talk about hubris in the context of Greek tragedy.) Wotan is the king of the gods, and he attempts to rule the world with order and justice, at least as far as he can conceive of them. He breaks a branch off the World Ash-tree and fashions a spear of power. Into the shaft of this spear he carves the laws by which he will rule, showing on one hand that he really does want to rule justly and not as a tyrant. But because his actions remain controlled by ambition and hubris, he becomes an unwitting mirror to Alberich. Wotan too renounces love in his way, seeking in its stead power over the world. As he says to Brünnhilde in Act II of *Die Walküre*,

When youth's delightful
pleasures had waned,
I longed in my heart for power;
and driven
by impetuous desires,
I won myself the world.

In the course of the events of the *Ring*, Wotan perceives the error of all he has done, and by renouncing any further attempt at recapturing the ring he performs his first act of contrition. The merit of this contrition allows him to be reborn as Amfortas, who has a chance to dedicate his life to spiritual quest. Amfortas inherits the koan of ambition and hubris, which was not entirely converted at the end of the *Ring*, because Wotan's renunciation alone was not enough to cleanse all the karma of his actions. More positive action is needed in order to cleanse that karma completely, and thus the reproductive karma left over at Wotan's death conditions rebirth in the person of Amfortas. The Spear of Amfortas is not only the spear of Longinus, the Roman centurion who pierced Jesus's side while he hung on the cross (the interpretation Wagner adopted as his own), it is also the spear of Wotan, a spear that had been misused for power. Amfortas, as Grail Guardian, is given the opportunity to use this Spear for selfless action in service of the Grail and in so doing to cleanse the old karma completely. However (albeit with the best of intentions), he uses the Spear for personal ambition, trying to conquer Klingsor in knightly combat out of pride and a desire for glory. As Gurnemanz tells the squires in Act I, "All too daring Amfortas, thus armed, / who could have prevented you / from vanquishing the sorcerer?"[4] This is the reason he loses the Spear and suffers the horrid wound that cannot be healed until the coming of the redeemer. Like Klingsor, who had reverted to karmic tendencies inherited from Alberich, Amfortas unwittingly reverts to a karmic tendency inherited from Wotan, mirroring Klingsor just as Wotan had mirrored Alberich. Amfortas's wound is the wound of compounded karma, and the terrible suffering he bears for so long is what is now needed to cleanse the karma first set in motion by Wotan in the *Ring*. With the return of Parsifal to Monsalvat, the period of suffering is over, and Amfortas is ready for redemption.

Brünnhilde-Kundry

The connection between Brünnhilde and Kundry is the most fascinating and complex of the four. Their koan is not so simple and direct as the others, for there was a dual nature to Brünnhilde which is reflected in the dual nature of Kundry. The koan that Kundry inherits from Brünnhilde is one of pride, anger, a deep sense of personal hurt, and a fierce, even warlike desire for revenge. All of these traits flared up in Brünnhilde during the events of the *Ring*, and particularly in *Götterdämmerung*. Although it is true that Brünnhilde's final forgiveness and self-

sacrifice greatly soften these traits, they are not completely ex-
punged, and enough traces still remain for Kundry to inherit.

Wagner himself gave Kundry past lives. As Klingsor calls
Kundry from her sleep in Act II of *Parsifal*, he says:

> Come up! Come up! To me!
> Your master calls you, nameless one,
> primaeval witch, rose of hell!
> You were Herodias, and what else?
> Gundryggia there, Kundry here![5]

According to an entry in Cosima's diaries of March 14, 1877,
Wagner briefly considered giving Kundry the name Gundrigia:
"At lunch he tells me: 'She will be called Gundrigia, the weaver
of war,' but then he decides to keep to *Kundry*."[6] Although no
Valkyrie in any of the sources used by Wagner is named Gundryggia, Gunn ("strife" or "battle") is one of Odin's principal
Valkyries. There is also another connection of Kundry to a former Valkyrie. One of her past lives was Herodias. In the Bible,
Herodias is the mother of Salome. When Salome dances for her
stepfather, Herod Antipas, he becomes so inflamed with desire
that he promises Salome anything she wants. She asks for, and
receives, the head of John the Baptist. In Heinrich Heine's 1847
poem "Atta Troll" it is Herodias who demands the head of John
and who must ride until Judgment Day with the Wild Hunt
of Odin, bearing and continuing to kiss the head. Wagner was
aware of Heine's poem; Heine was the author from whom Wagner first learned the story of the Flying Dutchman. In Teutonic
folklore, thunder was often thought to be caused by a horde of
wild horsemen galloping above the clouds. These riders were believed to be the dead heroes following the Valkyries to Valhalla.
Herodias in this context is part of Odin's Wild Hunt of Valkyries
and heroes, and thus we can see that in Wagner's own conception, at least one of Kundry's past lives was as a Valkyrie.

There is also an interesting, though partly playful, connection between Brünnhilde and Kundry that Wagner made him-

self. Amalie Materna, who had sung the role of Brünnhilde in the original 1876 production at Bayreuth, also sang the role in the 1881 Berlin production of the *Ring*, and Wagner hired her as his primary Kundry for the 1882 Bayreuth Festival. (Marianne Brandt and Therese Malten also sang some of the performances.) Toward the end of the festival, Wagner gave inscribed copies of his photograph to a number of his friends and performers. The inscription given to Frau Materna read, "Kundry here, Brünnhilde there, the work's bright jewel everywhere."[7] Even though Wagner is making a play on "Gundryggia there, Kundry here," referring to Materna's performances in both Bayreuth and Berlin, he was known to enjoy making plays on words and ideas that had both humorous and serious levels of meaning. In this light, his association of Brünnhilde with Gundryggia, and thus with Brünnhilde having been a former life of Kundry, can be taken seriously as well as playfully.

The dual nature of Kundry, that she serves both the Grail Brotherhood and their enemy Klingsor, stems from the karmic debt she inherited from Brünnhilde. Brünnhilde began her life serving Wotan as one of his Valkyrie daughters. Indeed, she even considered herself to be "Wotan's will." Thus she has an obvious karmic connection to Wotan. After her rebellion, Wotan kisses away her godhead and makes her mortal. She is awakened on the rock by Siegfried, and the two briefly share an idyll. When she is betrayed by Siegfried she plots revenge, and it is she who tells Hagen, the son of Alberich, where Siegfried is vulnerable. Hagen, armed with this knowledge, then kills Siegfried. This is Brünnhilde's karmic debt, for she directly participates in Siegfried's death.

Before Brünnhilde performs the final immolation, she communes with the Rhinemaidens and learns the truth about Siegfried's betrayal. She does forgive him, and with her own self-sacrifice she performs much of the contrition necessary in order to turn her karmic stream in the direction of salvation. But the final karmic debt of Siegfried's death must still be redeemed, and thus she takes what will be her final incarnation before enlightenment as Kundry.

Just as Brünnhilde served both Wotan and Alberich (through Hagen), so Kundry serves both the knights of the Grail and Klingsor. Brünnhilde was intrinsically good and would not have served Alberich and Hagen had she not felt so betrayed by Siegfried. Thus Kundry instinctively serves the Grail and serves Klingsor involuntarily, only when summoned by his magic. That his magic can work on her is due to the karmic bond Brünnhilde formed by plotting with Hagen. This bond is severed in Act II of *Parsifal.*

Siegfried-Parsifal

Siegfried's koan is naive pride and greed, along with an inability to feel compassion for others. Siegfried is intrinsically good and even noble, but he is also naive to a fault, selfish, prideful, and at times arrogant. His inability to feel compassion for the suffering of others precludes him from being able to accomplish the work of redemption.

Siegfried considers the world to be there for his taking. Anything he wants he takes, and there is no one who can stop him. He never even considers that there might be something wrong with this. It is only when he is dying, with a spear wound in his back, that he begins to see the world in its true light. Only then does wisdom begin to dawn on him. He sees Brünnhilde in her true light, as *Heilige Braut* (Holy Bride), not as something to take when he wants, trade when he wants, and forget about when it suits him. He has never done these things out of evil, only out of ignorance. In his dying moments this veil of illusion begins to lift. It is too late for him to come to full wisdom in this particular lifetime, but the fact that the veil lifts even partially is enough for him to be reborn as Parsifal.

When we first see Parsifal he seems to be Siegfried exactly. He is young, strong, and full of aggressive energy. Just like Siegfried, he bounds into the world considering it his for the taking. He is prodigious with arms and has made creatures and people fear him. He is ignorant of worldly ways, having grown up in the wilds away from men and society. Also like Siegfried, his father fell in battle before he was born, and he has a strong yearning for his mother.

But Parsifal is not the young Siegfried, for he has inherited the wisdom of Siegfried's final vision. Thus there is a seed in Parsifal that was not there in Siegfried as a youth. As Siegfried lies dying, the orchestra plays Brünnhilde's awakening music, and Siegfried sings:

Brünnhilde!
Holiest Bride!
Now wake! Wake from your slumber!

The orchestra recalls Brünnhilde's awakening on the rock from the third act of *Siegfried*, but this music is not just remembrance of a former event. It now becomes symbolic of Siegfried's spiritual awakening, commenting on the action, just as the chorus would have done in ancient Greek tragedy. This spiritual awakening is now just under the surface in Parsifal, needing only a catalyst to bloom and flower in this lifetime. That catalyst is Gurnemanz's admonishment at the killing of the swan. For the first time in the life-flux of Siegfried-Parsifal, true compassion for the suffering of another being is awakened. Although Siegfried had felt a kind of sympathy for, and kinship with, the animals of the forest, he had never felt genuine contrition for any of his own acts that had caused suffering in others. It is this vital contrition that Parsifal feels for killing the swan, and with it, he takes his first steps toward becoming the true redeemer.

～

We are now ready to embark on a detailed analysis of this interpretation. I will start with Greek tragedy.

CHAPTER 3

Tragedy as Mysticism

We have just seen how karma and rebirth form the main aspect of the link between the *Ring* and *Parsifal*. I would like to begin our detailed analysis by examining how karma is made, and later cleansed, from the point of view of Greek tragedy. This chapter will also show how the *Ring* and *Parsifal* as one work goes beyond tragedy, just as Dante went beyond tragedy with the *Divine Comedy*.

There have been many articles written on whether Wagner was writing tragedy or epic when he composed the *Ring*. Of course there are elements of both tragedy and epic in this great cycle, and arguing between them is to miss the point. The *Ring* is one of the grandest epics ever written. It is also tragedy.

Greek tragedy was one of the deepest and most profound influences on Wagner's creative life. He believed the Athenian civilization of the fifth century B.C. to be the apex of world culture, and we do not need to agree with him on this to appreciate the inspiration he derived from the art of this period. Of all the Greek arts, tragedy had the greatest impact on his own dramatic works.

Bryan Magee has done an excellent job of summarizing Wagner's view of the influence Greek tragedy had on his own art, and on the place he wanted his art to have in modern society:

The highest point ever reached in human creative achievement was Greek tragedy. This is for five main reasons, which need to

be considered together. First, it represented a successful combination of the arts—poetry, drama, costumes, mime, instrumental music, dance, song—and as such had greater scope and
expressive powers than any of the arts alone. Second, it took its
subject-matter from myth, which illuminates human experience
to the depths and in universal terms. "The unique thing about
myth is that it is true for all time; and its content, no matter how
terse or compact, is inexhaustible for every age." Third, both the
content and the occasion of performance had religious significance. But fourth, this was a religion of "the purely human," a
celebration of life, as in the marvellous chorus in the *Antigone* of
Sophocles that begins:

Numberless are the world's wonders, but none
More wonderful than man . . .

And fifth, the entire community took part.[1]

Much has been written, from Aristotle to modern writers,
on what constitutes tragedy and what the role of tragedy was
in ancient Greece. There is often disagreement on both points.
I will briefly explore both of these topics, not to choose one side
over another in the arguments, but to show how the tradition of
tragedy influenced Wagner and led him through the *Ring* and
into *Parsifal*.

Aristotle, in his *Poetics*, wrote, "Tragedy is the imitation of
noble action." Here the term "imitation" can be read as "expression" or "portrayal." Arthur Miller, is his essay of 1945 entitled
"Tragedy and the Common Man," wrote, "Tragedy is the consequence of a man's total compulsion to evaluate himself justly."
There have been countless other definitions in between. The truth
is that tragedy was, even for the Greeks, not just one particular
form or mode of expression that never changed. Not only were
Aeschylus, Sophocles, and Euripides different from each other,
but the individual works of each playwright differ from the others of that same artist. Aristotle used *Oedipus Rex* by Sophocles

as the model for his discussion, but *Oedipus* is unique. No other Greek play imitates it. It has often been said that all Greek tragedies are unorthodox, and this is true in that no two are exactly alike.

Even with Shakespeare, each play is different. You cannot take any one of his tragedies and say, "This is Shakespearean tragedy," because you immediately have to deal with the others, which in one way or another are different.

Therefore it is useless to try to manufacture a definition of tragedy that will hold up to all assaults. What is important is to understand the common threads and themes of tragedy, those aspects that run throughout the works we now deem great. By doing so we can understand the nature of tragedy and see its relation to the *Ring* and *Parsifal*.

Wagner wanted his music dramas to occupy in the society of his own time the same place that tragedy had held in Athens during the fifth century B.C. As I mentioned above, there is much disagreement over what the role of tragedy was in Greek society. Some say that tragedy was meant to make the "masses" conform to the social order by showing, through the fall of the tragic hero, the consequences of disobeying that social, and moral, order. Others say that tragedy prepared people for the (apparently) random catastrophes that inevitably befall humans in the course of their lives. Some say that tragedy prepared the common people for suffering: by showing them the suffering of "great ones," tragedy allowed commoners to better endure their own unhappy lots in the world.

Although all these views, as well as others, can be supported, they do not provide a complete picture, either separately or combined. In the course of this chapter I will offer another view, not in opposition to those just mentioned, but in addition to them. Like the myths and epics from which the stories of the Greek plays were derived, tragedy works on a multiplicity of levels simultaneously, and one views tragedy in as many lights as one is capable of comprehending. I believe that Wagner intuitively understood tragedy on its highest level, that of mysticism. The view of tragedy as mysticism may not be commonly held, but it is one of the keys to understanding the relationship between the *Ring* and *Parsifal*.

To understand the influence Greek tragedy, in all its aspects, had on Wagner, we must trace the development of tragedy from its origins to its apogee, and from there to Wagner.

Greek tragedy developed from the early Dionysian fertility rites. The word "tragedy" comes from the Greek word *tragoidia*, which means "goat song" (*tragos*, goat; *odias*, song). The purpose of the original ceremony was to invoke the spirit of Dionysus for the aim of producing a bountiful crop. A goat was sacrificed to Dionysus while the community danced and sang hymns to Dionysus. As these communities grew larger, it became difficult to train everyone to perform the ceremony correctly. The first step in the progression of these fertility rites into stage drama was the establishment of a trained group of dancers and singers that would perform in place of the whole community. The trained body of singer-dancers was the prototype of the chorus.

The next step in the progression was the elimination of the goat sacrifice. In its place the singing and dancing alone attempted to invoke Dionysus and give a blessing to the crops. At this point Dionysus was invoked in spirit, but not represented. The next stage came with the representation of Dionysus by a masked actor. Here was the prototype of the tragic hero.

Why was the invocation of a god linked with tragedy? The answer gives an important insight into the connection between tragedy and mysticism.

During the sixth and fifth centuries B.C. in the civilizations of the Middle East and Mediterranean, there was a movement away from the state religions and toward what are known as Mystery religions. Prior to the sixth century B.C., integration between the human and the divine was accomplished primarily through state religion. Through the observance of ceremonies performed by the state priests, the society was kept in harmony with the divine. The individual, as a member of society, was also integrated.

Over time, this outlook changed. Integration became the responsibility of the individual, not the state. Observance of state ritual remained necessary to show political allegiance, but one's own "salvation" was one's own choice. The Mystery religions provided the means of spiritual practice. This is not to say that Mystery religions did not exist before the sixth century B.C., for they did. It is simply to say that during this period there was a shift in emphasis away from the state religions and toward the Mysteries.

Each Mystery religion focused on a particular deity. Dionysus, Attis, Adonis, Mithra, Orpheus (here a deity), Demeter, Isis, Osiris, and others were sources of Mystery cults. The followers of each Mystery partook in the suffering, trials, sacrifice, death, and resurrection of its god. Christianity, which follows this same pattern, differed from the other Mystery religions of that era in that its deity was an actual historical personage rather than a character from myth. But otherwise much of the symbolism is the same. (We will discuss this further in chapter 4.) Spiritual integration, or salvation, was achieved through identity with the god, particularly in the god's resurrection after death. Each god had his or her own specific trial, but for the purpose of this chapter I will concentrate on Dionysus.

The identifying trial of Dionysus was dismemberment. Dionysus was a chthonic god, a god of the earth. *Chthonos* was one of the Greek words for earth, and the chthonic gods and goddesses were the gods of fertility and the underworld. Their opposite numbers were the sky gods, such as Zeus, Apollo, and Artemis.

There are at least two universal features of fertility gods, features found throughout world mythology: death and resurrection, and dismemberment. The fertility aspect of death and resurrection is easy to understand. Just as winter, the symbol of death, must come before spring, the symbol of rebirth, so must the fertility god die and be resurrected, symbolic of the seasonal cycles and their relationship to the planting, harvest, and replanting of crops.

The symbol of dismemberment is also worldwide. The god is literally torn to bits and scattered, just as seed is spread at sowing time. The reconstruction of the fertility god after this dismemberment is symbolic of the growing crops becoming ready for harvest.

There is, however, a much deeper symbolism to Dionysus and his trial, dismemberment, death, and resurrection. As Nietzsche describes at length in *The Birth of Tragedy*, Apollo symbolizes the principle of individuality. Dionysus symbolizes the shattering of the individual and the reintegration of the individual into the universal. Apollo represents the individual in his glory; Dionysus, the individual in his suffering. The dismemberment of Dionysus symbolizes the fragmentation of a world where the individual tries to assert his or her will over the will of the universe. Such an assertion will eventually lead to suffering, whose only cure is the merging of the individual will with the will of the universal. I will expand on this shortly, but right now it is important to understand the symbolism of the suffering, death, and resurrection of the god in order to see how the early fertility rites developed into tragedy.

In our discussion of this progression, we left off at the stage where a masked actor began to represent Dionysus as the singing and dancing invoked him. At first the actor simply stood and symbolized the invocation, his presence confirming that the rituals had succeeded in securing the god's blessings for the crops. But as time went on, the actor began to act out the trials of Dionysus. Here was the real prototype of the drama itself, for now the actor interacted with the "chorus." The next stage in the development was the introduction of other characters besides Dionysus. At first these other characters, well-known to the community from myth, were symbols of various aspects of Dionysus, rather than individual characters in their own right. Finally, in the union that Nietzsche called "the birth of tragedy," the characters were those not just from myth, but from epic poetry as well. To simplify Nietzsche's idea into one sentence, the birth of tragedy came with the union of the Dionysian arts of music and dance with the Apollonian art of epic poetry.

How does this pertain to Wagner?

It is easy to see the idea of unifying poetry and music. It is common knowledge that Wagner emphasized the union of poetry with music, and many believe he embodied that union to a greater extent than any other composer.

But the dichotomy of Apollo and Dionysus is far more complex than that of poetry and music alone. Apollo and Dionysus represent reason versus intuition, intellect versus sensuality, form versus formlessness, control versus abandon, and, as mentioned above, the principle of individuation versus that of absorption into the collective. It is this last concept, individuality versus absorption, that is the concern of Wagner, and it is the idea of reabsorption after the pinnacle of individuality that is the aim of mysticism. To understand this, let us examine first Greek tragedy, then mysticism, and finally the *Ring* and *Parsifal*.

Although there is no rigid form that every Greek tragedy follows, there are certain fundamental aspects that can be found, to one extent or another, in all of them. To begin with, Greek tragedy centers on the tragic hero. This hero is a man or woman who rises to a height far above the ordinary and who falls from that height through a combination of external events and acts of free will. The rise can come from birth, circumstance, action, or a combination of the three. The fall is precipitated by events that happen to the hero, along with the hero's reactions to those events.

In the study of tragedy we often speak of the hero's "tragic flaw." This is a weakness in the hero's otherwise virtuous character, the "vicious mole of nature" by which the fall is brought about. In Shakespeare these flaws are easily identifiable. Othello's jealousy, Hamlet's inability to act, Macbeth's ambition, Lear's foolishness—are all tragic flaws that every school student is taught early on. While approaching Shakespearean tragedy from the point of view of tragic flaws is elementary and even superficial (if one does not appreciate the complexity of characterization and drama Shakespeare has created), with Greek tragedy this approach is completely misdirected. Anyone trying to understand

Greek tragedy from the point of view of tragic flaws will end up confused and misinformed.

The Greek word that is key here is *hamartia*. This word, which has deep meanings and connotations, has sometimes been translated—inaccurately—as "tragic flaw." A more accurate translation would be "error in judgment" and "error in action." Further, the concept of *hamartia* is inextricably bound to the hero's virtue. That is, the aspect of his character that is his greatest virtue is the same aspect that leads to his downfall. Ajax's pride, Antigone's unwillingness to compromise her principles, Oedipus's demand for total knowledge, Hippolytus's utter devotion to Artemis, Prometheus's willful defiance—all constitute the greatest virtues of these tragic heroes. It is by their very virtues that these characters are brought down. It is not by flaws.

Yet still there is error. Were there no error, there would be no fall. So how do these virtues lead to the errors in judgment and actions that precipitate the falls?

Now we arrive at the crux of tragedy as mysticism. All of the qualities listed above are traits of individualism. They are qualities arising from the hero's *separation* from everything around him. The error comes from this separation.

How, then, are these qualities virtues? Two more Greek words must be introduced here, *arete* and *sophrosyne*. *Arete* is often translated as "virtue," but "virtue" alone does not contain the whole meaning and connotation of *arete*. Inherent in the idea of *arete* is what the ancient Greeks called "the will to greatness." It is the quality in human beings that aspires to greatness, that drives us to attain greatness, and that values the attainment of that greatness. The word *arete* thus contains in its full meaning what we might call "the virtue imbedded in the will to greatness."

Arete is the greatest attribute of the tragic hero, and it is also the root of his or her downfall. This paradox has led to great confusion among some commentators on tragedy; one, because they have not understood that this is the very paradox with which mysticism deals; and two, that tragedy is mysticism.

Often people think of Greek tragedy as "pessimistic" or "fatalistic." But there are many levels to tragedy. Certainly tragedy had social and political, not just religious or spiritual, meaning and purpose for the Greeks. But because I am concerned here with tragedy's spiritual aspects, I will address the ideas of fatalism and "poetic justice" so often mentioned in regard to Greek tragedy. I will use *Oedipus Rex* in this discussion because Oedipus is the best-known of the characters who seem to suffer far in excess of their error.

"Fatalism" implies a universe where people have little or no free will, their fates being either predetermined or in the hands of random and capricious forces (the gods). "Poetic justice" implies retribution in proportion to one's crimes. Let us see how each of these applies to Oedipus.

Oedipus is born with a prophecy already hanging over his head. The prophecy says that Oedipus will murder his father and marry his mother. His parents know of this prophecy, and, later, so does Oedipus. Oedipus is sent away at birth and raised by a foster father, Polybus. Oedipus grows up to be a man of great wisdom and virtue, loved by those who know him.

At a chance meeting on the road, Oedipus kills an old man who accosts him. That man is Laius, Oedipus's father, king of Thebes. So without knowing it, Oedipus has fulfilled the first half of the prophecy.

On his way to Thebes, Oedipus encounters the Sphinx and answers her riddle. He then proceeds to marry the widowed queen of Thebes, Jocasta, and assumes the reins of kingship. The second half of the prophecy is also fulfilled.

Where does Oedipus err? Certainly he kills a man in the heat of anger and passion. He does this knowing of the prophecy, though he does not know that Laius is his father. He also marries a widow, without first knowing who she really is. But are these crimes enough to bring upon him the total ruin and humiliation he suffers? Laius attacks *him*. It can be said that Oedipus kills in self-defense. In marrying Jocasta, Oedipus becomes a good and beloved king and rules with a wise and fair hand. But he is also the source of the terrible plague that besets Thebes, a plague that can be cured only by the removal of Oedipus as king.

The faults of Oedipus—brashness, pride, and metaphorical (and later actual) blindness—are certainly not faults that deserve the punishment he receives. It is as though the gods are set against Oedipus as soon as he is born, and that for all his virtues, his life is irrevocably destined for ruin. There is no poetic justice in *Oedipus*. Oedipus could have felt, like Lear, "more sinned against than sinning."

Is the play then a statement of fatalism? Did Sophocles believe that men are powerless, without free will, destined to be nothing more than puppets vulnerable to the whims of malicious and capricious gods? No. In spite of the prophecy that seems to doom him from the start, Oedipus still acts with free will. The gods don't make him kill Laius. The gods don't make him marry Jocasta. Oedipus, in grand defiance of predetermination, chooses his own life and his own actions. He acts unwittingly. He acts compulsively. He acts in ignorance. He acts with love and kind-heartedness. He acts both selfishly and selflessly. And in the end he is toppled from the greatest heights to the depths of ruin and death.

If, on one hand, *Oedipus* is not fatalistic, and yet on the other hand does not support a rational, predictable universe that metes out poetic justice, what is behind its vision?

Arete. Oedipus is an archetypal example of *arete.* His whole life is a great striving for greatness, to tower above his peers, to rule them, guide them, make them wise. His will to greatness is beneficent, not evil. He strives for greatness to improve his every attribute, to become a shining model for human achievement. And he ends up traveling the road to death completely alone, his eyes gouged out by his own hand.

If *arete* is both the virtue and the flaw in man, what is its counterpart?

The word *sophrosyne* means self-restraint. If *arete* leads to the great imbalance which eventually results in catastrophe, then *sophrosyne* is the balance in life which the tragic heroes lack. In Euripides, the *deus ex machina* or "god in the machine" who appears at the ends of *Hippolytus* and *The Bacchae* explains that the cause of the death of the hero is his one-sidedness. Hippolytus had given all his devotion to Artemis while denying Aphrodite, rather than dividing his devotions equally between the two. He thus incurs the jealousy and anger of Aphrodite, who plots the events which lead to his downfall. In *The Bacchae*, Pentheus tries to deny Dionysus and as a result is torn to pieces by the Bacchae or Maenads. (Here again we see the symbol of dismemberment.) Dionysus appears at the beginning of the play and at the end to say that no one can deny Dionysus, that all aspects of our psyches (the "gods") must be honored and held in balance. If they are not, the result will be retribution.

And yet, is *sophrosyne* alone the answer? Is it enough to see the tragic results of *arete*, and from there on to lead a life of restraint and temperance? One might avoid the catastrophic results of *arete*, but will the potential of one's life be fully realized by restraint alone?

Now we come to mysticism. Although there are many traditions of mysticism in many parts of the world, there is at least one aspect that is common to all and that I will use to define mysticism itself. Mysticism is the merging of the individual self into the universal, where one's identity no longer lies with the self alone, but with the Eternal, the Absolute, the great Unborn, God, whatever term we want to use for That which is greater than all of us. In Hinduism this is often spoken of as the merging of the *atma* with the *Atman*, or the individual "soul" with the "universal soul." In Buddhism this is enlightenment, or Nirvana, the state of complete absorption into the eternally shining light. In Christian mysticism it is the state of union with God. Buddhism describes it as "the drop slipping into the sea."

How does this pertain to *arete* and *sophrosyne*? One very important teaching of Buddhism can be phrased as follows: "The universe is not answerable to my own individual will." For all its glory and passion, what is *arete* other than the attempt to make the universe answerable to one's own individual will? Whether the intentions are "good" (Oedipus, Prometheus, Wotan), or

"evil" (Richard III, Macbeth, Alberich), the result is the same.
The character is attempting to force the universe to answer to his
or her own individual will. What tragedy shows, in its final light,
is that the universe never will be answerable to us, and that if we
lead our lives aiming the will to greatness toward the glorification
of self, the end result will be ruin. Oedipus falls not because he is
evil, not because the world is random and fatalistic, but because,
for all his greatness, even he can never exert his will over the will
of the divine. Oedipus is not conscious that he is doing this. But
this very ignorance, innocent enough as it may seem from one
point of view, is part of the delusion of self that leads not only to
misdirected *arete*, but also to the inevitable catastrophe which is
the result of that misdirected *arete*, the inevitable consequence
of error in judgment and error in action.

We saw earlier that Apollo represented the principle of individuation and Dionysus, the re-merging of the individual into
the collective. Does this mean that the frenzied Maenads of *The
Bacchae* are the "enlightened ones" we are to emulate? No. By
no means. For if Dionysus cannot be denied, neither can Apollo
be. If Artemis and Aphrodite must be honored equally (from
Hippolytus), so must Apollo and Dionysus be honored equally.
If mysticism is the merging of the individual with the universal,
what place does the individual have in that merging? What we
are asking, in essence, is, what is the positive use of *arete*?

This is the key to mysticism, and this key becomes part of the
link between the *Ring* and *Parsifal*.

We have seen the negative aspects of *arete*, portrayed so
vividly in Greek tragedy. The tragic hero, symbol of the greatest pinnacle of the individual and all his striving, is brought to
ruin by the forces around him that he can no longer control or
vanquish. But *arete* cannot be completely negative. If it were,
then all of human endeavor would aim at nothing more than
static mediocrity, which is, by the way, the negative aspect of
sophrosyne. If the positive aspect of *sophrosyne* is the balance
and harmony in one's life of all the disparate components of our
psyches and the ability to react to the vicissitudes of life with

temperance and wisdom, then what is the positive aspect of the will to greatness?

If that will to greatness and all its endeavor is aimed at glorification of the individual, trying to assert the individual will against the will of the universe, then the *arete* will result in tragedy. If, however, the will to greatness is aimed at the *merging* of the individual will with the will of the divine, the result, after assiduous training, is enlightenment. On the eve of his betrayal and capture, Jesus knows that "this cup shall pass from me." In his prayer to God, he asks that the cup pass "not as I will, but as Thou wilt."[2] Here is the *arete* transformed from the individual will to the will of God. And in this transformation, Apollo and Dionysus are merged. The individual's desire for great attainment is directed away from self-glorification and toward self-realization. But without this intense desire and effort there would be no spiritual progress, no training. As all mystical traditions admonish, enlightenment is the result of great effort, not sloth or indifference.

Greek tragedy leads us to the brink of the void. We are shown the folly and futility of personal glory. We are shown the suffering that results from the individual's separation from the divine, and his rebellion against the divine. We are made to examine the cause of this suffering and to meditate on its cure. We are made to gaze into the abyss, both within and without, and to reflect on the evanescence of human ambition and accomplishment. But are we led, in the plays themselves, along the specific road to redemption? No. We are directed; we have the way pointed to us, but we are not led to its end. Tragedy leaves us on our own to follow that road, having first shown us, in explicit terms, the wrong way. Is there, then, a step beyond tragedy? A step which will, more than just pointing the way, actually lead us all the way? Yes. With *The Divine Comedy* Dante did just that. In the *Inferno* Dante reveals the tragedy. He explains to us the errors of the characters and shows us in extraordinarily vivid images the retribution they received for their mistakes and wrong actions. But Dante's journey does not stop in Hell. He travels through Hell, up the mountain of Purgatory and into Paradise. In this way *The Divine Comedy* goes beyond tragedy, as it leads the reader step by literal step along the path to salvation after first portraying the tragedy and the reasons for the retribution. With the *Ring* and *Parsifal* as one work, Wagner accomplished the same great feat. The *Ring* is the most monumental tragedy ever created. And with *Parsifal*, as we were with the *Purgatorio* and *Paradiso*, we are led step by step down the path to salvation.

Along with its many other aspects and accomplishments, the *Ring* is a portrayal of misdirected *arete* on the grandest of scales. And the catastrophe that ensues is the inevitable and inexorable result of that misdirected *arete* leading to error in judgment and error in action.

Although Wotan is the central tragic hero of the *Ring*, other characters also undergo tragic action and suffering. Alberich, for a time, achieves fortune and power, only to have it violently stripped from him, hurling him lower than he was at the start, for he has renounced love and has only bitterness and rage to show for it. Siegmund defies all around him, fighting to the death every opposition he meets. He attains the hero's glory and suffers the hero's end. Siegfried also attains the hero's greatness of accomplishment and reputation, only to pay for them with his life. And of course Brünnhilde is a tragic character also, falling first from the heights of godhood as a consequence of rebellion; and falling again from her love with Siegfried through deception and her desire for revenge. These characters all rise to their heights through *arete* and fall as a direct result of that same will to greatness. And in keeping with the tradition of Greek tragedy, the quality in each of these characters that allows the rise to greatness is the same quality that brings the fall.

What is the first significant action Wotan takes? He breaks a branch from the World Ash-tree, and from that branch he fashions a spear, a spear by which he plans to rule the world. He carves the laws of the world into the shaft, and by those laws he makes himself ruler, subduing the forces around him with his might. Here is the classic example of *arete* being directed toward power. Wotan is not evil. He does not want the world to suffer. He believes that he is bringing order to the world, that as the king of the gods it is his prerogative to rule, and that all should obey him. He exerts his might over those who resist him and has a castle built to fortify his power. Every action he takes is an attempt to force the universe to be answerable to his own individual will. Even without specific evil intent, this action creates error, and as the consequences of this error compound, Wotan and all his aspirations are brought to ruin.

Alberich, Wotan's counterpart, has specific evil intent. Like Wotan, Alberich wishes to rule the world. Unlike Wotan, Alberich is not interested in bringing beneficent order to the world. He simply wants power and wealth for himself, regardless of the suffering this might create for others. Wotan rules by laws; Alberich, were he to attain complete power, would rule by only one law, Alberich's law. But here again we have *arete*, albeit a perverted version. We have a Richard III, an evil genius who has been rejected by the world and who therefore seeks redress through subjugating the very world that cast him out. The end result of Alberich's *arete* is the same as Wotan's: utter ruin.

Siegmund is a product of Wotan's attempt to force his will over the world. Although Wotan pretends that Siegmund is an agent of his own free will, we know, as does Fricka, that Siegmund was created to fulfill Wotan's ambition of recapturing the ring and in this respect is an agent of Wotan's will. This does not mean that the human being Siegmund does not have free will, because he does. It means that Siegmund, fighting heroically against all those forces opposed to him, and perhaps even being the most sympathetic character in the *Ring*, is still the product of misdirected *arete*, separate from everything around him, fighting his environment rather than living in harmony with it.

Siegfried, in Wagner's scheme of the *Ring*, is an agent of his own free will, and not Wotan's. But what does he do with this free will? He conquers. When he sees something he wants, he takes it. When he meets opposition, he kills it. Siegfried is by no means evil. He does not, like Alberich, consciously create suffering, taking enjoyment in the process. But he, like Wotan, is a classic example of *arete* aimed at individual glory. The concept of surrendering that glory in return for spiritual wisdom is beyond him. When he finally does attain insights into the true nature of love, it is too late, for he is dying. Like Oedipus and Lear, wisdom comes too late. The course of events, by then, is irrevocable.

Brünnhilde is the most complex character after Wotan, or perhaps along with Wotan. She is unique in that she falls twice, from two different heights. Her first fall comes from rebellion, one of the classic examples of tragedy. Aeschylus's Prometheus in *Prometheus Bound* is the archetypal rebel, followed by Antigone, Cordelia (in her way), Satan in *Paradise Lost*, and of course others as well. Brünnhilde follows in this tradition.

In each case, the rebel attempts to defy the existing law, trying to replace the dictate of that law with action emanating from the hero's own view of what is right. Even in those instances where the hero seems to *be* right, the act of rebellion is an act of *arete*. We certainly side with Prometheus, Antigone, and Cordelia, and even sometimes with Satan. We also side with Brünnhilde, knowing she is carrying out Wotan's inner desires.

But the rebellion is contrary to the existing law, and Brünnhilde pays the price. Because that price is not death, Brünnhilde lives to rise to another height, only to be cast down again. Awakened on the rock by Siegfried, she knows a joy and ecstasy she never knew as a god, and, significantly, never *could* know as a god. Free from the laws and the wills of the gods, she can experience life reborn, experience love in its purest state. She is human, the paragon of free will.

The tragedy comes through the use of that free will. At first the love of Siegfried and Brünnhilde is idyllic. But Siegfried enters the world of politics and machinations, and through ignorance he becomes accessory to deception. The victim is Brünnhilde, and when she discovers that Siegfried is involved, her passion for revenge is unquenchable. At no point does she try to understand why and how Siegfried could have done this, or what could have happened to him. She thinks only of her own hurt and desires to return this wound with violence of her own. (In this regard she follows in the tradition of Medea.) Like so many tragic heroes before her, her wisdom comes too late. By the time she has communed with the Rhinemaidens and learned the truth, Siegfried is dead, killed as a result of her own devices. There is nothing left for her but to wipe the slate clean, and this she does in the final conflagration.

If there is one universal trait that all of these characters possess, it is hubris, or pride. This is the trait all the Greek tragic heroes possess, in one way or another and to one extent or another, and it is a part of misdirected *arete*. Inherent in the Greek-tragedy concept of hubris is excessive pride that leads to retribution. This hubris is easy to see in Wotan and Alberich, but it is there in the others as well. Siegmund and Sieglinde revel in the pride of being Volsungs, separate from all others. Siegfried and Brünnhilde exult in the pride of love. It is a selfish love, albeit radiant and impassioned. But when, for example, Waltraute pleads with Brünnhilde to give up the ring for the good of the world, she refuses. And this defiance, so romantic and sympathetic, also rears up in Siegmund. When Brünnhilde, as the Valkyrie, appears to Siegmund to announce his death, he refuses to go to Valhalla if Sieglinde cannot go with him. This is perhaps Siegmund's most heroic moment, and yet it is another form of rebellion against the existing law. The root of this rebellion, the root of selfish action, is hubris. And it is this hubris, even when it is so well intended, that leads the will to greatness away from self-realization and toward the glorification of the individual, the root of tragedy.

This brings us to a very important aspect of mysticism. One of the most difficult truths of spiritual training to understand and accept is the giving up of self when the self seems to be "right." "Yes, I rebelled against the existing law, but that law was unjust." "Of course Brünnhilde keeps the ring; true love is more important than the politics of the world." Et cetera, et cetera, et cetera. All of these "ideals," no matter how well intended they may be, are only our own opinions of what should or shouldn't be. That is, they are rooted in self. And the real meaning of hubris is the putting of self above all else, including God. It is saying, "*my* will be done," not "*Thy* will be done." And this assertion of self may at times appear great and glorious and heroic, especially when represented by dramatic characters such as Brünnhilde and Siegmund and Siegfried, but in the end it will bring only tragedy, for the universe is not answerable to our own individual wills.

It is important to understand that the previous paragraph does *not* mean that we should turn a blind eye to injustice or refuse to offer help when an opportunity to help the suffering of the world is presented to us. It means that we must try to find the way of "*Thy* will be done," not "*my* will be done," when we contemplate action. We must be willing to let go of self. In this way we can help to cleanse the karma of the world, not make more of it.

This is how *Parsifal* differs from the *Ring*. This is how it leads us away from tragedy and down the road to redemption.

I mentioned before that the positive aspect of *arete* was the transformation of the will to greatness away from the glorification of the self and into the desire for self-knowledge, for union with the Eternal, the Absolute, with God. When the desire to assert one's will over the world is transformed into the desire to merge the individual will with the will of the divine, the energy and effort of *arete* are channeled into spiritual quest. And this quest is the heart of *Parsifal*.

The four characters who are reborn from the world of the *Ring* find themselves in the land of Monsalvat, the land of the Grail Castle. This castle has been built to house and guard the holy relics of Christ, the Grail and the Spear. The knights who have taken the holy vows of the Order of the Grail Brotherhood ride out into the world to help those in need, and the Grail, the castle, and its knights become symbols of a beacon of spiritual light shining forth on the world in an age of darkness.

Even though those who serve the Grail are in quest of enlightenment and not power, in the holy land of Monsalvat hubris is just as deadly as it was in the world of the *Ring*, and maybe even deadlier, for the stakes are higher. The knights who ride out on missions from God must be completely pure, or else they will become ensnared by the very sins they are trying to exorcise and redeem, leaving Monsalvat weak and prey to evil. The knights and, especially, their leader, are still susceptible to error if they stray from the path of training.

This is a very good lesson. No matter how sincere someone's spiritual training is, there is always the chance for error if one is not constantly vigilant. Christianity poses seven "deadly sins" which can be fatal to one's spiritual progress: anger, greed, envy, gluttony, lust, pride, and sloth. There is a passage in Sir Thomas Malory's *Le Morte d'Arthur* where the knights of the round table must joust with seven knights who are personifications of these seven deadly sins. Only Galahad is able to unseat all seven, meaning that only he has purified himself fully. All the others are still susceptible to temptation.

This is what we find in *Parsifal*. As Gurnemanz narrates, Titurel was a true, uncorrupted Grail King, but after he refuses to admit Klingsor to the Order, and Klingsor begins his attack of temptation, many knights of the Grail are ensnared and ruined. The overt temptation by which Amfortas and the others fall is seduction in the arms of Kundry, but there is a deeper and more dangerous temptation that catches them first: pride.

The Grail knights are guilty of pride without even knowing it. For example, when in Act I Gurnemanz finishes telling the squires about the loss of the Spear, one of them exclaims, "Ha! He who brought it back would win fame and joy!"[3] In his zeal to serve the Grail, this young man thinks of personal glory first. Here again is *arete* leading to error even when the intentions, ostensibly, couldn't be better. Amfortas, also in the thrall of his enthusiasm to serve the Grail, commits the same error of pride. Gurnemanz tells the squires:

> When Titurel, much burdened with age,
> had conferred sovereignty on his son,
> Amfortas could not wait
> to subdue this plague of sorcery.[4]

And earlier, Gurnemanz had said to them:

O wondrous-wounding
hallowed spear!
I saw thee wielded
by unhallowed hand!
All too daring Amfortas, thus armed,
who could have prevented you
from vanquishing the sorcerer?[5]

Here is Amfortas going out into the world to conquer. He uses, or attempts to use, the holy Spear to force the world to conform to what he believes is right. And through this error of pride and willfulness he becomes susceptible to the powers of Klingsor and loses the Spear.

Buddhism speaks of what is called victim-victimizer karma. This refers to a karmic entanglement between two beings that continues over a number of lifetimes. The victim in one life who is harmed by the other becomes the victimizer in the next life, and the original victimizer in the first life becomes the victim in the second, and this relationship can continue to trade back and forth, lifetime after lifetime until both are willing to stop it and forgive what has been done in the past. We see an example of this with Wotan-Amfortas and Alberich-Klingsor.

In *Das Rheingold*, Wotan violently tears the ring from Alberich's finger, hurting Alberich in the process (though, of course, much more emotionally than physically). Alberich is humiliated, but Wotan is completely unconcerned with his suffering. In the next lifetime it is Klingsor who violently steals the Spear from Amfortas, dealing him a terrible wound that will not heal. Just as the gold must be "won back" and returned to the Rhine, so must the Spear be won back and returned to the Grail Castle. Each has stolen a symbol of power from the other, and the enmity that existed in one lifetime carries over into the next. Neither is able to let go of his injury and forgive, and thus each bears a terrible wound—Klingsor, his wound of castration; and Amfortas, the wound that will not heal.

Klingsor is also guilty of pride, not just lust. As we saw in the last chapter, Klingsor once had truly sought atonement for his sins, and desired admittance into the Grail Brotherhood. But he was not pure enough, and so admittance was denied him. At that point he could have accepted the rejection as a teaching that he needed to do more training before he could be ready for Grail membership. He could have reacted with humility, showing willingness to train on his own until such time as he would be ready for membership. But his pride could not bear the rejection, so he succumbed to the delusion that there was a short cut or easy way to training. He therefore castrated himself, thinking that this would gain him entrance to the Grail assembly. Titurel was outraged by this act and scornfully rejected him. Klingsor then reacted with anger and a desire for revenge, vowing to capture the Spear and Grail by force if he could not win them through virtue. Thus he perpetuated the negative karma that, as Alberich, he had started in the *Ring*, causing great harm to both himself and others.

Because Brünnhilde's forgiveness of Siegfried and her self-sacrifice at the end of the *Ring* cleansed a great deal of the karma associated with pride, the traces left over for Kundry to inherit are subtle. Unlike Amfortas and Klingsor, Kundry is not seeking any kind of power or control over others. But there is one layer of pride still left in her that she must convert before she can experience final redemption. Buddhism calls this "wanting enlightenment on your own terms, not on the terms of the Eternal."

A large part of spiritual training is giving up the self. And part of giving up the self is letting go of having things your own way and on your own terms. This goes for enlightenment itself. Enlightenment does not come on our terms, it comes on the Eternal's terms, and we have to be willing to accept that. This is sometimes explained in Christianity by a humorous analogy: The new missionary says, "I'm willing, Lord, to go anywhere you want me to go, except to such-and-such a place." We all know where the new missionary gets sent.

In the famous Act II scene between Kundry and Parsifal, Parsifal has rejected Kundry's kiss, and is the only one who has ever done so. She knows, because Klingsor told her, "He who braves you, saves you as well."[6] She recognizes Parsifal as the redeemer, but she will not accept the redemption he offers her. She wants redemption, but only in the way that she can conceive of it: through sexual love. She is too fearful to let go all the way and let all of the self fall away. Parsifal asks her for the way to Amfortas, but she is unwilling to tell him, to share the compassion of redemption with one who she feels is unworthy.

> KUNDRY: So it was my kiss
>> that gave this all-seeing vision?
>> Then let my loving embraces
>> give you the Godhood you look for!
>> The world's redemption, is this your charge?
>> It's God who made this moment,
>> for it let me perish evermore,
>> my wound unhealed forever!
>
> PARSIFAL: Redemption, wanton one, take of it now.
>
> KUNDRY: Let me, divine one, then love you.
>> Salvation such as that I want.
>
> PARSIFAL: Love and redemption I can offer
>> If the way to Amfortas is revealed.
>
> KUNDRY: No! Never shall you find him!
>> Leave that lost one, and let him perish,
>> so unholy, vile, lecherous,
>> fit but for laughter, laughter, laughter, ha-ha!
>> He fell by the spear that he owned!
>
> PARSIFAL: Who dared, though, to wound him with that holy
>> spear?
>
> KUNDRY: He—He!
>> Who gave me reason to laugh.
>> His curse, ha, it gives me strength.
>> Against you too I turn the spear,
>> since you show pity where none is due!

> Ha! Madness! Pity? Pity for me?
> Were you just one hour mine!
> Were I just one hour yours!
> And then, after, I would reveal the path.
> PARSIFAL: Away, iniquitous wretch![7]

Kundry tries to embrace Parsifal, but he shoves her away. Kundry then tries to curse him and calls on Klingsor to cast a spell on him. Klingsor is powerless over Parsifal, hurling the Spear at him to no avail. Parsifal seizes the Spear and makes the sign of the cross, and Klingsor's castle disintegrates, the garden becoming a wilderness. Kundry, "shrieking, sinks to the ground." Parsifal turns and says to Kundry, "You know / where you can find me once again."[8] As Parsifal leaves, Kundry raises her head and stares after him.

Because Kundry will not let go of this final layer of pride, it has to be wrenched from her, as it is in the final events of Act II. As she stares after Parsifal, she longs for him, but no longer sexually. Her longing is for redemption. And this she finally finds in Act III.

The fault of hubris is rooted in attachment to self. When self is truly given up, hubris vanishes, for there is nothing left to fuel it. This is the advancement made from Siegfried to Parsifal. But it does not come easy.

As we saw at the end of the last chapter, when Parsifal first appears he seems to be Siegfried exactly. He has all of Siegfried's attributes: youth, strength, courage, fearlessness, brashness, arrogance, inherent goodness, naiveté, skill with weapons, and a total lack of understanding that actions have consequences. But his readiness to change is very close to the surface, and when Gurnemanz points out to him the great error of his killing the swan and the suffering it has caused, Parsifal is truly contrite. He breaks his bow into pieces and throws away his arrows. This is a very significant act, for it is the exact opposite of Siegfried's great act, the reforging of Notung (which together with the killing of the dragon Fafner formed the two pillars of his fame). At this very point the *arete* begins to convert from individual glory to true spiritual humility and quest. When Parsifal first enters and is asked by Gurnemanz if it was he who had shot the swan, Parsifal boasts with pride, "Yes, I! In flight I hit all that flies."[9] Parsifal, like Siegfried, is proud of his martial prowess and completely unaware of the suffering it causes to others. But when Gurnemanz severely chastises him for his deed and makes him look on the bloody, lifeless body of the bird, Parsifal feels an emotion that Siegfried was never able to experience. Gurnemanz makes Parsifal understand that the forest of Monsalvat is sacred, that the beasts "approached you without fear, / greeted you friendly and tame."[10] He tells Parsifal that the swan was seeking its mate, to circle over the lake and thus to consecrate the bath of Amfortas. And now it is dead, killed by a "wild childish shot from your bow."[11] When Parsifal truly realizes what he has done, he breaks the bow, a weapon, like Siegfried's Notung, that he has made himself. With this action he begins the reversal of the direction of his karmic stream. No longer will violence be considered heroic. No longer will greatness be measured by physical prowess. From here on, although there is certainly a long way still to go, greatness will be measured by spiritual accomplishment, and that greatness will be expressed by humility, not by pride.

The key to all of this here is the ability to feel the suffering of another as though it is your own. At this point one has made a great stride in the letting go of self, albeit a painful one, and with the letting go of self the spiritual path becomes open. Siegfried was the personification of self, and of selfish action in the world. Parsifal begins the conversion of self, and the first step, an all-important step in the karmic stream of Siegfried-Parsifal, is the renunciation of violence.

Back in February 1991, while the Gulf War was still going on, I heard a lecture by the author Walter Wink on the subject of the demonic, how it was viewed in the time of Christ and how it is viewed now in modern society. At the end of the lecture there was a question-and-answer period, and the last question turned out to be the best: "What do you think is the most dangerous manifestation of the demonic in our society today?" Wink replied, "The most dangerous manifestation of the demonic in our society today is the belief in the myth of the redemptive power of violence."

This is a very profound statement. The "myth of the redemptive power of violence" is exactly what it says, a myth. Violence can never redeem. It can, in the short run, *appear* to redeem, but in truth it does not. It can make something happen to someone else instead of you, but this is not redemption. This is the perpetuation of the victim-victimizer karma I talked about before. Who now is on top will be on the bottom in the future, and who is on the bottom now will be on top in the future. And this cycle will continue to go round and round and round until violence is seen and acknowledged for what it really is, a great error in judgment and error in action. He who lives by the sword will die by the sword, and individuals as well as societies who continue to believe in the myth of the redemptive power of violence, and who act on that belief, will continue to perpetuate the karma of violence rather than converting it. And they will experience the consequences thereof.

The conversion of Parsifal begins with his recognition of the suffering he has caused to the swan. This conversion continues with his ability and willingness to feel his own mother's sorrow when Kundry tells him of Herzeleide's grief at the time Parsifal left her. And when he observes the Grail ceremony and hears Amfortas's last cry of agony, he clutches at his own heart, feeling Amfortas's suffering as though it were his own. There is still further to go, and intellectually Parsifal does not understand what he has just witnessed, but he is already well on the road to enlightenment.

Parsifal is not yet completely purged of violence, for when he is attacked by the knights at Klingsor's castle he does defend himself. But there are two things to note here. One, he does not kill any of the knights—he only wounds them. He does only enough to defend himself and keep himself from harm. And two, he does not carry his own weapon with him when he leaves the Grail Castle, for he has already broken it. He will never again carry a weapon into the world with the intention of using it for violence and conquest. He fights the knights with the sword of Sir Ferris, whom he has disarmed.

The great moment of awakening comes with Kundry's kiss. We will talk further about this in chapter 6, but here Parsifal has awakened not only to the suffering of Amfortas, but also to the suffering of the whole world. Parsifal is not only close to his own final enlightenment; he is becoming ready to perform the role of redeemer. He is now ready to take the next step in the renunciation of violence. After Klingsor's castle collapses, Parsifal wanders for many years before he finds his way back to Monsalvat. He carries the Spear with him, but though often attacked, he never uses the Spear for violence.

> Then I was forced to despair
> of holding unsullied the treasure
> to defend and guard which
> I earned wounds from every weapon;
> for I dared not wield this
> itself in conflict;
> unprofaned
> I have borne it beside me
> and now bring it home,
> gleaming clean and bright before you,
> the holy Spear of the Grail.[12]

Though possessed of great martial skill and of the Spear itself, he never uses these to conquer or suppress, or even to defend himself. He never uses the Spear or its power to assert his will over anyone else. When he arrives in Monsalvat and is told by Gurnemanz that he is in the sacred forest on Good Friday and that arms are forbidden, he immediately plants the Spear in the ground, lays down his sword and shield, and removes his helmet. He then kneels in prayer before the Spear, later allowing Gurnemanz and Kundry to disarm him. This is

an example of true spiritual humility. When Gurnemanz says
to him,

> Lay down your weapons!
> Do not offend the Lord, who today,
> bereft of all arms, offered His holy blood
> to redeem the sinful world![13]

Parsifal does not take this as a challenge. He immediately lays
down his weapons and kneels in prayer. Here is the greatest and
most accomplished warrior in the world not hesitating to obey
a spiritual command. Compare this to Siegfried's reaction when
he is confronted by Wotan as the Wanderer at Brünnhilde's rock.
When Wotan gives him genuine and sound advice, Siegfried
responds with impatience and arrogance, eventually threaten-
ing to kill Wotan if he does not get out of his way. With Parsifal this assertion of self and its attendant karma of violence has
been converted and cleansed. Hubris has been uprooted. *Arete*
no longer serves the self, but rather the spiritual welfare of the
whole world.

All of Parsifal's actions at this point are in service of the Grail,
not of his own desires, ambitions, or whims. Parsifal has attained true selflessness, something the *Ring* characters, for all
their heroism, never do. Even Brünnhilde, who does perform an
act of selflessness, does so at a time when she is powerless to do
anything else. Parsifal's acts of selflessness come at a time when
he could have, had he so desired, tried to conquer the world. Instead he serves the world, performing the ceremony of the Grail
for the benefit of all beings and healing the wound of Amfortas,
a wound that had its root in pride and violence.

Greek tragedy held up a mirror to its own time, showing the
society of that time what was true and what was false in the world.
Drama alone could not transform individual action; only the individual can accomplish that transformation in his or her own life.
But tragedy, by showing the way toward this transformation, performed a religious function in Greek society, a function far more

profound than the archaic ceremonies of the state priests.

It was this function that Wagner wanted to emulate. Like tragedy, the *Ring* and *Parsifal* held up a mirror to society and the individual. Like the old state religion of Athens that had degenerated into political ceremony, so had Christianity, in Wagner's view, become bereft of its mystical heritage, consisting only of outmoded ritual. Wagner wished his "festival plays" to take the place of organized, politicized religion, and to assume the place in society that the Greek dramas had held more than two thousand years earlier.

Like the characters from Greek tragedy, Wagner's characters are more than just individuals wrestling with the forces of the world. They are archetypal representations of the deepest aspects of our own psyches. Buddhism teaches that everything in the universe is a manifestation of our own inner nature. By understanding that inner nature completely, we come to live in harmony with the world instead of against it. This is the accomplishment of Parsifal.

Wagner gave musical and dramatic expression to the primal emotions in all of us that are suppressed, or at least regulated, for and by society in order that we may live together. Wagner lets them loose, opening all the doors to our deepest consciousness. This is exactly what Greek tragedy had done. Our inner psyches are laid bare, all the forces unleashed, and in the process we come face to face with our own true nature. It is then up to each of us to accomplish the transformations necessary to convert those aspects of ourselves that cause suffering into aspects of ourselves which help to heal it. And this is the transformation from the *Ring* to *Parsifal*. The *Ring* left off where Greek tragedy left off. With the *Ring*, the error is revealed. With *Parsifal*, the error is redeemed.

$\sim$

There is, of course, much more to talk about concerning the *Ring* and *Parsifal*, and this will be done in chapter 6. In this chapter we have seen how Wagner, like Dante, went beyond tragedy, showing us the tragedy first, and then taking us down the actual path of redemption, rather than just pointing the way. It is *Parsifal* that takes us down that path, and because the central symbol in this opera is the Grail, I want to devote a separate chapter to the background and symbolism of the Grail, where we will have the opportunity to examine the different versions of the Grail legend, their sources, and their roots in sacred kingship and the Mystery religions. This will allow us to have a better understanding of Wagner's use of the Grail symbolism in *Parsifal*, and of how his use of this symbolism relates to the interpretation of the *Ring* and *Parsifal* as one work. Chapter 4 is thus devoted to the Grail. In chapter 5 we will discuss Wolfram von Eschenbach's *Parzival* and the influence it had on Wagner. This will prepare us for the final analysis in chapter 6.

CHAPTER 4

Wagner and the Grail

The subject of Wagner and the Arthurian/Grail legends is a fascinating one. Many people immediately associate Wagner with the Teutonic myths and sagas, not always realizing how important the Arthurian cycles were to him as well. Wagner was extraordinarily well-read and insightful about the traditional Grail legends in particular, and he incorporated many aspects of these stories and their symbols into both *Parsifal* and the *Ring*.

As we saw in chapter 1, the *Ring, Tristan, Die Sieger,* and *Parsifal* were all developing in Wagner's mind at the same time. Wagner first read Wolfram von Eschenbach's *Parzival* and *Titurel* poems in 1845. *Lohengrin* followed, and then the first draft of *Siegfrieds Tod* in 1848. In 1852 he completed the four-opera poem of the *Ring*. He began sketching *Tristan* at the end of 1854, sketched *Die Sieger* in 1856, and wrote his first sketch for *Parsifal* while still in the process of composing *Siegfried* in 1857. Thus we cannot separate the *Ring* from the Grail stories in terms of the inspiration in Wagner's own mind. Wagner eventually broke off the composing of *Siegfried* in June 1857 in order to concentrate on *Tristan*, but the other works were always in his mind as well. Wagner at one point even contemplated having Parsifal come to the bedside of Tristan, and a connection in Wagner's mind between the wound of Tristan and the wound of Amfortas can be seen in a letter he wrote to Mathilde Wesendonck on May 30, 1859. Speaking of the story of *Parzival*, he wrote:

Looked at closely, it is *Anfortas* who is the center of attention and principal subject. Of course, it is not at all a bad story. Consider, in heaven's name, all that goes on there! It suddenly became dreadfully clear to me: it is my third-act Tristan inconceivably intensified.[1]

The sources that Wagner used did not come from Germany alone. They came also from France, Britain, Ireland, Wales, Greece, and India. The "golden age" of the Grail legend took place roughly between 1180 and 1240, when the earliest and most influential versions of the story were committed to writing. Most scholars agree that the sources of these stories are much older than the written texts still extant, but they do not all agree about which version of the tale was original or definitive, or even whether there ever was one particular version that can be called definitive. There are three main camps concerning the origin of the stories: one holds that the origin goes back to very early fertility rituals, Mystery religions, and Hindu scriptures; another believes that the legends are originally Celtic; and the third maintains that the origin was specifically Christian. The truth is, the *symbols* that we find in the traditional legends have their origin in ancient fertility rites and Mystery initiations, as well as the Hindu Rig Veda. The origins of the *form* of the stories as we have them now can be found in the old Celtic tales and in certain passages of the Hindu *Mahabharata*. By the time of the twelfth- and thirteenth-century romance writers, the stories had become Christianized, their pre-Christian or "pagan" symbols and symbolism reinterpreted in the context of Christianity.

As far as Wagner is concerned, what matters is not the specific origin for these legends, but rather his own interpretation of the story and how he used it in the context of *Parsifal*.

Wagner himself believed that the stories were pagan. He even complained about this to Mathilde in the May 1859 letter quoted from above: "One notices, unfortunately, that all our Christian legends have a foreign, pagan origin."[2] But as usual, he took what he wanted from all the various sources available to him and fashioned his own unique version of the tale. The result was a work that combines pagan, Christian, and Buddhist symbolism into one integrated whole.

The earliest extant written account of the Grail legend is an unfinished poem by the French romance writer Chrétien de Troyes titled *Le Conte del Graal* (sometimes in the plural *Li Contes del Graal*), also referred to as *Perceval, the Story of the Grail*. Chrétien died somewhere between 1185 and 1190, leaving his epic poem unfinished at 9,235 lines, the last of them incomplete. Four authors wrote continuations of the poem: Manessier, Gerbert de Montreuil, and two anonymous authors who wrote what are known as the First Continuation and the Second Continuation. The Second Continuation was formerly attributed to Wauchier de Denain, but modern scholars no longer make this association and consider the work to be anonymous. It should be mentioned that these "continuations" often differ significantly from Chrétien's original, and thus they are not always literal and exact continuations of his own concept, but rather different versions of the tale in their own rights.

Robert de Boron's *Joseph d'Arimathie*, completed about 1200, is best known for developing the version of the story that relates how the Grail as a Christian relic originally came to Britain. Robert was a Burgundian knight for whom the Grail was the chalice that Christ used for the Eucharist at the Last Supper. The Grail is not a Christian relic in Chrétien. It is a large dish that emits a brilliant light, but it has no specific Christian connotations except that it bears a wafer. After Robert's poem, the Grail became a Christian relic with most, but not all, of the Grail authors. Also relating the story of Joseph of Arimathea is a poem from the second half of the thirteenth century, *Sone de Nansai*.

Although Wolfram von Eschenbach's *Parzival* was Wagner's main source for *Parsifal*, Wagner adopted Robert's view of the Grail as his own. In Wolfram, the Grail is not a Christian relic. It is a magic stone with both Christian and Arabic properties, which include providing food, drink, eternal youth, and spiritu-

al wisdom and direction for the knights who possess it. Wagner
had written to Mathilde in the same letter mentioned above:

> The Grail, according to my *own* interpretation is the goblet used
> at the Last Supper in which Joseph of Arimathea caught the Sav-
> iour's blood on the Cross. What terrible significance the connec-
> tion between Anfortas and this miraculous chalice now acquires;
> *he*, infected by the same wound as was dealt him by a rival's spear
> in a passionate love intrigue,—his only solace lies in the bene-
> diction of the blood that once flowed from the Saviour's own,
> similar, spear-wound as He languished on the Cross, world-re-
> nouncing, world-redeeming and world-suffering![3]

This is part of Wagner's seamless integration of sources and
influences: no one work alone provided Wagner with all his material.

There are a number of anonymous French versions that are not
continuations of Chrétien and with which Wagner was familiar.
The most famous is a huge five-part work by different authors
called the Vulgate Cycle. It was composed perhaps between 1225
and 1240, although the dates of 1215–1235 are also given. The first
part of this cycle is the *Estoire del Saint Graal* (History of the Holy
Grail), though this part may have been written last. Based largely
on Robert's tale, it expands the history of the Grail and how it
came to Britain. The second part, known as the Prose *Merlin*,
does not concern a Grail hero, but the third and fourth parts
do, the Prose *Lancelot* and the *Queste del Saint Graal* (Quest of
the Holy Grail). The *Queste* is believed to have been written by
a cloistered Cistercian monk, though we do not know his name.
The fifth part, *La Mort Artu*, concerns the death of Arthur. The
remaining anonymous French versions are the *Didot Perceval*,
Grand Saint Graal, and *Perlesvaus, le Haut Livre du Graal* (the
High Book of the Grail), "book" here meaning "history" or "account." *Perlesvaus* was probably completed by 1210.

The most famous of the German versions is Wolfram's *Parzival*, but there are also Heinrich von dem Türlin's *Diû Crône*

(Jeweled Crown), c. 1220, and Wolfram's *Titurel*. *Parzival* was written possibly between 1198 and 1212, though some scholars estimate 1200–1210.

The anonymous Welsh *Mabinogion* contains among its eleven tales the story of Peredur, the Welsh name equivalent to Perceval. Although the earliest complete manuscript of the collected tales that we have, the White Book of Rhydderch, dates from about 1325, the stories are certainly much older and often find their own origins in the old Irish legends and tales of heroes and gods. *Mabinogion* scholars believe that the individual stories were committed to writing as early as 1100, but no manuscripts from that period have survived. The earliest fragment of a *Mabinogion* story that we have dates to 1225.

The English version of the Grail legend best known to Americans comes from Sir Thomas Malory's *Le Morte d'Arthur*, which he completed probably in 1470, not long before he died. This was edited and published by William Caxton in 1485, the year that Richard III was defeated at Bosworth Field. This battle marked the end of the War of Roses and inaugurated the Tudor dynasty. Malory took a great deal of the material for his work from the Vulgate Cycle, and the part of his book which deals with the Grail story is taken primarily from the *Queste del Saint Graal* and thus is considered more a retelling (or even a translation) of the thirteenth-century tale than a work that introduces any important new material on its own. His accomplishment as a writer, however, is still highly respected by scholars, and some of his passages concerning the quest of the Grail are among the most beautiful in Arthurian literature.

If we want to put the years 1180–1240 into brief historical context, we would find the figures of Henry II, Eleanor of Aquitaine, Richard the Lion-Hearted, King John, Robin Hood, Saladin, and Philip Augustus of France; the construction of Notre Dame Cathedral in Paris; and five Crusades, including the Albigensian Crusade against the Cathars in southern France. It was a time of great artistic creativity and social and political change, and through the Crusades it was also a time of an extensive exchange of ideas between East and West.

The word "grail" comes from the Old French *graal* (dish). Scholars find the root of this word in the Latin *gradatim* (degrees). A *gradale* was a dish used to serve delicacies to the nobility "in degrees," that is, one after another. From *gradale* came *graal*, with the variations *greal* or *greel*. The "Holy Grail" became the San Greal. A later etymology suggested *sang real*, which means "royal blood" or "kingly blood," but the original idea of the Grail itself was a dish used to serve food. Whether the Grail was described as a dish, platter, cauldron, magic stone, or chalice (depending on the version of the story), it had the power to provide bountiful food to its guests and long life to those who beheld it. It also possessed the ability to heal the wound of the Grail King when its quest was achieved by the worthy redeemer.

In order to appreciate and understand the fundamental symbols in these stories, which exhibit a consistent inner similarity despite their outward variations, it is necessary to understand the tradition of sacred kingship and the relationship of this tradition to the ancient fertility rites and to the later Mystery initiations and rituals. What we will find is that the Grail legends as we have them now retain a memory of both the old fertility rites and the secret Mystery ceremonies. We will also find that Wagner incorporated various aspects of all these traditions into the *Ring* and *Parsifal*.

In 1890 Sir James Frazer published the first edition of his landmark work *The Golden Bough*. This book has remained the definitive work on the subject of sacred kingship, but Frazer was far from being the first European to understand, or have knowledge of, this tradition. Wagner was fully aware of it, as was Wolfram. Nevertheless, Frazer's work had an enormous influence on the scholarship of his day.

Frazer began his study when he pondered a particular ancient ritual that had taken place in the sacred grove of Diana near the village of Nemi in Italy. A runaway slave, carrying a bough of a sacred tree (the Golden Bough), challenged a man to a fight to the death in the sacred grove. After vanquishing his opponent, the former slave remained in the grove and became its guardian, reigning as King of the Wood until a stronger man could, in turn, slay him. Frazer posed the question, "Why did this take place, and what did it mean?" His quest for the answer took him to the examination of cultures, both ancient and modern, all over the world. *The Golden Bough* was the result of that examination.

The core of what he found was the tradition of sacred kingship and its relation to the fertility rituals and beliefs of ancient cultures. He found that this tradition existed, in one form or another, in all areas of the world, in all cultures, in all times of history, even up to modern times. He found this tradition in both "primitive" cultures as well as in "civilized" ones. And it is this tradition that forms the initial basis for the stories of the Grail.

In the last chapter we saw that the Dionysian fertility rites had both a practical and a spiritual purpose. The practical purpose concerned the welfare of the land and the crops, and the spiritual purpose represented the mystical merging of the individual with the universal. Death and resurrection had both an agricultural and a spiritual symbolism. The tradition of sacred kingship had a similar dual purpose, the welfare of the land and crops and the integration of the society with the divine.

The sacred king took a number of forms. He could be the actual hereditary king of the tribe, nation, or empire, in which case he was considered both human and divine together. In ancient China, for example, the emperor was the Son of Heaven, the link between heaven and earth, and between society and God. Ancient Chinese society was seen as a pyramid with the emperor at the top, touching both earth and heaven.

The sacred king could also be a person who had not inherited his title, but who had been chosen for the role by the community. This person, like the divine hereditary king, was considered to be the embodiment of the spirit of fertility, the human incarnation of the fertility god and the god of vegetation, and the one responsible for the spiritual and agricultural welfare of the land.

Thirdly, the sacred king could be a man who won the right to be king by defeating and killing the current king. And fourthly, the sacred king as fertility spirit could be an actual god.

The sacred king's own personal welfare and reproductive ability were linked to the welfare and productivity of the land and community, whatever form that community might assume, large or small. It was believed that if the sacred king became sick or feeble, the society would likewise lose its vitality, and if the sacred king lost his reproductive ability, the land also would cease to be fertile. Thus great pains were taken to ensure the protection and health of the king. Our word "taboo," for example, is related to a Tongan word, *tabu*, which means forbidden. It was *tabu* for the sacred king of the tribe to do certain things, in the interest of his protection from harm, and in the interest of not upsetting the very delicate balance between heaven and earth that the sacred king was believed to hold and control. We can see this idea extending from African tribal customs to the emperor of old Japan, the Mikado. The Mikado was not allowed to touch the ground, be exposed to the sun, be touched by anyone except his wife or doctor, and so on. We can see remnants of this tradition even into the twentieth century with the last emperor of China. We can also see this tradition in the European "divine right of kings," where the kings were considered to rule by divine decree and used the term "we" when speaking about themselves because God was a part of their divine rule. Frazer found this tradition, in one form or another, in every part of the world.

Even though each society took great care to protect its sacred king from harm, the eventual old age and death of the human man was inevitable. Thus each society needed a way to ensure that its sacred king was always healthy and vigorous. One way, mentioned above, was to have the king reign until a stronger successor was able to kill and replace him. Thus the society was always assured of having the strongest man as its king.

Another common way was to limit the time span that a king could reign. This could be a fixed number of years, or until the king began to show signs of aging or weakening. A common fixed time span was one year, but seven years, nine years, and twelve years were also known. At the end of this time span the king was ritually put to death, and it was believed that through this ritual death the soul and powers of the former king were transferred to his successor before they could diminish in their capacity. In this way the fertility of the land and the spiritual vitality of the society were assured.

It was believed that if serious harm or death came to the sacred king before the spirit of fertility was transferred, the society would experience catastrophe in the form of bad crops, drought, the animals dying or being unable to reproduce, and the women of the society becoming unable to bear children. This event became known as the Waste Land. It was both an agricultural and a spiritual disaster. Both land and spirit were barren. And in the majority of the Grail legends it is precisely this catastrophe, the Waste Land, that we encounter. The Grail King is grievously wounded, and his kingdom lies in waste. It is the task of the questing knight to heal the wound of the Grail King and restore his land to fecundity.

At this point it is necessary to examine the nature of the wound the Grail King suffers. In most versions of the story the wound is referred to by a euphemism, "pierced through the thigh[s]." In *Parzival* it is referred to explicitly:

> One day the king rode out alone—and sorely did his people rue it—in search of adventure, rejoicing in Love's assistance. Love's desire compelled him to it. With a poisoned spear he was wounded so in the jousting, your sweet uncle, that he never again was healed, pierced through the testicles.[4]

The wounded Grail King is castrated. When we hear of the Maimed King, he is a castrated king. He is a sacred king who has lost his powers of reproduction, and as a result his kingdom is a Waste Land. There are many references in the various Grail stories and in mythology in general to a man "pierced through the thigh[s]." Whenever this reference appears, it signifies that the man is castrated.

Castration of the sacred king was more than just a symbol of agricultural and spiritual barrenness. Sometimes it was literal. As mentioned above, when the term of the sacred king's reign was over, the king was ritually killed. As time went on, some societies (and kings in power) changed the custom, allowing various mitigations. One change was to castrate and/or revile the old king rather than killing him. In the ritual castration it was believed that the power of fertility was thus transferred from the old king to the new.

Another mitigation was to offer a substitute sacrifice. Rather than killing the actual king, another man was killed instead. It could be a condemned criminal, a slave, or any other person, who then represented the dying god. As Frazer says, "We must not forget that the king is slain in his character of a god, his death and resurrection, as the only means of perpetuating the divine life unimpaired, being deemed necessary for the salvation of his people and the world."[5]

The final stage of the mitigation was to kill an effigy of the god or king, not to harm an actual person. The effigy could be burned, drowned, reviled, or dismembered, in ceremonies and festivals that Frazer found continuing into his own time.

When the spirit of fertility was seen to abide in a specific god, the fertility rites of the society sought to invoke and supplicate that god in order to ensure continued agricultural prosperity. We have already talked about Dionysus in this context, but there were many other gods in various cultures. I will use Adonis and his Phrygian counterpart Attis as examples, for there is a poignant aspect of the Adonis/Attis myth that relates to the Grail legends and Wagner's Siegfried. Adonis was a beautiful youth beloved of Aphrodite. He was wounded in the thigh by a wild boar and died of his wound. In her grief Aphrodite supplicated Zeus for a boon, which was granted. Adonis was allowed to spend half of each year with Aphrodite among the Olympians, but the other half he had to spend in the underworld with Persephone. In the version of the story concerning Attis, rather than being wounded in the thigh by a boar, Attis castrates himself and bleeds to death from the wound beneath a pine tree. Here we have the basis for the relationship between castration and its euphemism, being pierced through the thigh or thighs.

Adonis represented the spirit of life and fertility, and his wound in the thigh by the boar represented castration, that is, the suspension of his reproductive powers, and thus the suspension of the reproductive fertility of the land. He is allowed to leave the underworld for half the year; the other half he spends beneath the earth. Just as the seed spends part of the year in the ground, so does Adonis spend part of the year in the underworld. And just as the seeds sprout and push up from the earth to become bountiful crops, so does Adonis rise from the underworld to spend part of the year on Olympus with Aphrodite and the other gods. There is also the symbolism of winter and summer, where Adonis's loss of reproductive power represents the land in winter, while his resurrection from the underworld represents the fecundity of the land in spring and summer. In the Greek rites of Adonis his death was ritually mourned and his return to life celebrated—another variation of the death and resurrection of the god.

We see a relationship between the god of life and fertility to the human sacred king both in the aspect of castration and the presence of the wild boar. The boar appears in various myths, and being wounded by the boar, especially when the wound is specified as being in the thigh, constitutes castration. Hagen tells Gutrune that Siegfried was killed by a boar, and even though we know that it was Hagen who killed Siegfried and that Siegfried was not literally castrated, the old mythological reference still finds its way into Wagner's version of the story. (We will also see Siegfried as sacred king in chapter 6 when we discuss his scene with Wotan as the Wanderer in Act III, Scene 2 of *Siegfried*.)

Castration was not the only way to pass the reproductive power of one king to another. Sometimes the wounds to the old king entailed putting out one of his eyes, smashing his front teeth, parading him in a cart through the streets while the people of the community reviled him, strapping him to the underside of a horse and again parading him in front of the people, and so on. We find references to sacred kingship throughout the various Arthurian stories, though in most cases the authors do not know what they are dealing with. This is why many of the events in these stories seem inexplicable. The old myths contained the actual ceremonies and rites of the sacred kingship practices. In the process of time these myths became the basis for the medieval romances, but the authors (except for Wolfram) no longer understood all aspects of the stories. Thus, for example, we have Malory telling the story of Lancelot in the cart, and Sir Lionel strapped under a horse and being beaten. Often knights are guarding sacred trees or lakes or fords, and they fight anyone who passes. If the traveler wins, he becomes the new guardian of the sacred site. These stories make no sense in the context of medieval knighthood, but they do make sense in the context of the old practices of sacred kingship. It is not uncommon in Malory and other authors to have one knight say to another, "Return here in one year's time and we will fight." Here again we see a remnant of the old practice, where one year was the length of a sacred king's reign. The idea that the old myths contained the actual ceremonies and rites of the ancient fertility and nature practices will be very important when we get to the explanation and interpretation of the Grail stories themselves.

The Fisher King

In almost all of the Grail stories there are two main characters, the questing knight and the Grail King, also known as the Grail Guardian. The knight is always from King Arthur's court, but the Grail King can be known by any one of three titles: the Fisher King, the Rich Fisher, or the Maimed King. (Very occasionally the term "Lame King" is used.) The Maimed King refers to a king who is castrated, usually confined to a litter, and in constant agony from his wound, which will neither heal nor bring death. The Maimed King must wait for the appointed redeemer for the healing of his wound. The redeemer is the one who successfully achieves the quest of the Grail.

Sometimes in the Grail stories the term "Grail King" refers to the very old father of the Fisher King, the father being kept alive at a great age by the power of the Grail. (Titurel is an example of this.) The father has transferred the authority and responsibility of guarding the Grail to his son, the Fisher King, and both reside at the Grail Castle. For the sake of simplicity and clarity I will not worry about this distinction in our discussions, and thus the terms Grail King, Grail Guardian, Fisher King, Rich Fisher, and Maimed King all refer to the same personage: the one who is in charge of guarding the Grail at the present and who is wounded and waiting for the redeemer to heal him.

In light of the tradition of sacred kingship that I have been examining, it is easy to see why the Grail King is called the Maimed King. He is a sacred king who has lost his reproductive and regenerative powers, and whose land (in most versions of the story) lies in ruin as a result. His country has become a Waste Land, both agriculturally and spiritually. What, then, are the origins of the terms Fisher King and Rich Fisher? Why is a Grail Guardian termed a Fisher?

The fish and the dragon, or serpent, are both symbols of life that can be found all over the world. I will discuss the dragon shortly, but for now I will look at the tradition of the fish as a symbol for food and prosperity.

I mentioned at the beginning of this chapter that some scholars posit a pre-Celtic origin for the Grail legends, some a Celtic origin, and some a Christian one. The best-known purveyor of the pre-Celtic view is Jessie Weston, who published her groundbreaking book *From Ritual to Romance* in 1920. Like Frazer before her and Campbell after her, Weston researched traditions in many different cultures and found a fundamental unity of practice and belief, of ritual and myth. In her chapter on the Fisher King she writes:

> In my opinion the key to the puzzle is to be found in the rightful understanding of the *Fish-Fisher* symbolism. Students of the

Grail literature have been too prone to treat the question on the
Christian basis alone, oblivious of the fact that Christianity did
no more than take over, and adapt to its own use, a symbolism
already endowed with a deeply rooted prestige and importance.

. . . So far as the present state of our knowledge goes we can affirm with certainty that the Fish is a Life symbol of immemorial
antiquity, and that the title of Fisher has, from the earliest ages,
been associated with Deities who were held to be specially connected with the origin and preservation of Life.

In Indian cosmogony Manu finds a little fish in the water in
which he would wash his hands; it asks, and receives, his protection, asserting that when grown to full size it will save Manu
from the universal deluge. This is Jhasa, the greatest of all fish.[6]

The symbol of the fish is also primary in Celtic mythology.
In Celtic myth there are four "divine" animals, that is, animals
whose appearance signals a meeting with the land of fairy, or the
land hidden behind the mists. Symbolically this is the land of
inner spiritual quest, one withdrawn from the outer world of the
senses and worldly attachment. These four animals are a hart, a
boar, a hare, and a salmon. When a traveler in a forest sees or
comes upon one of these creatures, it means he is about to have
an experience with the invisible world. Just as Jhasa spoke to
Manu, so do the salmon found in Celtic adventures often speak
to the humans who encounter them.

One of the most famous of the Irish heroes, and the prototype
for King Arthur (his Fianna being the prototype of the Knights
of the Round Table) is Finn Mac Cumhail. One of the stories
concerning the young Finn is his service to an old man, Finn
Eger, who has been sitting by the Boyne River for seven years
watching for the Salmon of Lynn Feic. It has been foretold that
Finn Mac Cumhail would be the one to catch the fish, and indeed the young Finn does. He is charged with watching the fish
while it roasts over a fire but is told he must not eat it. While it is
cooking he reaches out his hand and touches it, and in doing so
burns his thumb. He quickly puts his thumb in his mouth to cool

the pain and immediately becomes possessed of all knowledge. (Compare this with Siegfried tasting the dragon's blood and being able to understand the voice of the forest bird. Drawing his sword from the dead Fafner, he smears blood on his hand. He quickly draws his hand away, exclaiming, "Like fire burns the blood!" He puts his fingers in his mouth to suck the blood from them and finds that he can comprehend the voices of nature.)

One of the best-known of the Grail scholars who favor a Celtic origin of the legends is Roger Sherman Loomis. Loomis contends that the Grail itself is based on what is often called the Celtic "cauldron of plenty," and that the immediate prototype of the Fisher King is Brân the Blessed, from the *Mabinogion* story "Branwen Daughter of Llyr." Brân originally was the son of the old Celtic sea god Lir (or Llyr, later to become Lear), and is often associated with the more recent Celtic sea god Manannan Mac Lir, after whom the Isle of Man is named. (Mac Lir means "son of Lir.") In the *Mabinogion* story, Brân is a mystical king of the Britons, part god and part human, who possesses a magic cauldron that can bring the dead back to life.

Branwen is Brân's sister, said to be the most beautiful maiden in the land. Brân makes an alliance with the king of Ireland, giving him Branwen in marriage and the magic cauldron as a gift. But when the Irish neglect the alliance, Brân raises an army and invades Ireland. In the ensuing battle the cauldron is destroyed, and Brân is wounded in the foot by a poisoned spear. (Compare the wound of Achilles in the *Iliad*.) In one legend the bard Talyessin relates that he was with Brân that day and that the wound to Brân was in the thigh, which again would equate with a castrated sacred king. In the story itself there is a character named "Pierced Thighs," who is not described but who could be Brân himself. The battle between the Irish and the Britons causes both kingdoms to become waste. The Irish are all killed, and only the wounded Brân and seven of his men survive. (One of the seven is Brân's nephew Pyrderi, a probable variation on Peredur. Another of the seven is Talyessin.) Branwen dies of a broken heart when she realizes that two kingdoms have been destroyed because of her. Brân commands his men to cut off his head, which they do. The head remains preserved in a charmed state of animation for seven years, while his seven surviving men reside with it in Harlech. After seven years have passed they set out for Gwales (Grassholm), where they spend eighty years in an enchanted castle, experiencing agelessness and joy. When one of the seven breaks the enchantment they all have to leave. They take the head to London, where it is buried in the White Hill facing across the channel toward France, standing guard for Britain against all dangers.[7]

Although there is no direct mention of Brân as a Fisher King in this story, we have his ancestry as a sea god, and Loomis and others see Brân as the prototype of Chrétien's specifically named Fisher King.

It is certainly true that fish symbolism occurs in Christianity as well as in the ancient pagan traditions. Jesus calls both Peter and Andrew to him with the words, "Follow me, and I will make you fishers of men."[8] The fish itself is often used as a symbol of Christ: the acronym *ichthus* comes from the Greek prayer "*Iesous CHristos Theou HUios Soter*" (Jesus Christ, Son of God the Savior). *Ichthus* (ἰχθύς) is the Ancient Greek word for fish. The Buddha also is thought of as a "rich fisher" because he helps rescue people from the ocean of Samsara and shows them the way to salvation by crossing over to the other shore.

There are many other examples that can be given, but the important point is that the fish, like the Grail itself, was a symbol of both physical and spiritual food, a symbol of plenty providing abundant life, and a symbol of material and spiritual regeneration. And thus it is logical for the Grail Guardian to be referred to as a Fisher King, just as he is also called the Grail King.

This brings us now to the symbol of the dragon.

One of the most vivid and common images in Western myth and religion is that of the knight killing the dragon. Many children grow up knowing the story of St. George, and we all hear the fairy tales where the maiden is chained to a rock by the sea as a sacrifice to the giant sea monster whom the warrior-hero must slay in order to rescue the maiden. From India to England, from Indra to Hercules to Beowulf to Siegfried, the greatest exploit of the hero is dragon slaying. I will discuss Siegfried and Fafner at length in chapter 6, but right now I will look at the myth in general and at its origin as it relates to the symbolism of the Grail legends.

Many interpretations of the knight, or hero, killing the dragon have been offered. Religiously, dragons, and monsters in general, can represent the guardians of the higher stages of understanding. Before the initiate, or seeker, can progress to the next level of experience and awareness, he must pass through the portals and their guardians. No one who is afraid or not ready can be allowed to pass. Thus, the slaying of the monsters in this context represents overcoming the fear of spiritual quest. This is one of the purposes of the gargoyles on great cathedrals. They represent the guardians of the inner chambers, the inner sanctums. Only those who have conquered fear can truly enter into the divine presence.

Psychologically, it has been said that for the boy passing into manhood, the dragon represents the fear of the feminine, and this fear must be slain before the woman can be won. The slaying of the dragon thus becomes not just the overcoming of the fear of the feminine and the readiness for marriage, but also the passage from boyhood to manhood and the readiness to take on the responsibilities of adult life.

In those early religions of the Near East and Europe where God, or the Eternal, was often represented in female form as the Great Mother, a common icon was of the Tree of Life accompanied by a woman and a serpent. Both woman and serpent were symbols of life, as the woman gave birth and the serpent shed its skin, emerging anew, reborn, like the phoenix. When first Judaism, and later Christianity, attempted to assert the male image of God over the female image, the serpent became the symbol of the Devil, and the woman the bearer of original sin. In this context, the knight killing the dragon became the symbol of Christ's victory over Satan.

While these and other interpretations can be valid, they do not point to the original symbolism. It is that original symbolism which will provide the starting point from which I will begin my step-by-step construction of the meaning of the Grail legends. For it was the original slaying of the cosmic dragon Vritra by the great warrior god Indra that released the waters upon the world and freed it from the Waste Land.

The Tavatimsa Heaven

In order to have a full understanding of the mythologies of India and Europe and the influence they had on the *Ring* and the Grail legends as I will be interpreting them, it is helpful to understand the Buddhist view of the various heaven worlds, because this will give us a context for much of what happens in the *Ring* specifically and in mythology in general. It should be pointed out that the Buddha himself did not expound any particular cosmology, and a belief in any such cosmology is not necessary for the practice of Buddhism. However, Buddhism does teach that there are various realms of existence besides this one here on earth.

In Buddhism there is no such concept as an eternal heaven as opposed to an eternal hell. While Buddhism does enumerate many worlds into which our karma can be born, all these worlds are impermanent. Only Nirvana is permanent, and as we have seen before, Nirvana is beyond all rebirth and is entered when all karma is cleansed. Thus, by definition, any world into which karma is born in order to *be* cleansed is impermanent. This goes for the hell worlds as well as for the heaven worlds.

Buddhism teaches the existence of six *lokas*, or places of karmic rebirth. In Sanskrit *loka* means "place." It is related to the Latin word *locus* and our word "location." The six *lokas* are the human realm; the animal realm; the realm of *pretas*, or hungry ghosts; the heaven realms; the realm of the Asuras; and the hell realms. The hell realms are worlds of great suffering, and a life in one of these worlds may last for a very long time, but Buddhism teaches that when the karma that led to a birth in one of these realms is finally burned or exhausted, the next rebirth will be out of the hell realm and into whichever other world is necessary for the further cleansing of karma. Thus in Buddhism there is no such thing as eternal damnation.

As far as the heaven worlds are concerned, Buddhism teaches that they begin with the six heavens in the realm of desire. The Devas, or heavenly beings, who reside in these six realms are sometimes referred to as "desire gods." Beings in these spheres are still subject to sexual desire, greed for wealth and fame, and so on. Because these desires are often satisfied, these realms are considered heaven realms, but there is suffering too, as no impermanent realm is free from suffering. The Devas are mortal, even if their lives last a long time by earthly standards, and thus they may seem "immortal." It is often said in Buddhist and Hindu references that a hundred years of earth time are but one day in the life of a Deva. In spite of this, their lives in the heaven realms are finite, and it is said that there is great suffering at the death of a god.

These six heaven realms, where the Devas are born as male and female, are the lowest of the heaven worlds. Above them are the high meditation realms, the *rupalokas*, or realms of form, and above those the *arupalokas*, or formless realms. In these worlds there is no sexual desire, and thus beings in these worlds are born without distinction of sex. Rebirth in these realms is only for those who on earth, or in some other realm, cleansed the karma of sensual desire and who attained through assiduous training the ability to meditate at a very deep level. There are sixteen planes in the *rupalokas* and four planes in the *arupalokas*. Each plane corresponds to the level of meditation one learned to cultivate in one's previous birth. In the *arupalokas* mind exists alone, without matter. The beings born in these meditation heavens work out there whatever very subtle karma is left to cleanse and then from these abodes enter Nirvana.[9]

In this discussion of mythology, the planes I am concerned with are the six heavens of the realm of desire. Rebirth in these realms is for those who have cultivated various excellent merits, but unlike the meditation heavens, rebirth into the desire realms is not necessarily from high spiritual attainment (though it can be). Narada Thera says of these planes:

> The last six are the realms of the Devas whose physical forms are more subtle and refined than those of human beings and are imperceptible to the naked eye. These celestial beings too are subject to death as all mortals are. In some respects, such as their constitution, habitat, and food they excel humans, but do not as a rule transcend them in wisdom. They have spontaneous births, appearing like youths and maidens of fifteen or sixteen years of age.[10]

The first of these heavens is called Catummaharajika in Pali. It is the world of either terrestrial spirits or low celestial beings, invisible to the human eye, but whose presence can often be felt or detected. These spirits are often considered to be the guardian deities of various places on earth and are often worshipped in animistic and polytheistic religions.

The second is the Tavatimsa heaven, meaning literally "thirty-three." This realm consists of eight celestial heavens in each of the four quarters, north, south, east, and west, with one heaven in the center that is the abode of the king of the gods. This king is known as Shakra in Buddhism, Indra in Hinduism, Zeus in Greek mythology, and Odin in Teutonic mythology. Odin is, of course, Wagner's Wotan.

It is the Tavatimsa heaven that corresponds to the Olympian world of the Greek gods, and Asgard of the Teutonic gods. Mount Sumeru, the abode of Indra, is Mount Olympus. Indra wields the great lightning-bolt weapon *vajrayudha*, just as Zeus and Odin hurl their lightning bolts and the Celtic sun god Lug wields his "flaming spear." What are known as Titans in Greek mythology, Giants in Teutonic mythology, and Fomorian Giants in Celtic mythology are known as Asuras in Hinduism and Buddhism. The Asuras are the enemies of the Indian gods, just as the Giants and Titans are the enemies of the European gods. In fact, even in the Indian myths the Asuras are sometimes referred to as both titans and giants. In Buddhism, the Asuras are considered to be beings who occupy a lower region than the gods, and who in the excess of pride are jealous of the position and wealth of the gods. They try to storm heaven and take it by force rather than earn rebirth there through generating proper merit. Thus the Asuras are the ones who make war on the gods, and, especially in the Hindu myths, it is one of Indra's duties as king of the gods to lead the fight against the Asuras.

There is an interesting reference in legend to the number thirty-three and King Arthur. Manly P. Hall, in his book *Orders of the Quest: The Holy Grail*, mentions that in what he calls the "old records," the original Round Table had thirty-two seats around the table, including Arthur's seat and the Siege Perilous. In the middle of the table was a place for the Grail itself, and thus there were thirty-three places. Hall goes on to relate this to the thirty-three degrees of Freemasonry, where thirty-two degrees are earned and the thirty-third is bestowed by grace.

The third heaven is called Yama, "that which destroys pain."

The fourth is the Tushita heaven. This is an important realm in Buddhism, for it is the heaven in which the Buddha-to-be resided before he was born on earth to become the Buddha Shakyamuni. Buddhism teaches that Bodhisattvas who are poised to become Buddhas reside in this realm until the time is right for their birth on earth where they will attain Buddhahood. Maitreya, the coming Buddha, is said to be residing in the Tushita heaven at this moment. This is also the heaven where the Buddha's mother, Maha Maya, was reborn following her death on earth.

The fifth heaven is called Nimmanarati and is the world of heavenly mansions.

The sixth and final heaven in the realm of desire is called Paranimmitavasavatti, "the Realm of the Devas who make others' creation serve their own ends."[11] This can be described in another way as the heaven where one enjoys the fruits of the labor of others.

It is the Tavatimsa heaven that I will most often be talking about in reference to the various myths of our discussion, but we should remember the others as well when we encounter passages describing otherworldly encounters, mansions, and paradises.

With this in mind we can now begin our construction, from the ground up, of an interpretation of the Grail legends that will lay the groundwork for our examination of the *Ring* and *Parsifal*.

The World of the Grail

Not only do scholars pose three different origins for the Grail legends (pre-Celtic, Celtic, and Christian), but the stories themselves differ in many ways, and even the actual Grail itself is described variously as being a dish, platter, cauldron, magic stone, or chalice, or is even left undescribed. The 1982 book *Holy Blood, Holy Grail* suggested that Jesus was married to Mary Magdalene, who was pregnant at the time of the Crucifixion. After this she was taken by Joseph of Arimathea to France, and thus the Grail in this light was not an external vessel of any kind, but the actual womb of the Magdalene, which indeed contained the Sang Real, or Kingly Blood: the child of Christ. With all these variations, we can see that there is no definitive object that can be proven to have been the Grail, and because the written accounts we have are versions of earlier, orally transmitted tales, there is no definitive version of the story that we can say for sure was the original. Therefore, where do we begin?

We begin first by concentrating not on the differences between the various versions of the stories, but on the similarities. Can we paint a general picture of the Grail legends? Do certain themes run consistently throughout the stories? Are the themes and symbols there consistent enough for us to construct a basic model? The answer is yes.

A questing knight, riding from King Arthur's court, is directed to or comes upon an enchanted castle, one that cannot be seen or reached by ordinary people. This castle, though appearing in the world, is not of this world, but of a world beyond. Within this castle are housed sacred objects, which in the later versions become Christian relics: the Grail, a spear, and often a sword and a cup as well. In some versions the sword is broken, and part of the hero's task is to mend it. The king of this castle and of the lands around it is the Guardian of the Grail, and the welfare of the land and the protection of the Grail are in his charge. This king is maimed, castrated, and confined to a litter (or, in some versions, dead and lying on a litter). His lands are desolate, his kingdom a Waste Land. The cause of the Waste Land is usually (but not always) a "Dolorous Stroke," an actual act, with either a spear or sword, that maims the king and sends his land into barrenness. The questing knight spends the night in the castle and witnesses many marvels. He sees people there who, he is told, are of great age, but who seem either to be youthful or no more than forty. He is the invited guest of the Grail King, and he participates in a great feast and is allowed to see the procession of the Grail. Many tables are prepared for a large number of guests, and when all are seated the procession of the Grail begins. Maidens enter bringing candles, tablecloths, and golden and jeweled goblets. When all is ready, a special maiden or queen brings in the Grail itself, and as it is borne through the room, all at the feast are supplied with limitless food and drink, each guest receiving the food he or she most desires. Even though the food is served by squires and servants, the source of this bounty is the Grail, regardless of which particular form—dish, platter, chalice, or stone—it may take. As a part of this procession a squire enters bearing a bleeding spear that drips blood from its tip. All of this is witnessed by the questing knight. It is incumbent upon this knight to perform the needed act of redemption, an act that will both heal the wounded king and restore his land to fertility. In some versions this act entails asking the proper question about the Grail and the Spear. In other versions this act is a particular deed, such as Galahad touching his fingers to the blood of the Spear and anointing the legs and body of the king. In some versions the knight succeeds, in some he only partially succeeds, in others he fails. In the versions where he fails, he sleeps in the castle after the banquet is over and wakes the next day to find the castle empty; he leaves the castle, only later to find out that he has failed. He then vows to find the Grail King again in order to perform the needed task, but the castle has disappeared, and he wanders for many years trying to find it once more so that he may heal the king and the land and win back his own honor. When the knight does succeed, he either remains at the castle to become the new Grail King or, as in the case of Malory's Galahad, becomes the Grail Guardian for one year in the holy city of Sarras, after which he is then taken up into heaven with a supreme vision of the deepest secrets of the Grail.

We certainly see here a number of references to the old practice of sacred kingship. We see the idea of the king's health tied to that of his land, the wasting of the land when the king has lost his reproductive powers, the succession of the old sacred king by the new one, and even the exact limit of a sacred king's reign (Galahad's period of one year in the city of Sarras). In addition to these, we see other symbols and events that cannot have been of Christian origin. Remembering that the years in the West of 1180 to 1240 were years where the religious authority of the time was the medieval Roman Catholic Church, it would not have been possible for the main participants in a Christian religious ceremony to have been women, but this is the case in the Grail stories. The Grail Bearer is almost always a woman, as are many of the others who prepare for the feast, though squires also help with the preparations. The main objects are the Grail and the Spear, and although these came to be seen as the cup Jesus drank from at the Last Supper and the spear that Longinus used to pierce Jesus's side when he hung on the cross, in the earliest written version we have, that of Chrétien de Troyes, the Grail is not a chalice or a Christian relic, and there is no mention of Joseph of Arimathea. Besides, nowhere in Christian ceremony, liturgy, or art do the Cup and the Spear appear together as they do in the Grail ceremonies. The whole event takes place not in a church, but in a castle, a castle that is otherworldly. In addition, the symbolisms of castration and waste land are specifically pagan and have no place in Christian symbolism. And finally, the Catholic Church of the time declared the stories to be heretical. It has even been suggested that the reason for the relative lack of new versions of the stories after 1240 was due to Church suppression. It is true that a number of recent authors have proposed that the Grail stories contain an "underground code" supporting an apostolic succession that rivaled the Catholic Church of that time, which would have led the Church to repress them. (I will discuss this in the last section of the present chapter.) However, even if we acknowledge this possiblity, it is still the case that the basic elements of the Grail legends long pre-date Christianity.

It is therefore clear that even though the versions of the stories we are dealing with became "Christianized," Christianity itself cannot have supplied the original inspiration or symbols for the Grail legends themselves. The question then becomes, where do we look?

Roger Loomis, in his book *The Grail: From Celtic Myth to Christian Symbol*, does a very good job of showing how the stories evolved from the old Irish and Welsh legends into the tales as we have them now. However, he does not take into consideration the fact that the Celtic myths themselves are not *sui generis*, that is, Ireland and Wales did not produce these myths out of their own cultures exclusively. The symbols and events of the Celtic myths, as well as those of the Grail legends, can be found in the mythologies of both Europe and India, and from times far pre-dating the Celts. To give one very brief example, the story of Perceval-Parsifal being raised in a forest ignorant of the ways of the world finds its origin in the *Mahabharata* tale of Rishyaçringa, the young Brahmin raised by his father in an isolated forest hermitage, ignorant of the outside world and even of the existence of women. He spends his time in religious devotion. A drought has stricken a neighboring land, and its king learns that as long as Rishyaçringa remains chaste, the drought will continue. The king's daughter is sent, by way of a raft fitted in great luxury, down a river to bring Rishyaçringa to her father's kingdom. She waits until his father is absent, then lures him to the raft and from there takes him to her father's land, where the two are married. At the consumation of the marriage the drought is ended, and rain falls in abundance. Jessie Weston says of this part of the story: "The circumstances under which Rishyaçringa is lured from his Hermitage are curiously paralleled by the account, found in the *Queste* and Manessier, of Perceval's temptation by a fiend, in the form of a fair maiden, who comes to him by water in a vessel hung with black silk, and with great riches on board."[12]

Therefore we come back to our question: where do we look?

We know that we have part of the answer in Frazer's *The Golden Bough*—but only part of the answer, certainly not all of it. Sacred kingship alone will not give us an origin for the Grail stories. Since Celtic culture was Indo-European, we can begin by looking at those Indo-European myths that pre-dated the Celts.

The earliest written texts we have from any Indo-European civilization are the Vedas from India. These are a collection of religious hymns whose exact origin cannot be dated, but which comprise the earliest written scriptures we have from India. Chief of the Vedic gods was Indra, the giver of rain to the earth, the chariot-driving warrior king of the gods and wielder of the mighty *vajrayudha*, the thunder-lightning bolt. And his greatest deed, the source of his fame, was the slaying of the cosmic dragon Vritra.

The story of Indra and Vritra has two general versions, the first coming from the Rig Veda, and the second from the much later *Mahabharata*, the great epic poem from which comes the well-known *Bhagavad-Gita*. I will very briefly relate both tales, for both help to form the initial basis for the Grail legends.

According to the first version, Vritra had imprisoned the seven great rivers of India, hoarding the waters for himself, so that the earth became a waste land. Hurling his *vajrayudha*, Indra slew Vritra, thus releasing the imprisoned waters and replenishing the earth. Jessie Weston describes a passage from the Gerbert continuation where Perceval has been partially successful in his quest, having asked the proper question at the Grail Castle, but having been unable to mend a sacred broken sword. Having asked the question was enough to restore the fertility of the land:

Coming to a castle he is received by a solemn procession, with great rejoicing; through him the folk have regained the land and goods which they had lost. The mistress of the castle is more explicit. Perceval had asked concerning the Grail:

"All this was done by what he said,
This land whose streams no waters fed,
Its fountains dry, its fields unplowed,
His word once more with health endowed."

Like Gawain he has "freed the waters" and thus restored the land.[13]

Here we have an exact parallel between the effect of Indra's deed and that of Perceval. However, this is only the beginning.

The version of Indra's story related in the *Mahabharata* is more complex, and Indra is not the pure hero he is in the Vedas. Originally a heralded warrior god, esteemed for his feats of arms, Indra in the *Mahabharata* is portrayed as a god who errs from an excess of pride, one who is in need of contrition and repentance. In this second version of the story Indra is drunk with pride and refuses to rise and properly greet the Preceptor of the gods, Brihaspati. Brihaspati perceives Indra's arrogance and leaves the assembly of the gods. As a result their power begins to weaken, and the Asuras see their chance and attack. The other gods seek the advice of the great Brahma, who advises them to find and employ another Preceptor. They choose the young and highly respected ascetic Visvarupa, who agrees to become their teacher. The power of the gods returns, and the Asuras are repulsed.

But Visvarupa's mother was from the Asura clan, and for this reason Indra is suspicious of him and does not trust him. He tries to discredit Visvarupa by tempting him with women, but the young ascetic is not moved and holds to his vow of celibacy. Out of distrust Indra then kills Visvarupa, and this causes the lands to become barren. Here we have the prototype of the Dolorous Stroke, an act of violence that causes the lands to become waste.

The father of Visvarupa, Twashta, desires vengeance against
Indra, and out of sacrificial flames he creates the great Titan Vritra, who becomes Indra's mortal enemy. Vritra and Indra engage
in combat, and at first Vritra gains the upper hand. The gods
appeal to Vishnu, who enters the *vajrayudha* of Indra. Indra
engages Vritra on a beach by the ocean, and Indra dives into
Vritra's mouth and gullet and cuts his way out. He then flings
his *vajrayudha* into the ocean's foam, and through the power of
Vishnu the foam becomes a deadly weapon that gives the final
death blow to Vritra. With his death the lands are restored, but
Indra is ashamed of his actions and realizes the need for penance.
Only after the penance is properly completed is he returned to
his position as king of the gods.

Needless to say, the version of the story I have just told is ex-
tremely brief and condensed, but it is enough for us to perceive
the essential aspects of the story, which are important for our
discussion of the origin of the Grail legends. If we take both the
Rig Veda version of the tale and the *Mahabharata* version, we
see the elements of the Dolorous Stroke, the Waste Land, the
freeing of the waters, and the redemption of the land, along with
two important parallels to European mythology. First, we just
saw that in the fight Indra dove into the belly of Vritra and cut
his way out. Following is Joseph Campbell's narration of one of
the stories about Hercules:

> The Greek hero Herakles, pausing at Troy on his way homeward
> with the belt of the queen of the Amazons, found that the city
> was being harassed by a monster sent against it by the sea-god
> Poseidon. The beast would come ashore and devour people as
> they moved about on the plain. Beautiful Hesione, the daughter
> of the king, had just been bound by her father to the sea rocks
> as a propitiatory sacrifice, and the great visiting hero agreed to
> rescue her for a price. The monster, in due time, broke to the sur-
> face of the water and opened its enormous maw. Herakles took
> a dive into the throat, cut his way out through the belly, and left
> the monster dead.[14]

We have here an exact parallel to Indra's dive into the throat and belly of Vritra. The word *vritra*, by the way, means "cloud." On the agricultural level, then, the cloud has hoarded the waters, and Indra pierces it with his thunderbolt, thus releasing the rain on the world and giving it fertility. In India the serpent is also seen as a representation of a river, because a river winds through the landscape like a snake. Thus the dragon has a symbolic relationship to water and its fertilizing power.

On the spiritual level, the demon-dragon encircling the world and hoarding the waters, rendering the earth a waste land, represents the delusion of ignorance, maya, imprisoning the True Self, our own true spiritual self. The waste land is a spiritual waste land, barren of enlightenment. The hero, representing on the highest level both the Savior and the True Seeker, kills the dragon, thus freeing the True Self. The True Self is released from its imprisonment by delusion and comes forth into its true state of enlightenment. When the monster comes out of the sea, the True Self, or divinity, is represented by the beautiful and pure maiden. The hero slays the sea monster, thus freeing the divinity. We will see this aspect of the maiden representing the mind of enlightenment when we discuss Siegfried's awakening of Brünnhilde and the awakening of Kundry in chapter 6.

The second parallel of Vritra to European mythology concerns Vritra's form as both dragon and Titan. He is called variously dragon, Titan, and evil giant. We have therefore a prototypical reference to a giant taking the form of a dragon and guarding the treasure hoard. The treasure in this case is not Fafner's gold, but the waters themselves, certainly a treasure to an agrarian society. The hero who kills the guarding dragon thus frees the treasure for the use of the world. In this context the killing of the dragon is an act of compassion for the world, and an act of spiritual transformation for the seeker after enlightenment.

We have now established as part of our basis for the origin of the Grail legends the tradition of sacred kingship and the myth of Indra freeing the waters and thereby redeeming the barren land. The direction of the next step is to be found in the significance of the symbolism of diving into the maw of the monster. This symbolism is to be found in mythologies worldwide. Mishe-Nahma, King of Fishes, swallows the Algonquin hero Manabozho; Jonah is swallowed by the whale in the Old Testament; Finn Mac Cumhail is swallowed by a monster. Joseph Campbell has explained this symbolism:

> This popular motif gives emphasis to the lesson that the passage of the threshold is a form of self-annihilation. Its resemblance to the adventure of the Symplegades [the "Clashing Rocks" that Jason and the Argonauts had to pass through to enter the Hellespont] is obvious. But here, instead of passing outward, beyond the confines of the visible world, the hero goes inward, to be born again. The disappearance corresponds to the passing of a worshiper into a temple—where he is to be quickened by the recollection of who and what he is, namely dust and ashes unless immortal. The temple interior, the belly of the whale, and the heavenly land beyond, above, and below the confines of the world, are one and the same.[15]

This leads us to our next step. Fertility symbols and rituals are part of the Grail origins, but there is a whole other world to these legends, namely, the secret and the mystical. In the above quotation Campbell mentions that the worshiper passes into a temple, there to undergo a transformative experience. This is precisely what we have in the Grail stories. The questing knight passes the threshold from this world into a world beyond, to be initiated into secret mysteries, and to be granted a mystical vision denied those who are not willing to follow this quest, the path of spiritual realization. The Grail Castle is the temple, the knight the initiate. How much of what he sees he understands and can put into practice is symbolized by the knight's success, partial success, or failure, depending on the particular version of the story.

Our next step leads us to Jessie Weston's thesis that the origins of the Grail legends lie in a combination of two traditions: the

symbols and rituals of ancient nature cults, and the secret practices of the Mystery religions.

As we have seen, the old fertility rites had a dual purpose,
one agricultural and one spiritual. Weston expains them as
the *exoteric* rites, where the rituals were performed publicly
and which all could attend, and whose aim was primarily the
material benefit of the community; and the *esoteric* rites, "rites
open only to a favoured few, the initiates, the object of which
appears, as a rule, to have been individual rather than social,
and *non*-material. In some cases, certainly, the object aimed
at was the attainment of a conscious, ecstatic, union with the
god, and the definite assurance of a future life. In other words
there was the public worship, and there were the Mysteries."[16]
Samuel Angus, in his well-known work *The Mystery-Religions*,
confirms this idea in speaking of the resurgence in popularity during ancient times of the chthonic gods: "These views
precipitated the mind toward the Mystery-Religions, which,
originally nature cults, had conserved elements of chthonic
and telluric ritual and which also were professedly eschato-
logical religions."[17]

Because the Mystery rites were secret, we do not have a
large body of written accounts of the actual ceremonies, but
there were those who underwent initiation in these rites and
who left written accounts of what they felt could be made public without violating the vow of secrecy. It is very clear from
the accounts we do have that the ceremonies and initiations
of the Mystery religions contained elements closely related to
the objects and events we find in the stories of the Grail. The
Mysteries of Adonis/Attis supply the closest parallel to the
Grail stories, and two examples can be given here. A Christian
writer, Firmicus Maternus, who at one time had undergone
initiation into a Mystery religion, writes: "On a certain night
the image is placed, lying on its back, on a litter, and the devo-
tees mourn it with rhythmic lamentations. At length, when
they have satisfied themselves with this pretended lamenta-
tion, a light is brought in."[18] The image of the slain god placed

on a litter is, of course, the dead or castrated Fisher King of
the Grail legends.

Speaking of the Attis rites in general, Weston writes:

> But now what do we know of the actual details of the Attis mys-
> teries? The first and most important point was a Mystic Meal, at
> which the food partaken of was served in the sacred vessels, the
> tympanum, and the cymbals. The formula of an Attis initiate was
> "*I have eaten from the tympanum, I have drunk from the cymbals.*"
> As I have remarked above, the food thus partaken of was a Food
> of Life—"*The devotees of Attis believed, in fact, that they were eat-
> ing a magic food of life from the sacred vessels of their cult.*" . . . In
> the Attis initiation the proof that the candidate has successfully
> passed the test is afforded by the revival of the god—in the Grail
> romances the proof lies in the healing of the Fisher King.[19]

It is easy to see the relationship between the tympanum and
the Celtic cauldron of plenty. Although it is true that in the Grail
stories the guests at the banquet do not eat directly out of the Grail
itself, it is the Grail that provides the food for all. Angus states:

> In nearly all the Mysteries an *agape*, or sacramental meal, pre-
> ceded initiation. . . . These sacramental meals, therefore, were not
> sacramental in the primitive magical sense. They rather signal-
> ized the reception of the neophyte communicant as a member of
> the religious guild or Mystery-church, and served as a token of
> the communion of the Mystery-saints, forming the main bond of
> brotherhood among the cult members. They were also in some
> way not merely the symbol but the outward means or sacrament
> of union with the patron god.[20]

There are further similarites between the nature cults/Mys-
teries and the objects and references that we find in the Grail
romances. In the two main ceremonies of the Church of Isis, the
Blessing of the Vessel of Isis and the Passion and Resurrection
of Osiris, "Women in white raiment led the procession," and the

procession included priests bearing the "chest with the venerable mysteries," a "golden boat-shaped lamp," and a "golden vase."[21]

There is also the important symbolism of the Bleeding Spear. In the Grail stories the Grail itself is carried in by the Grail Maiden, and a squire bears the Spear. In some versions the blood flows from the Spear's tip and runs down the hands and sleeves of the squire; in other versions the tip drips three drops of blood, or sometimes just one drop. Weston holds that the Grail, carried in by a maiden, and the Spear, carried in by a squire, had originally been sexual fertility symbols. Campbell, supporting Weston's conclusion, associates the processions of the Grail and Spear with ancient Mystery rites. He then gives his own interpretation of the Spear and Grail:

> The lance that pierced Christ's side is, by analogy, the boar that slew Adonis and, like the boar, a counterpart of the slain divinity himself, in whom opposites are transcended: death and birth, time and eternity, the slayer and the slain; also, male and female. Accordingly, the lance in Christ's wound is comparable to the *lingam* in the *yoni* (or as the Buddhists say, "the jewel in the lotus"), and the blood pouring from the wound (the *yoni*) is equally pouring from the lance (the *lingam*), as the one life-substance of the god: for the two, though apparently separate, are the same. And that is the lesson of the bleeding lance symbolically borne about the great hall, with blood running down the length of its shaft and over the bearer's hand into his sleeve. It tells of the lance by which the Maimed Fisher was wounded: Anfortas on his bed of pain, Christ upon the Cross; announcing the sense of mystery to come, of the Grail, the Perfection of Paradise, in which opposites are at one.[22]

There is an interesting entry in Cosima's diary from October 29, 1872, where Wagner speaks to Cosima about the Bleeding Lance and its relation to the Mysteries: "In the afternoon R. told me that he had been thinking about the bloody lance in *Parzival* and had been led by it to the Greek mysteries. 'The Greeks were very right to leave the people all their superstitions, simply linking fine festivals to them, while wisely confining the mysteries to initiates.'"[23]

There are also specific references in the Grail legends to the Deva worlds I talked about earlier when I mentioned the Buddhist heavens. Loomis writes about the Irish and Welsh legends that were prototypes of the Grail romances:

> Even in those stories concerned with historic kings of Ireland, the main theme is often a visit to a country or mansion where, as Professor Dillon has put it, "there is neither sickness nor age nor death; where happiness lasts forever and there is no satiety; where food and drink do not diminish when consumed; where to wish for something is to possess it; where a hundred years are as one day." In other words, it is the pagan Elysium, the abode of the immortals.[24]

Note, for example, the *exact* correlation of the time period of one hundred years to one day that we found in the Buddhist and Hindu views of the time relationship between earth and a Deva realm. Loomis continues:

> Among the immortals who presided over such blissful mansions one recognizes the sun-god Lug and the sea-god Manannan Mac Lir. The sagas which describe the lavish hospitality extended to privileged mortals in these divine abodes form a group which goes under the name of *echtra*, "adventure." This group is of the greatest importance for our study since it furnishes some of the basic patterns for the visit to the Grail castle.
> . . . A pious legend tells how St. Collen visited the castle of Gwyn son of Nudd and found his host seated on a golden throne, surrounded by minstrels making music and by the comeliest men and maidens in the bloom of youth. On the table were the most luxurious delicacies that the mind could desire.[25]

Note here the mention not only of the feast, but also of the "comeliest men and maidens in the bloom of youth." Narada Thera had said that Devas usually appeared as youths of fifteen or sixteen. Also, we can remember that the fifth heaven in the realm of desire, the Nimmanarati, is the world of heavenly mansions.

In keeping with this aspect of the Grail legends, it should be mentioned that these stories do not contain references only to heaven worlds. The mortals who encounter these otherworldly realms also encounter hell worlds, or realms of suffering. One adventure that appears in many of the Grail stories is that of the Perilous Chapel. Occasionally it appears as the Perilous Grave-yard, but the general idea is the same:

> Students of the Grail romances will remember that in many of the versions the hero—sometimes it is a heroine—meets with a strange and terrifying adventure in a mysterious Chapel, an adventure which, we are given to understand, is fraught with ex-treme peril to life. The details vary: sometimes there is a Dead Body laid on the altar; sometimes a Black Hand extinguishes the tapers; there are strange and threatening voices, and the general impression is that this is an adventure in which supernatural, and evil, forces are engaged.[26]

The encounter of the Perilous Chapel happens before the knight has reached the Grail Castle. The hero in question must spend the night in the Perilous Chapel and fight the Black Hand, and then, as in the Manessier version, must sprinkle the walls of the chapel with holy water, after which the enchantment will cease. The hero is usually told that many knights have hitherto been slain by the Black Hand.

Weston believes that these stories of a mortal having encoun-ters in worlds beyond this one are not fiction or myth, but had their basis in actual experiences. Of course, in time these experi-ences, and the individuals who had and related them, became fictionalized and mythologized, but she affirms her belief that they are grounded in reality.

> Visits to the Otherworld are not *always* derivations from Celtic Fairy-lore. Unless I am mistaken the root of this theme is far

more deeply imbedded than in the shifting sands of Folk and
Fairy tale. I believe it to be essentially a Mystery tradition; the
Otherworld is not a myth, but a reality, and in all ages there have
been souls who have been willing to brave the great adventure,
and to risk all for the chance of bringing back with them some
assurance of the future life.[27]

Many more examples of this connection could be given, but
for our purposes in this chapter it is enough to have established,
as a background to our discussion of Wagner, the relationship
between the Grail stories and the practices of sacred kingship,
the old nature-fertility cults, and the Mystery religions. Our next
step is to see how legends which were founded in pagan practices became Christianized, as Wagner adopted the view that the
Bleeding Lance and the Grail were the Christian relics of the
spear of Longinus and the cup of the Last Supper.

The Christianization of the Grail

We have seen that the nature-fertility cult and Mystery religion
practices entailed the suffering, sacrifice, death, and resurrection of a patron god, and the identification on the part of the
worshipers with that god. We easily see in these practices and
beliefs a correlation to Christianity. Samuel Angus writes: "A
Mystery-Religion was a religion of Redemption which professed to remove estrangement between man and God, to
procure forgiveness of sins, to furnish mediation. Means of
purification and formulae of access to God, and acclamations
of confidence and victory were part of the apparatus of every
Mystery."[28]

This statement could just as easily apply to Christianity. But
the truth is there is much more than just a similarity between
Christianity and the Mystery religions. Christianity was the actual fulfillment, on a historical as well as a religious level, of the
promises and beliefs of the Mystery religions. According to Angus, the world of the Near East and Mediterranean was not only

ready for the coming of one such as Jesus, it was waiting for it, and all the symbols were already in place:

> The Mysteries contributed largely to the conservation of the material which Christianity has recast. . . . Sacrifices were not overlooked in the Mysteries. In spite of the philosophic protest against bloody sacrifices, the prevailing view in the theology of antiquity was that "without shedding of blood there is no remission of sin." . . . The ideal of a Messianic era retreated more and more before that of a Messianic personage. Moreover, among pagans there was a nascent consciousness that the time was ripe for the epiphany of a God-man.[29]

Weston writes:

> That Christianity might have borrowed from previously existing cults certain outward signs and symbols, might have accomodated itself to already existing Fasts and Feasts, may be, perforce has had to be, more or less grudgingly admitted; that such a *rapprochement* should have gone further, that it should even have been inherent in the very nature of the Faith, that, to some of the deepest thinkers of old, Christianity should have been held for no new thing but a fulfilment of the promise enshrined in the Mysteries from the beginning of the world, will to many be a strange and startling thought. Yet so it was, and I firmly believe that it is only in the recognition of this one-time claim of essential kinship between Christianity and the Pagan Mysteries that we shall find the key to the secret of the Grail.[30]

Indeed, there is no symbol or belief in Christianity that did not previously exist in some other religion of that place and time, whether pagan cult, myth, or Mystery religion. Virgin birth; baptism; death and resurrection; remission of sin through sacrifice; eternal life for the believer or the initiated and eternal suffering for the nonbeliever or the uninitiated; original sin; the need for atonement and redemption; sympathy for the suffering of the god, participation in and the sharing of the passion of the god, and a similar sharing in the joy of resurrection; salvation through spiritual rebirth and regeneration—all these were already there in the old religions. The symbol of the Madonna and child, for example, was taken from the Egyptian representation of Isis holding her infant son Horus. The specific term "Mother of God," used by Christians to honor Mary, was one of the titles of Isis. Communion through consuming the body and blood of the god, represented by bread and wine, was centuries old in the Mysteries of both Mithra and Dionysus.

Even the idea and symbol of the Crucifixion existed previously in religions throughout the world. Frazer describes the way in which the gods and goddesses of Vegetation were also tree spirits. Part of the rituals of the sacrifice, death, and resurrection of these divinities involved the actual hanging, either of human victims, animals, or effigies, from trees and killing them. This was particularly true of the rites of Attis, Odin, and Artemis, and of the Bagobo people of the Philippines. For brevity I will cite just four examples, though there are many others.

Attis, born of a virgin and who died beneath a pine tree, was loved by Cybele just as Adonis was loved by Aphrodite. When Attis died he was mourned by Cybele, and she was comforted by the flute music of the satyr Marsyas. In his pride as a musician Marsyas challenged Apollo to a contest; upon losing, he was tied to a pine tree and killed.

Frazer describes the sacrificial rites of the Bagobos: "The victim was led to a great tree in the forest; there he was tied with his back to the tree and his arms stretched high above his head, in the attitude in which ancient artists portrayed Marsyas hanging on the fatal tree. While he thus hung by the arms, he was slain by a spear thrust through his body at the level of the armpits."[31]

Also striking in the parallel to Christ on the cross is a passage from the *Elder Edda* concerning Odin. Odin himself says that he hung

Nine whole nights on a wind-rocked tree,
Wounded with a spear.
I was offered to Odin, myself to myself,
On that tree of which no man knows.[32]

Frazer says of the fertility rites of Odin, "The human victims dedicated to Odin were regularly put to death by hanging or by a combination of hanging and stabbing, the man being strung up to a tree or a gallows and then wounded with a spear."[33]

Finally, there is the example of Indra in the *Mahabharata* version of the killing of Vritra and the Preceptor Visvarupa. Ashamed of his actions, Indra tried to flee the consequences of those actions, personified by the Gorgonlike female monster Brahmincide: "with teeth projecting terribly, of an aspect furiously contorted, tawny and black, with disheveled hair, appalling eyes, and a garland of skulls around her neck, bathed in blood, clad in rags and in the bark of trees."[34]

Indra flees to a lotus stalk, but Brahmincide catches him and attaches herself to him, and he cannot escape her. Finally, in repentance, Indra bows to Brahma the Creator, "who, knowing the crime, commenced to ponder the question of how the King of Gods might be set free."[35] Campbell says of this episode: "There is thus an echo, here, of Prometheus; an echo, also, of Christ crucified, with the sins of the world upon his shoulders. Christ on his cross; Prometheus nailed to the world mountain; Indra in his lotus stem!"[36]

Incidentally, we see in the description of Brahmincide (so named because in this version Vritra was also considered to be descended from Brahmins in addition to Asuras) a similar description to that of the Loathly Damsel, who appears to Perceval in those versions of the story where he has failed the test. She points out to him his fault, whereupon he becomes contrite and vows to find the Grail again and succeed. We find out in some of the versions (though not in Wolfram) that she is also the Grail Maiden, who in that guise is seen as a woman of surpassing beauty. I will talk more about this symbolism in the next chapter, for this dual nature is related to the dual nature of Kundry mentioned in chapter 2.

As to the subject of Christianity, it can now be seen that all the various symbols that we find in this religion already existed. Jesus thus lived, taught, and died in the context of parables and symbols that the people of his place and time could readily recognize and understand. The best of all the current teachings and beliefs were brought together and embodied in one historical man, and the worst of those beliefs and practices, such as magic, superstition and sacrifice, were discarded, for now the supreme sacrifice had been made, and the way to salvation was open for all those who believed in Christ's resurrection.

Because the common pagan symbols I have spoken of were already in place and were incorporated by and into the Christian religion, it was easy for the romance writers to transform the Grail symbols, originally pagan, into Christian symbols. The Bleeding Lance became the spear of Longinus. When the Grail was conceived as a dish, it became the dish from which Christ ate the Passover lamb on the eve of his betrayal (see Malory's *Le Morte d'Arthur*). When the Grail was conceived as a magic stone, the story was told that this stone was brought to earth from heaven by those angels who had remained neutral when there had been war in heaven between God and Lucifer. When the Grail was conceived as a cup or chalice, it became the cup from which Jesus drank at the Last Supper. When the sword, which continues to appear as one of the sacred objects in the Grail Castle, needed a Christian context, it became the sword used to cut off the head of John the Baptist. And when the pagan tradition of the Fisher King needed a Christian lineage, the founder became Joseph of Arimathea.

The Spear and Grail thus became Christian relics, and the need arose for a story to explain how these relics came from the East to Britain. In the first few centuries after Christ's death there were a great many scriptures and accounts of his life written, and at first there was no official canon. In 185 Bishop Irenaeus chose the four Gospels that we now have as what he believed to be the "true" ones, but it was not until the Epistle of Athanasius, Bishop of Alexandria, in 367 that the books of the New Testament as we now know it were listed as the official canon. The early Catholic Church came to adopt Athanasius's list, even though different versions of this early canon continued to exist in different parts of the empire. Once the Church had decided on a canon, the writings outside that canon were declared apocryphal and were suppressed by the early Church, insofar as it had the power and ability to do so. The Church could not suppress everything, however, and stories concerning Joseph of Arimathea and Nicodemus were circulated throughout the following centuries.

Joseph of Arimathea appears in all four Gospels of the New Testament. He appears alone in the first three but is mentioned along with Nicodemus in the Gospel of John. It is also only in John, among the four Gospels, that mention is made of a Roman soldier piercing the side of Jesus with a spear, though this soldier is not named. He *is* named in the Gospel of Nicodemus.

The Gospel of Nicodemus, also referred to in Arthurian scholarship as the *Evangelium Nicodemi*, is attributed to Nicodemus himself, though some scholars believe that it was a forgery written around the end of the third century or beginning of the fourth century. We can never know for sure whether Nicodemus wrote this work or it was forged by a later hand and attributed to him. The content of this Gospel, at one time known as the Acts of Pontius Pilate, begins with the Jewish leaders accusing Jesus before Pilate and continues through Jesus's Crucifixion and his Resurrection to his disciples on earth. It also relates at length his journey into hell and his raising of the faithful from there into heaven.

Even though the early Church did not include this Gospel in its new canon, it remained very influential in the early Christian world and was one of the works the Church could not suppress. It is common knowledge, for example, that Longinus is the name of the soldier who pierced the side of Jesus. That he is not named in any of the four canonical Gospels, but only in the Gospel of Nicodemus, shows how well-known and accepted this work was.

Most important for our discussion is the expansion in this work on the character of Joseph of Arimathea.

Nicodemus was one of the rulers of the Jews who had testified before Pilate in favor of Jesus, and who thus incurred the wrath of the other leaders, who were demanding that Jesus be put to death. After Nicodemus and Joseph had placed the body of Jesus in the sepulchre, they were both confronted by those leaders. Nicodemus stands up to them and affirms his faith. Joseph goes farther, condemning the leaders for their actions. Infuriated, the leaders cast Joseph into prison, sealing the lock.

When these leaders later find Joseph absent from the chamber but the seal on the lock unbroken, they become very afraid, for during this time they are hearing other reports concerning Jesus's Resurrection. Joseph is eventually found at his home in Arimathea, and when he is questioned about his escape, he says that while he was praying during the night, four angels surrounded the prison. The resurrected Jesus appeared to him and lifted him from the ground, eventually taking him back to his house in Arimathea and telling him not to be afraid.

The Gospel of Nicodemus became the basis for a whole group of legends surrounding the character of Joseph. Joseph does not appear in Chrétien, but he does appear in many of the later versions of the Grail story. As might be expected, the versions dealing with Joseph's story differ in detail, but the general pattern is that Joseph took the Grail to the Cross and collected the blood of Christ as it dripped from his body. The Grail is either the cup of the Last Supper or the dish from which he ate the lamb, or is simply called the Grail, depending on the particular version. When Jesus is dead Joseph takes his body and places it in the sepulchre, just as the canonical Gospels relate. Joseph escapes prison, as mentioned above, and is later banished by the Jewish leaders from his homeland. He journeys across Europe and eventually reaches Britain, where he builds a castle to house and protect the Grail, entrusted to him by Christ himself. He has a son, Josephus, who becomes his successor as the Grail Guardian. All the Grail Guardians are thus descended from Joseph, including Perceval and Galahad. Joseph becomes the first Fisher King, and in *Sone de Nansai* he is wounded by God in the standard fashion, in the thighs, in order to test his faith. During the time that he is maimed, the kingdom of Logres (England) lies under a spell where nothing will grow and no woman can bear children. He is eventually healed by a knight, and we see the author drawing together the legends of the Fisher King and the story of Joseph. Also in this poem Joseph is the Guardian not only of the Grail, but also of the spearhead of Longinus. Josephus becomes the first ordained bishop of Christendom, and, as in the other versions, the pagan and Christian traditions are brought together.

In Malory the Spear and the Grail are together in a castle where King Pellam, a descendent of Joseph, is the Grail Guardian. King Pellam holds a large feast, and Sir Balin comes there to avenge two deaths perpetrated by the invisible knight Sir Garlon. At the feast Sir Garlon can be seen. Balin slays him in the castle, but because Garlon is Pellam's brother, Pellam must avenge his death. In the ensuing fight between Balin and Pellam, Balin's sword breaks, and he runs through the castle, pursued by Pellam, looking for a weapon. At last he enters the chamber which holds the relics, as well as a great bed covered with a cloth of gold. A figure is lying on the bed, and on a table of pure gold with legs of silver stands "a marvellous spear strangely wrought."[37] Without knowing that this is the sacred spear, Balin grabs it and strikes King Pellam. This is the Dolorous Stroke, which causes three kingdoms to fall into ruin. The "most part of the castle" also falls,[38] and outside people lie dead, "slain on every side".[39]

And King Pellam lay so, many years sore wounded, and might never be whole till Galahad the Haut Prince healed him in the quest of the Sangrail, for in that place was part of the blood of our Lord Jesus Christ, that Joseph of Arimathea brought into this land, and there himself lay in that rich bed. And that was the same spear that Longinus smote Our Lord to the heart. And King Pellam was nigh of Joseph's kin, and that was the most worship-

ful man that lived in those days, and great pity it was of his hurt,
for through that stroke, turned to great dole, tray and tene.[40]

We see not only the traditions of the wounded Fisher King
and the Waste Land combined with Christian symbolism, we
also see that the Spear and Grail have become Christian relics,
and that the Grail King Pellam was descended from Joseph. In
later chapters Malory shows that Galahad, too, is descended
from Joseph, and thus the old traditions of Sacred King–Fisher
King–Grail Guardian now have a Christian parallel in the lineage from Joseph of Arimathea through succeeding generations
of Grail Kings down to the present Grail quester.

We also see in the above quotation that the spear of Longinus
was the spear used in the Dolorous Stroke, an association Wagner himself was to make. In this way Wagner bypassed Wolfram
and Chrétien, using the tradition started by Robert de Boron for
his own interpretation of both the Spear and Grail.

Prior to their Christianization, the Grail legends contained
elements of both heroic legend and Mystery initiation. In their
highest Christianized form, they became symbolic representations of the path to enlightenment, to salvation. The quest of
the Holy Grail is the quest for spiritual illumination. Only the
fittest knights, such as Galahad and Perceval/Parzival, are worthy enough to achieve this quest. But even in their Christianized forms, these stories never lost their link to the old heritage.
Throughout the Arthur and Grail legends there are references to
the penalties for trying something out of pride for which one is
not ready. Trying to draw swords that are not meant for you and
sitting in seats or lying on beds that are for the worthy only bring
severe consequences, usually in the form of immediate death or
being pierced with a sword or spear that comes out of nowhere.
We see not only a memory of the Mysteries, where proper fit-
ness and initiation were necessary for the revelation and contemplation of the secrets, but also an awareness of the need for
serious and genuine training in order to be granted the gift of
religious experience. The Grail legends contain more than just

romantic representations of the search for spiritual Truth. They
retain remembrances of the actual practices and experiences of
the ancient Mysteries, even when the outward form of the search
portrayed is Christian. Sometimes the Grail is the dish from
which Jesus ate the Passover lamb. Sometimes the Grail is the
cup from which he drank at the Last Supper. At other times the
exact nature of the actual vessel is not revealed at all. It doesn't
matter. As Roger Loomis concludes: "To behold the Grail openly
is not to see a sacred vessel in an earthly castle, but the Beatific
Vision, vouchsafed by God's grace only to those who have fitted themselves by discipline and contemplation for the ineffable
experience."[41]

The Bloodline of the Grail

Earlier in the chapter I mentioned two ideas that have been written about fairly extensively over the last two or three decades.
One is that Jesus was married to Mary Magdalene and had a child
or children by her, and that this bloodline exists even today. The
other is that the traditional Grail stories contain an underground
code supporting a succession, either political and/or spiritual, that
rivaled the Catholic Church of that time, a succession based on
the surviving bloodline of Jesus. We can see evidence of this, for
example, in *Parzival*.

Even though Wolfram eventually describes the Grail as a
stone possessing wondrous properties, the first description of
it we are given during Parzival's initial visit to the Grail Castle
leaves us with an image that at first seems incongruous: "After
them came the queen. So radiant was her countenance that everyone thought the dawn was breaking. She was clothed in a
dress of Arabian silk. Upon a deep green achmardi she bore the
perfection of Paradise, both root and branch. That was a thing
called the Grail, which surpasses all earthly perfection."[42]

The image of root and branch cannot be immediately reconciled with that of a stone. However, in light of the possibility that
the Grail represented the actual bloodline of Jesus, the image

suddenly makes sense, especially in the context of the underground code I have mentioned. The image of a vine is used as a symbol for the bloodline: a vine can grow, develope multiple branches, and even undergo grafting. Thus Wolfram is making an allusion to the bloodline of Christ, using a symbol that would have been recognized by the supporters of this lineage but not, at least at first, by the Catholic Church.

If we accept the reality of such a lineage, then we certainly see one reason for the eventual Church suppression of the Grail legends. If these romances, even in coded form, were supporting a succession that rivaled the Catholic Church, then the Church would have done all in its power to stamp out such a lineage, or at least the support for this descent. There are those who believe that the Albigensian Crusade against the Cathars in southern France was indeed an example of such an act. The years of this Crusade, from 1209 to 1244, coincide very closely with the writing and popularity of the Grail stories.

It is not the aim of this book to take sides in the current debate over whether Jesus fathered children whose descendants survive to this day. Such a discussion would take us too far afield from the thesis I am developing in regard to Wagner. There is, however, a pertinent interpretation of the symbol of a bloodline.

In Zen Buddhism we speak of the Bloodline of the Buddhas. This is not a physical bloodline, but rather a spiritual lineage. It represents the transmission of the Truth from master to disciple, generation after generation, beginning with the Buddha himself and continuing down to the present day. This transmission lineage will of course have many branches, because one master might have more than one Dharma heir, and thus each master may generate several branches of the succession. In my own monastic order we can trace our transmission lineage from our own master back to the Buddha himself, from generation to generation, in an unbroken line. This line is the Bloodline of the Buddhas, where the blood represents the transmission of the Truth.

This idea is one of the meanings of the Grail and its quest. The Grail symbolizes the true, spiritual apostolic succession, where the Sang Real, or Holy Blood, is the transmission of the Truth from master to disciple, generation to generation. The Grail King passes on the lineage to the questing knight, who in achieving the quest of the Grail shows himself worthy to be a vessel for the Truth. Thus the tradition of the Fisher Kings is a tradition of transmission, and the blood relationship of the questing knight to the Grail King that we find in so many versions of the legend becomes symbolic of the spiritual relationship, where the knight becomes the spiritual descendant of the Grail King and eventually becomes the new Grail King himself, carrying on the lineage and the transmission.

In the final analysis, no one particular origin or interpretation of the Grail legends can be proved absolutely. But this doesn't matter. They are, in their highest form, symbolic representations of the path to enlightenment and salvation. This is how Wagner treated them, and this is how they are relevant and important to our discussion of the *Ring* and *Parsifal*. Wagner was concerned with the actual path to redemption portrayed as grandly as possible through artistic symbol. There is no doubt that he saw the Grail as the symbol of the highest achievement in spiritual quest, and *Parsifal* as the final culmination of his life's work.

CHAPTER 5

Parzival

Wolfram von Eschenbach was born around 1170 and died at least by 1220, if not a few years earlier. He was a Bavarian knight, and one of his patrons was Hermann, Landgrave of Thuringia, whose residence was the castle Wartburg. Walther von der Vogelweide, a knight-poet who was an acquaintance of Wolfram's and who is mentioned in *Parzival*, appears along with Hermann and Wolfram himself in Wagner's *Tannhäuser*.

Wolfram wrote *Parzival* probably between the years 1198 and 1212, though the years often given are 1200–1210. It is not possible to date manuscripts of this era exactly, for no records were kept. *Parzival* was composed in rhymed couplets, and the whole poem comprises 24,810 lines. The poem is divided into sixteen books, and each book is divided into sections of thirty lines each, the number of lines that Wolfram fit onto each of his manuscript pages.

Although Wagner, in his letters, made many disparaging comments about Wolfram and *Parzival*, saying that Wolfram's treatment of the subject matter was trivial and superficial, the truth is that Wagner took much more from the Bavarian master than he was ever willing to admit. *Parzival* is considered to be one of the great poetic masterpieces of the Middle Ages, standing easily along side of *The Divine Comedy*, and scholars overwhelmingly agree that it is the greatest of all the treatments of the Grail legend.

Wagner first read *Parzival* in 1845 while at Marienbad. *Lohengrin* was the first result of that reading and inspiration, but the

story of the knight Parzival remained with Wagner throughout
the following years, and he took it up again in 1857, writing, as
we saw earlier, a prose sketch for the opera that has now been
lost.

He struggled with the idea for two years, during which time he
continued to work on *Tristan und Isolde* and, at least in his mind,
Die Sieger. In the letter to Mathilde Wesendonck of May 30, 1859,
that I quoted from before, Wagner was not sure he wanted to go
through with the project of *Parzival* and only half-humorously
wrote, "And—am I to undertake such a task? God forbid! Today
I take my leave of this insane project; Geibel can write about
it and Liszt can compose it!—When my old friend Brünnhilde
leaps into the funeral pyre, I shall plunge in after her, and hope
to die a Christian! So be it! Amen!"[1]

Part of the reason Wagner was reluctant to carry the project
through to completion was the length and complexity of Wolfram's poem. Wagner felt that, by itself, *Parzival* could not be the
basis for an opera, and that he would have to start almost from
scratch to write a libretto based on a work that had far too many
individual episodes to put into an opera. The other issue Wagner
struggled with was how to make Parsifal, and not Amfortas, the
center of the drama. Wagner wrote to Mathilde in the May 30,
1859, letter:

> And then there is a further difficulty with Parzival. He is indis-
> pensably necessary as the redeemer whom Anfortas longs for:
> but if Anfortas is to be placed in his true and appropriate light, he
> will become of such immense tragic interest that it will be almost
> impossible to introduce a second focus of attention, and yet this
> focus of attention must centre upon Parzival if the latter is not
> simply to enter at the end as a deus ex machina who leaves us
> completely cold. Thus Parzival's development and the profound
> sublimity of his purification, although entirely predestined by
> his thoughtful and deeply compassionate nature, must again be
> brought into the foreground. But I cannot choose to work on
> such a broad scale as Wolfram was able to do: I have to compress

everything into *three* climactic situations of violent intensity, so that the work's profound and ramified content emerges clearly and distinctly.[2]

We all know that Wagner eventually solved this problem by making Parsifal the central character from the beginning, and that indeed Wagner was able to compress the story into three acts, the second, especially, of "violent intensity."

While a full analysis of Wolfram's *Parzival* is a book-length subject in itself, we can, in the context of this chapter, look at the most important aspects of this great poem and see how they influenced Wagner's creation of his own *Parsifal*, and how these aspects became part of the *Ring* and *Parsifal* as one work.

Wolfram's primary source was Chrétien's *Le Conte del Graal*. Many of Wolfram's episodes follow Chrétien quite closely, and Wolfram even says in the last section of his poem:

If Master Chrétien de Troyes did not do justice to this story, that may well vex Kyot, who furnished us the right story. The Provençal [Kyot] correctly [*endehaft*] tells how Herzeloyde's child won the Grail, as he was destined to do, when Anfortas had forfeited it. From Provence to Germany the true facts were sent to us, as well as this adventure's final conclusion. I, Wolfram of Eschenbach, shall tell no more of it than the master told there.[3]

Who was Kyot? Wolfram declares Kyot to be his main source for the story of the Grail and for his knowledge of the lineage of the Grail family. For a long time scholars maintained that they could find no proof that any such person as Kyot ever existed, and many believed that Wolfram had simply invented Kyot in order to give his story authenticity. It was common for authors of Wolfram's time to name a source as authority for their tales, and many of the Grail romance writers name sources we cannot confirm now. Wauchier says that his source was Bleheris, but scholars cannot confirm his existence for sure. Often the authority of a *grant livre* (great book) is given, though we no longer possess any such book. Chrétien himself cites as his source a book given to him by his patron, Count Philip of Flanders. Scholars agree that the book existed, but no copy has survived. Loomis shows that although Chrétien and the First Continuation were sources for Wolfram, they were not the only sources, for Wolfram includes details that agree with other versions of the Grail story but do not appear in Chrétien. Wolfram could not have read these other versions, specifically *Peredur Son of Evrawg, Perlesvaus, Sone de Nansai,* and the *Queste,* since these other versions were written after *Parzival.* Therefore, there had to be a source or sources now lost to us that provided material for all these different authors. Although scholars until recently doubted the existence of Kyot, they did not doubt that Wolfram had at least one other source besides Chrétien and the First Continuation, and possibly more than one. In *Holy Blood, Holy Grail,* Baigent, Leigh, and Lincoln affirm that Kyot was not only a real person, he was in fact the well-known Guiot de Provins, a troubadour, monk, spokesman for the Templars, and enemy of the Catholic Church. They believe that Wolfram met Guiot at Mayence, Germany, in 1184 at the chivalric festival of Pentecost, where Friedrich Barbarossa that year conferred knighthood on his (Friedrich's) sons.

We saw in the last chapter that in some of the Grail stories the Grail hero succeeds in his quest, healing the Maimed King and restoring the Waste Land to fertility; in some of the versions there is only partial success, such as in the First Continuation and Gerbert's continuation, where Gawain in the former and Perceval in the latter asks the question and therefore restores the land, but fails to mend the broken sword, leaving the task incomplete; and finally there are versions where the hero fails to ask the question, thus failing in his mission. The seminal version of the failure is Chrétien's *Le Conte del Graal.*

Because Chrétien did not live to finish his poem, we don't know whether he had planned to give Perceval a second chance to succeed. All we have is the failure. I will give a brief summation of Chrétien's version.

Perceval is brought up by his widowed mother in the Barren Forest. One day Perceval sees a group of King Arthur's knights riding through the forest, and after talking to them and finding out who and what they are, he desires to be made a knight by the great king. He runs home to tell his mother what he has seen and what he wants to do. In great sorrow she tells him that his father had once owned lands in the kingdom of Uther Pendragon, King Arthur's father. One day in battle Perceval's father "Was wounded between the legs / And his whole body was crippled."[4] Uther also died, and his kingdom became ravaged. Perceval's father was carried on a litter to the house he owned in the Barren Forest, where he remained for years until Perceval's two older brothers were ready to become knights. The older brother went to the king of Escavalon to become knighted, and the younger to King Ban of Gomeret. As both were returning home they fell in combat and were killed, and their father died of grief upon hearing the news.

Right away we have the symbols of castrated king and waste land, but Chrétien does not pursue any elaboration or any connection between Perceval's father and a Grail King.

Perceval leaves his mother, who swoons and collapses in grief. But Perceval, looking back and seeing her on the ground, turns forward anyway and spurs his horse "Into the dark forest."[5] After finding Arthur's court he is given training and knighthood by the friendly Gornemant de Goort, who becomes Gurnemanz in Wolfram. (Wagner's Gurnemanz is a combination of Wolfram's Gurnemanz and the hermit Trevrizent.) Gornemant gives Perceval instruction in manners as well as in arms, and one of his admonishments to Perceval is not to talk too much, for "Too much talking / Is sinful."[6]

After leaving Gornemant, Perceval comes upon a castle and is given lodging there for the night. There is very little to eat, and the maiden of the castle, Blanchefleur, tells him that she and her lands are under attack by a knight who wants to force himself upon her. Perceval fights for her and defeats both this knight and his steward, sending them to Arthur as prisoners. The castle is freed of the siege, and Perceval and Blanchefleur fall in love. In *Parzival* this episode is related in greater detail, Blanchefleur being renamed Condwiramurs. Parzival marries Condwiramurs, but Perceval does not marry Blanchefleur; they simply have a brief love affair. Perceval desires to know if his mother is alive or dead and, in spite of Blanchefleur's pleas for him to stay, sets out for his home. One day he is riding by the bank of a river and sees two men in a boat, one of them fishing. He asks where he might find shelter for the night, and the fisherman directs him to his own house. Perceval follows the directions and comes upon a great castle. The drawbridge is down, and he enters through the gate.

Two squires disarm him and then take him to greet his host. The king is reclining on a couch, and apologizes for not being able to rise to greet his guest. Perceval assures him he is not offended. The king then bestows a marvelous sword on his guest, saying, "Good sir, this was destined for you, and I desire you to have it."[7] Perceval then takes a seat beside the king, and they witness a squire entering the hall bearing a white lance with a white point, from which a drop of red blood runs down onto the squire's hand. Two more squires enter bearing golden candelabra with ten candles in each. Then "a damsel came in with these squires, holding between her two hands a grail (graal).[8] She was beautiful, gracious, splendidly garbed, and as she entered with the grail in her hands, there was such a brilliant light that the candles lost their brightness, just as the stars do when the moon or sun rises."[9]

Another damsel enters holding a silver carving dish, and the grail is described as being of refined gold and set with many very costly jewels. The lance and the grail pass before the king's couch and enter another chamber: "The youth watched them pass, but he did not dare to ask concerning the grail and whom one served with it, for he kept in his heart the words of the wise nobleman. I fear that harm will come of this, because I have heard say that one can be too silent as be too loquacious. But, for better or for worse, the youth put no question."[10]

Squires then serve a great feast, and with each course the grail again passes before them. Still Perceval does not ask about the grail. He thinks to himself that he will wait until morning and then ask one of the squires about the wonders he has seen. Finally the king tells Perceval that it is time for bed and bids him remain in the hall, but "because of my infirmity I must be carried."[11] Four servants then come and bear the couch and the king away. Perceval sleeps that night in the hall, but when he wakes the next morning the hall is empty and no one is to be found. The doors of all the chambers, open the night before, are now all closed, and no one answers Perceval's knocks or calls. He finds his horse and armor ready for him and leaves the castle, intending to find a squire outside whom he can ask concerning the events of the night before. But there is no one, and the drawbridge closes behind him, forcing his horse to leap the rest of the way to the ground.

He sees fresh hoofprints on a path and follows them, thinking he will find someone who can answer his questions. He comes across a maiden mourning over the headless body of a knight. He asks her who killed her knight, and she replies that a knight had killed him that morning. But she then notices that Perceval's horse is freshly groomed, and she knows that there is no lodging anywhere for twenty-five leagues in any direction. Perceval tells her that he had enjoyed the best lodging he had ever had right nearby. "Ah, sir, did you lie then at the dwelling of the rich Fisher King?"[12] Perceval tells her about the fisherman in the boat: The maiden said: 'Good sir, he is a king, I assure you, but he was wounded and maimed in a battle, so that he cannot move himself, for a javelin wounded him through the two thighs. He is still in such pain that he cannot mount a horse, but when he wishes to divert himself, he has himself placed in a boat and goes fishing with a hook; therefore he is called the Fisher King.'"[13]

Here we see an example of Chrétien not fully understanding the tradition of Fisher Kings, and therefore inventing a reason why they were so called. But we again see the wounding in the thighs and the inability of the king to be healed. Perceval then tells the maiden that he had spent the evening before with this man. She asks him if he saw the bleeding lance.

"Did I see it? Yes, by my faith."

"Did you ask why it bled?"

"I said nothing about it."

"So help me God, learn, then, that you have done ill. Did you see the grail?"

"Yes, indeed."

"And who held it?"

"A maiden."

"And whence did she come?"

"From a chamber."

"Whither did she go?"

"Into another chamber."

"Did no one precede the grail?"

"Yes."

"Who?"

"Only two squires."

"What did they hold in their hands?"

"Candelabra full of candles."

"Who came after the grail?"

"Another maiden."

"What did she hold?"

"A little carving-dish [*tailleor*] of silver."

"Did you not ask anyone where they were going?"

"No question came from my mouth."

"So help me God, that was worse. What is your name, friend?"

Then he, who did not know his name, divined it and said that his name was Perceval of Wales. He did not know whether he told the truth or not, but it was the truth, though he did not know it. When the damsel heard it, she rose and faced him, saying angrily: "Your name is changed, good friend."

"What is it?"

"Perceval the wretched! Ah, unfortunate Perceval, how un-
lucky it was that you did not ask all those things! For you would
have cured the maimed King, so that he would have recovered
the use of his limbs and would have ruled his lands and great
good would have come of it! But now you must know that much
misery will come upon you and others. This happened to you,
understand, because of your sin against your mother; she died
of grief for you."[14]

Perceval asks her how she knows that his mother is dead, and
the maiden answers that she is Perceval's cousin and was present
when his mother was buried. Perceval invites her to travel with
him, but she declines. Chrétien does not name this maiden, but
in *Parzival* she is Sigune.

Perceval defeats a number of famous knights and sends them
to Arthur as prisoners, the defeated knights going there of their
own accord owing to the code of chivalry. When Perceval finally
reaches Arthur's court himself, he is received with a hero's wel-
come, and there is great joy in his company. On the third day
after his arrival, all are assembled at court, and a damsel riding
on a tawny mule enters the assembly: "Never was there a creature so loathly save in hell." She is described as having the features of various animals, and her general appearance is hideous:
"Never had such a creature come to a royal court."[15] This is the
Loathly Damsel who features in many of the Grail stories, as well
as in other Arthurian tales and in the old Irish legends. Chrétien
does not name her, but in Wolfram she is Cundrie *la sorcière*, the
Messenger of the Grail. She comes before the whole assembly
and denounces Perceval for not asking the question:

"Ah, Perceval, Fortune is bald behind, but has a forelock in front.
A curse on him who greets or wishes you well, for you did not
seize Fortune when you met her. You entered the dwelling of
the Fisher King; you saw the lance which bleeds. Was it so painful to open your mouth that you could not ask why the drop of
blood sprang from the white point of the lance? When you saw

the grail, you did not inquire who was the rich man whom one served with it. Most unfortunate is he who when the weather is fairer than usual waits for even fairer to come. It was you, unfortunate man, who saw that the time and the place were right for speech, and yet remained mute. You had ample opportunity, but in an evil hour you kept silence. If you had asked, the rich King, who is now sore troubled, would have been wholly cured of his wound and would have held his land in peace—land which he will never hold again. Do you know what will happen if the King does not hold his land and is not healed of his wound? Ladies will lose their husbands, lands will be laid waste, maidens, helpless, will remain orphans, and many knights will die. All these calamities will befall because of you!"[16]

The damsel then turns to Arthur and tells him of Castle Orgulous, where 566 knights of fame dwell, each with his lady-love, and that if any knight journeys there he will not fail to find combat. She also tells of Montescleire, where a damsel is besieged, and if any knight wants to win supreme glory, he would raise the siege and deliver the maiden. Gawain immediately jumps up and says that he will go to Montescleire. Giflet says that he will go to Castle Orgulous. Perceval swears that he will not lie two nights in the same lodging or turn down any combat until he has found out whom one serves with the grail and why the lance bleeds.

Fifty more knights swear that they will undertake any adventure of which they hear, and we see an early version of the famous scene in the *Queste* and in Malory where the Grail appears in a vision of light and holy radiance in Arthur's hall at Pentecost, where all 150 knights of the Round Table vow to undertake the quest of the Grail. Although Chrétien's scene cannot compare in majesty or religious profundity to Malory's or that of the *Queste*, we can still see the influence his story had on the later romances.

At this point in *Le Conte del Graal* the adventures of Gawain are related, and when Chrétien returns to Perceval, five years have passed. Perceval has forgotten God, though he continues to follow the path of chivalry and has defeated and sent to Arthur's court many knights of fame. "Throughout this time he did not think of God."[17]

Perceval then encounters a group of pilgrims, one of whom asks him why he is bearing arms on the day that Jesus Christ died. Perceval has lost all track of time and asks what day it is. He is told that it is Holy Friday, and then he is given a sermon on how Jesus was betrayed and died on the cross, and how he lived and died for the sins of humanity. Then he is told that the small group of five knights and ten ladies has just come from a holy hermit, to whom they had made their confession. Perceval is very moved and asks the way to the hermit. He is directed to the hermit's dwelling and finds him, along with a priest and another ministrant, in a small chapel, where they are about to celebrate Mass. Perceval disarms and falls on his knees in the chapel, asking for forgiveness and counsel. The hermit, who remains unnamed here but who is Trevrizent in *Parzival*, asks what Perceval's sin was, and Perceval tells him about not asking the question at the house of the Fisher King. The hermit then reiterates that the sin Perceval committed was the sorrow he caused his mother, and that was the reason he did not ask concerning the grail and the lance. He then tells Perceval that the reason he has survived these five years was a prayer his mother had said for him, commending him to God. Because of the power of that prayer, God for her sake had saved Perceval from death and prison. The hermit then tells Perceval whom one served with the grail, though he does not say why the lance bleeds:

> "And great was your folly when you did not learn whom one
> served with the grail. It was my brother; and his sister and mine
> was your mother. And believe me that the rich Fisher is the son
> of the King who causes himself to be served with the grail. But do
> not think that he takes from it a pike, a lamprey, or a salmon. The
> holy man sustains and refreshes his life with a single mass-wafer.
> So sacred a thing is the grail, and he himself is so spiritual, that
> he needs no more for his sustenance than the mass-wafer which

comes in the grail. Fifteen years has he been thus without issuing from the chamber where you saw the grail enter. Now will I enjoin penance on you for your sin."[18]

The hermit then tells Perceval what penance is necessary and how he should serve God from now on. Perceval accepts the terms of the practice and stays with the hermit for two days:

And Perceval learned, once again,
    That Our Lord had died that Friday,
    Crucified high on the Cross.
    He made his Easter communion
    Humbly, in perfect simplicity.
    And here the story breaks
    Away from Perceval,
    About whom the tale turns silent:
    I'll speak a good deal of Gawain
    Before Perceval is mentioned again.[19]

This ends up being the last that we hear of Perceval or the grail in *Le Conte del Graal*. We don't know what Chrétien may have planned or what the book given to him by Count Philip might have contained, but we do know from the last line that he intended to return to Perceval's story.

From this point until the end the poem concerns Gawain. Gawain at one point, in order to fulfill a vow, is asked to bring the Bleeding Spear to a particular castle, but there is no mention of the grail in this request. Chrétien did not get far enough even to finish this episode. We have the four Continuations, but as I mentioned before, they are often very different from Chrétien and therefore do not represent an actual conclusion to his version of the story. We saw earlier that in the First Continuation and Gerbert, the hero does ask the question, though he fails to mend a broken sword. In Chrétien the mending of a sword was never required of Perceval in order to heal the Grail King. Furthermore, in the First Continuation the hero is not even Perceval, but Gawain. In the Second Continuation, the one formerly attributed to Wauchier but now considered anonymous, Perceval arrives after Gawain has failed. Perceval succeeds in mending the broken sword and is then welcomed by the Fisher King as the lord of his house, but we again see that this version cannot be a literal continuation of Chrétien because Gawain was not the one who originally failed and who needed Perceval to succeed in his place. In Manessier's Continuation there are two kings: the Fisher King, whose daughter bears the Grail, and the King of the Waste Land, whose daughter bears the carving dish. This second king has been killed by Partinal, Lord of the Red Tower, with a sword that broke into pieces at the stroke. The king's daughter brings the broken sword to the Fisher King's castle, telling her uncle that the knight who could repair the sword would avenge her father's death. The Fisher King is wounded through the thighs like other Grail Guardians, but the wound this time comes from his own carelessness in handling the fragments of the sword. He also needs revenge to be taken against Partinal in order to be cured. Perceval undertakes the task of mending the sword and avenging the murder and the wound. He finds a smith who mends the sword, then rides on and kills the Lord of the Red Tower. When he returns to the Grail Castle the Fisher King is on his feet, cured of his wound. While this might make a good story in and of itself, it is obviously not a continuation of Chrétien's story. Is there, then, any version of the story that does continue and complete the original?

Believe it or not, the best and truest continuation of Chrétien is *Parzival*.

Scholarship does not ordinarily speak of Wolfram's great poem as a "continuation" of *Le Conte del Graal*, for it certainly exists as a masterpiece in its own right and is therefore not a "continuation" of anyone else's story. I mention it in this context because it does, in fact, draw Chrétien's unfinished tale to a true, satisfactory, and profound conclusion. The great questions left at the end of *Le Conte del Graal* are, "Will Perceval find the Grail Castle again, will he get a second chance, and will he succeed this time where he failed before?" These questions are answered in *Parzival*.

The first two of *Parzival's* sixteen books concern Gahmuret (here spelled with an "h") and his adventures in Arabia. After winning great fame he is eventually killed in a joust, though without being wounded in the thighs. Herzeloyde (Wagner's Herzeleide) gives birth to Parzival two weeks after hearing of her husband's death.

These first two books and their adventures do not exist in Chrétien, who begins his poem with the childhood of Perceval in the forest, Wolfram's Book III. Chrétien's poem ends, in the middle of a line, after Gawain has survived the trials at the castle called The Rock of Champguin (Wolfram's Castle of Wonders) and sent a messenger to Arthur's court. This corresponds to about halfway through Wolfram's Book XIII. Wolfram's conclusion of the story does not depend on any known or extant source. We may remember that he attributed the ending to Kyot. How much of it may have been his own invention and how much he borrowed from Kyot we will probably never know. The important thing is that Wolfram concluded his story by seamlessly finishing the adventures of Gawain (who does not, by the way, ever go to the Grail Castle) and then returning to the story of Parzival. Parzival is eventually led to Munsalvaesche by Cundrie, the Grail Messenger, where he again views the Grail and this time asks the proper question. Anfortas is healed of his wound, and Parzival becomes the new Grail King.

Although much of *Parzival* follows Chrétien, the episodes in Wolfram are more fleshed out, more full-bodied, and imbued with a deeper purpose and more consistent meaning. The characterization is much more lifelike and real, and there are times when Wolfram seems more like a modern novelist than a twelfth- or thirteenth-century romance writer. With him there is more conscious design, more unity of concept, and greater structural consistency than with Chrétien. A large part of his genius is the way he successfully welds together so many adventures and episodes into one unified and meaningful work.

An excellent example of this is Wolfram's treatment of the

question test. At first sight, one is tempted to view the asking of a question in order to heal the Maimed King as Wagner had viewed it, silly and meaningless. Wagner had written to Mathilde, "The thing about the 'question' is that it is *so* utterly preposterous and totally meaningless. I should simply have to invent everything here."[20] In Chrétien it does not make much sense. Perceval is told by Gornemant not to speak too much, and Perceval, obeying his instruction, does not. Then he is told that the reason he did not ask the question is because he sinned in causing his mother's death by leaving her. Admittedly, this does not add up, and it is a weakness in Chrétien's story. It is as though he has inherited the theme of the question test but does not understand it, and simply puts it in. This was typical of the French romance writers of that time.

Wolfram handles this aspect of the story with much more purpose and meaning. Parzival, like Perceval, remembering Gurnemanz's admonition, did not ask about the lance or the Grail. But Wolfram lets us know that Parzival is unsettled after the feast and the procession. Wolfram writes that when the attendants have left Parzival alone to sleep, he "did not lie alone. Until the dawn of day deep distress was his companion. Future suffering sent him its heralds in his sleep, so that his dream was no less terrible than his mother's dream in the night when she yearned after Gahmuret with such forebodings."[21]

After Parzival leaves the castle the next morning he comes upon Sigune. When she learns that he did not ask the question, she cries to him in anguish:

> "Oh, alas, that my eyes behold you, . . . since you were too faint of heart to ask a question. Yet you saw such great marvels there—to think that you could fail to ask when you were in the presence of the Grail! . . . You had the fangs of a venomous wolf, so early did the gall take root in you and poison your loyalty. You should have felt pity for your host, on whom God has wrought such terrible wonders, and have asked the cause of his suffering. You live, and yet are dead to happiness."[22]

Wolfram here introduces the theme that he will carry throughout his work, which Wagner also used: the theme of compassion leading to the redemption of suffering. In the above passage the gall is the poison of pride, and as Wolfram develops the idea throughout the poem, it was this pride and its attendant lack of compassion that caused Parzival not to ask the question. Sigune says, "You should have felt pity for your host," but Parzival was concerned only with outward courtesy and with finding out later about the externals of what he had seen. He had not been able to feel the suffering of Anfortas enough to be moved by it, and thus to inquire about its cause and how it could be relieved. We will see in the next chapter that this aspect of the story is an essential ingredient in the transformation of Siegfried into Parsifal.

Where did the tradition of the question come from? Chrétien did not invent it. And even though Wagner ridiculed it, he actually did incorporate it, albeit subtly, in an important way in *Parsifal*.

Loomis has found two sources. He explains that the old Irish *echtra* are adventures where a mortal hero "visits a supernatural palace, is hospitably entertained, witnesses strange happenings, and sometimes wakes in the morning to find that his host and his dwelling have disappeared."[23] One of these *echtra* concerning King Conn of the Hundred Battles (a king who reigned in the second century A.D.), which Loomis says predates 1056, is called *Phantom's Frenzy*. Loomis explains that this title is very hard to translate, and that it means "the supernatural being's ecstasy." Loomis relates the story:

> King Conn . . . lost his way in a mist. A horseman (the phantom) approached, welcomed him, and invited him to his dwelling. Conn, accompanied by a poet of his household, came to a golden tree and a house with a white-gold ridgepole. Entering, the two saw their host already arrived and seated on a throne. He revealed himself as Lug. A young woman, who wore a golden crown and who was called the Sovranty of Ireland, served Conn

with huge ribs of meat. Then, filling a golden cup with ale, she asked Lug, "To whom shall this cup be given?"

"Pour it," said Lug, "for Conn."[24]

As Loomis points out, this story alone is not enough to create the question test, for here there is no test, just the question. Therefore he relates a second source, a folktale from Ireland collected by Rev. Caesar Otway and published in 1841. Loomis summarizes this story as follows:

There lies off the coast of Erris an enchanted isle, crowned with a lofty castle, which is visible once every seven years. The king of this castle has sometimes been seen on the mainland as a small, royally dressed man of pleasant presence. "It is supposed that if *rightly* asked, this hide-and-go-seek potentate will tell the questioner where he can find untold heaps of gold, but the querist must be very particular, for if he ask as he should do, the wealth will be obtained by the one, and the enchantment will be removed by the other; but if not, the king vanishes never to return, amidst wild laughter resounding from the ocean wave, at the folly of him who might have wealth, but had not the wit to win it."[25]

We can certainly see a parallel to the Grail stories in this tale, especially if we combine it with the story of Conn. Consider what Sigune tells Parzival before she knows of his failure to ask the question:

"Tell me, did you see the Grail and its lord, forsaken by joy? Let me hear good tidings. If he has been released from his evil, may you be blessed for that fortunate journey. You shall reign over all things, whatsoever the air touches, all creatures, tame and wild, shall serve you, and the utmost of power and riches shall be yours."[26]

And a little while later:

"You shall have all your uttermost wish on earth. There is no one
so rich that he can compare with you in splendor if you did ask
the question as was right."[27]

Then Parzival utters the tragic line, "I did not ask."

We must remember that just as the fertility rituals had both a
worldly purpose and a spiritual one, so do stories such as these
have a worldly level and a spiritual level. When these stories
speak of "riches" and "gold," they refer to earthly wealth on one
hand, but also to spiritual wealth on the other. On the highest level, when we hear of the Rich Fisher, and of Parzival receiving great wealth and splendor, the reference is to spiritual
wealth. This is why Sigune says to Parzival, "There is no one
so rich that he can compare with you in splendor." When one
has true spiritual wealth, that is, the wisdom and compassion of
enlightenment, there are no earthly riches to be compared with
it. People understand these tales on whatever level of insight
and understanding they have. A worldly person will think of
the pot of gold at the end of the rainbow. A spiritual person will
see enlightenment.

Another aspect of the question test that I would like to mention is based on my own intuition, not on any research or legend
I have found. Thus I cannot prove that the question test came
from the source I am about to discuss, but it is something that I
believe is possible, based on my own monastic experience.

In the last chapter we saw how the Grail legends were based
in part on the tradition of the Mystery religions. Just as the Mystery initiate underwent a process of spiritual passage, so does
the Grail hero undergo a process of passage. We saw on page 108
that in the Mystery initiations the success of the initiate in his
ceremony was symbolized by the resurrection of the patron god.
In the Grail legends, the hero's success is symbolized by the healing of the Fisher King. In many of the Grail stories, the question
is an integral part of the hero's success or lack of it. Where would
a question fit in with a Mystery ceremony?

Because the most secret aspects of these ceremonies were not revealed, I can only use my intuition here. But I can make an educated guess.

In the monastic order I was a part of there is a ceremony called Shosan, which is a Japanese word that can be translated as "Spiritual Examination." I am sure that Christian monasticism has similar ceremonies. In Shosan, either the abbot or one of the most senior monks stands at the head of the ceremony hall, and one by one, in reverse order of seniority, the monks of the community come up and ask the Celebrant a question. This should never be an idle question or a mere philosophical query, but a question that comes from the heart of one's training. That is, one should ask what one most needs to know at that moment in order to further one's spiritual progress. If the question is properly asked, one's level of training and understanding will be revealed to the Celebrant, and based on his or her long monastic experience and deep meditation at that moment, the Celebrant will know what answer needs to be given. The answer that comes is what that particular monk needs to know most at his or her present stage and level of progress.

It is very possible that the asking of such a question was part of the Mystery ceremonies, where the initiate showed whether or not he or she was ready for the higher initiation. If the question was not properly asked, then the initiate was not ready to go on. If the question *was* properly asked, then the initiate showed that he or she was spiritually prepared to go on to the next level. In the Mystery of Mithra, for example, there were seven levels. One would have to pass a test, or a series of tests, to rise to the next step. And if in the Mysteries the successful passing of the test was symbolized by the resurrection of the patron deity, then in the Grail romances the successful passing of the test was symbolized by the healing of the Fisher King. Thus a properly asked question in the Mystery initiation would resurrect the deity, and in the Grail romances it would heal the king, whereas the failure to ask would leave the king still wounded, and the Grail hero "uninitiated."

We see a version of this, albeit a simple one, in Act I, Scene 2 of *Siegfried*. Wotan as the Wanderer comes into Mime's cave while Siegfried is out in the forest, and in return for hospitality he offers to forfeit his head if Mime can ask him three questions that he cannot answer. Mime, though desperate to know how to reforge Notung, tries only to trick Wotan rather than use the opportunity to ask what he most needs to know. Mime asks Wotan three questions to which he, Mime, already knows the answers. When Wotan answers them correctly, he then asks Mime three questions, with Mime's head at stake. Mime answers the first two, but the third question is "Who will reforge Notung?" Mime cannot answer this question, and it is the question that Mime should have asked Wotan. Wotan had told Mime:

> Many fancy
>   wisdom is theirs,
>   but what they most need,
>   that they don't know.
>   When they ask me,
>   freely I answer:
> wisdom flows from my words.

But Mime failed to ask the right question. And Wotan says to him,

> Thrice you asked me your questions,
> thrice I answered you right:
>   but what you asked
>   was meaningless;
> you gave no thought to your need,
> failed to ask what you required.
>   Now when I tell it
>   you'll feel despair.
>   Your wily head
>   I can claim as my prize!
> So, Fafner's dauntless destroyer,
> hear, you wretched dwarf:

"One who has never
learnt to fear—
he makes Notung new."

But Mime has gained the wisdom he needed too late, for his head is forfeit. Mime had committed the classic error of one who is still tied to greed and desire. He thought he knew everything he needed to know and that there was no one who could tell him anything. He had said to Wotan at the start:

Useless knowledge
many ask for,
but I know all that I need.
And my wits are good;
I want no more.
So, wise one, be on your way!

When one is in true spiritual training, one must be willing to let go of self and stand open before the Eternal, accepting the teaching that is given. When one stands before the Eternal, one must be willing to ask, without attachment to self, what one needs to know most. Holding back is a sign of attachment to self, and in that attachment one is not yet ready for the higher teaching. In those Grail stories where the hero fails to ask the question, the hero holds back, even when he desires to know about the wonders he is witnessing. Gurnemanz had never told Parzival not to ask *any* questions. He had said, "Do not ask too many questions."[28] That Parzival did not ask was due to his not being ready for the true Grail secrets. Five years later, after the great suffering he experiences and the wisdom he learns, he is ready. And here Chrétien's story is completed. Parzival *does* get a second chance. He does find the Grail Castle again, and he does ask the question that heals the Fisher King. We will never know if this is what Chrétien intended, but in the end it doesn't matter. It is what happens in *Parzival,* and the great story of Perceval is complete.

Another important aspect of *Parzival* is Wolfram's handling of the Waste Land. In various other versions, as we have seen, there is a physical Waste Land that must be redeemed along with the Fisher King. In *Parzival* there is no actual Waste Land to be brought back to fertility. The Waste Land in Wolfram is a spiritual waste land, one that affects both the community of Munsalvaesche and Parzival himself. Wolfram, to a far greater extent than most, if not all, of the other Grail writers, treats the suffering of his characters in vivid and realistic terms. In *Parzival* we do not feel emotionally removed from the characters and events by the distance of time and style. Thus, when Wolfram describes the suffering of Anfortas and of the people who live at Munsalvaesche, especially their sorrow after Parzival has failed, we are immediately and acutely aware that this suffering is the true Waste Land, and we feel this way also with Parzival and the suffering he undergoes in his five-year search to find the Grail Castle once again. The Waste Land becomes symbolic of the time in our life when we are without God, when we are either wandering aimlessly pursuing worldly desires or searching for God but unable to find the True Source, symbolized here by the Grail Castle and the Grail itself. Wolfram very skillfully handles Parzival's denunciation at the court of Arthur for having failed the question test. Just as the Loathly Damsel had denounced Perceval in front of all the knights, so does Cundrie denounce Parzival. Parzival is humiliated, for this denunciation comes at the height of his fame as a warrior and hero and in front of the very assembly whose admiration he most desires. Wolfram emphasizes in this scene the emptiness of worldly pursuit and the absolute necessity of spiritual quest. Parzival leaves Arthur's court vowing to redeem his honor by finding the Grail Castle again and this time healing the wounded king.

It is just before meeting the hermit Trevrizent that Parzival begins his conversion. For five years he had wandered, not entirely unlike the Jews in the desert (the Old Testament equivalent of the Waste Land). He has performed many deeds of chivalry, but he has not found the Grail Castle. One morning he is riding armed, not knowing what day it is. He meets a group of pilgrims who ask him why he is armed on Good Friday, and he tells them that he does not know what day it is: "'Sir, I have no idea when the year began nor how many weeks have passed. Not even what day of the week it is—of all that I know nothing. I used to serve one whose name is God until He in His charity doomed me to shameful disgrace. My mind had never wavered from Him Who I was told would give me help. Yet now His help has failed me.'"[29]

Parzival is still wandering in his own spiritual waste land, blaming God for his own failure. Yet within Parzival there is the merit of his quest, the search to find the Grail Castle (the True Source) and to succeed where before he had failed. And this merit begins to flower when he meets the pilgrims. He is moved by their devotion and humility, and he begins to doubt his own hardness and rejection of God. This is the beginning of his conversion, his saying to himself, "I could be wrong." Whenever we are able to let go of self long enough to accept the idea that we could, in fact, be wrong, we begin to open ourselves to the truth. Whenever we begin to let go of our opinions, our delusions, our anger and sense of hurt, we become able to start seeing the world as it actually is, rather than as we thought it was. And thus we become open to, and able to receive, spiritual teaching. This is beautifully described in *Parzival*. Parzival deems himself unworthy to travel with the pilgrims, "for I hate Him Whom they love with all their hearts and from Whom they look for help."[30] But as he rides away from them, he has a change of heart.

Away rides Herzeloyde's son. His manly breeding inclined him to virtue and compassion. And since the young Herzeloyde had bequeathed to him true loyalty, repentance arose in his heart. Now for the first time he thought on his Creator, how He had made the whole world and how mighty was His power. "What if God will give help to overcome my sadness?" he said. "If ever He wished a knight well and if ever a knight earned His reward, if He deems shield and sword and true manly combat to be worthy enough of His help that His help may heal my sorrow, if today is His day for helping, then let Him help, if help He can!"[31]

Parzival then performs a very simple but very important act of contrition and selflessness. He gives himself over to That which is greater than all of us. He lets go of the reins of his horse and allows himself to be taken wherever the horse may lead.

> "If God's power is so great that it can guide both horse and beast, and men as well, then I will praise His power. If God's art possesses such help, then let it show this Castilian of mine the road that is best for me. Thus His kindness shall show its help.—Now go, whichever way God chooses!" And he let the reins fall loosely over his horse's ears and urged it on vigorously with his spurs.[32]

The horse leads Parzival to the hermitage of Trevrizent, who is living the holy life of a monk, although he is not ordained by any order. It is Trevrizent who tells Parzival of the details of the Grail. Trevrizent was one of Anfortas's brothers and lived in Munsalvaesche. When Anfortas was wounded Trevrizent left the castle and began his life as a hermit. As Wolfram says of him, "God had turned his thoughts toward making ready to meet the heavenly host."[33] Parzival confesses to Trevrizent, and he gives Parzival his counsel. He warns Parzival against pride and directs him on how to travel the spiritual path. Parzival stays with him for fifteen days, living as the monk does, and when the time for parting comes, Trevrizent says to Parzival, "Give your sins to me. In the sight of God, I am the guaranty for your atonement. And now do as I have bidden you, and follow that course undaunted."[34] We will see in the next chapter that this very letting go of pride and delusion and the willingness to follow the quest of the Grail wholeheartedly and with purity of intent are at the heart of the transformation from Siegfried to Parsifal.

It is time now to discuss what Wagner finally did in terms of adapting *Parzival* to operatic form. In spite of telling Mathilde that he wanted no part of it, he ended up forming it into his final masterpiece, and by the time he was done, he owed much more to Wolfram than he later wanted to admit.

Parzival and Wagner

Both *Parzival* and *Parsifal* are portrayals of the path to enlightenment, from naiveté and innocence through many trials and sufferings and finally on to spiritual wisdom and understanding. Both base the success of this journey on the ability of the hero to let go of self and feel compassion for the suffering of others.

Wagner begins his story after Parsifal has already left his mother. Wagner follows the Perceval/Parzival story, having Parsifal's father, Gamuret, die in battle and his mother, Herzeleide, raising him in the wilds in order to keep him from becoming a warrior. But one day he sees men riding on beautiful horses, and he desires to be one of them. Wagner does not mention King Arthur at this point, but the rest of the details are close to Wolfram's version of the tale. In writing an opera libretto, Wagner necessarily had to condense a great deal of Wolfram's poem, and thus characters such as Gawan (the German Gawain) and Sigune, who are prominent in Wolfram, either get a quick mention by Wagner or are left out entirely.

Sigune does not appear, and instead it is Kundry who tells Parsifal that his mother is dead. Gawan searches for healing balm for Amfortas, but does not appear as a character. Wagner's Gurnemanz, as I mentioned before, is a combination of Wolfram's Gurnemanz and Trevrizent. The most significant difference between Wagner and Wolfram is that in Wagner Parsifal is not married.[35] There is no mention of Condwiramurs, and in Wagner's scheme of the opera, celibacy is a requirement for Parsifal's final enlightenment. In this regard Parsifal is the counterpart of Galahad, not Parzival.

Wagner does adopt one aspect of marriage from Wolfram: the Grail King is allowed to marry and have a son so that his line of Grail Guardians can continue. Even though Parsifal is not married, Titurel was, and his son is Amfortas. In Wolfram

Titurel is the first Grail King, and he has a son named Frimutel. Frimutel is the father of Anfortas, Trevrizent, Schoysiane
(mother of Sigune), Herzeloyde, and Repanse de Schoye, the
Grail Maiden. While Parzival is staying with Trevrizent, he
asks him,

> "Who was the man lying there before the Grail? He was quite
> grey, but his skin was bright and fresh."
>   "That was Titurel," answered his host. "He is your mother's
> grandfather. He was the first to be entrusted with the banner of
> the Grail and the charge of defending it. He has a sickness called
> podagra, a lameness for which there is no help. Yet he has never
> lost his fresh color, for he sees the Grail so often that he cannot
> die. They cherish him, bedridden though he is, for the sake of his
> counsel."[36]

We can see here a remnant of the tradition of the Lame King
as well as the Maimed King. Anfortas is specifically maimed and
is the one who needs healing. But the old tradition of lameness
is also preserved here by Wolfram in Titurel's illness.

Frimutel was killed in a joust, and thus his eldest son, Anfortas, became the Grail King. (Wagner also specifies Titurel
as the first Guardian, but he eliminates Frimutel and simply
has Titurel be the father of Amfortas.) Trevrizent explains to
Parzival how the Grail Order both requires celibacy and allows
marriage.

> "Maidens are appointed to care for the Grail," said his host. "That
> was God's decree, and these maidens performed their service be-
> fore it. The Grail selects only noble company. Knights, devout
> and good, are chosen to guard it. . . .
>   "Nephew, I will tell you something more, whose truth you
> may well believe. A twofold chance is often theirs: they both give
> and receive profit. They receive young children there, of noble
> lineage and beautiful. And if anywhere a land loses its lord, if
> the people there acknowledge the Hand of God and seek a new

lord, they are granted one from the company of the Grail. They must treat him with courtesy, for the blessing of God protects him.

"The men God sends forth secretly; the maidens leave openly."[37]

Trevrizent next describes how Herzeloyde was sent out in this fashion to be the wife of King Castis, but he died soon after the marriage, and she eventually married Gahmuret. Trevrizent continues:

> "Thus the maids are sent out openly from the Grail and the men in secret, that they may have children who will in turn one day enter the service of the Grail, and, serving, enhance its company. God can teach them how to do this.
>
> "Any man who has pledged himself to serve the Grail must renounce the love of women. Only the king may have a wife, and she must be pure and his in lawful marriage, and those other knights whom God has sent as rulers to lands without a lord."[38]

In other words, only the king and those knights sent out to be lords are allowed to have wives. The knights who serve at Munsalvaesche must remain celibate.

Wagner adopted this view of the Grail Order and its stipulations for both *Lohengrin* and *Parsifal*. Along with this, he adopted the cause of Anfortas's fall, although he reworked it in his own fashion. Trevrizent relates to Parzival how Anfortas fell, and these passages constitute another example of how Wolfram deals with human nature not only realistically, but also compassionately. Although Anfortas is the Grail King and is thus allowed to marry for the purpose of having children to carry on the line of Grail Kings, he is not allowed to have amorous relations out of romantic desire. But being a young man, he naturally had such desires, a matter Wolfram treats very openly and with a great deal of acceptance. Anfortas and Parzival are not perfect in the same way that Galahad is in the *Queste* and Malory. Galahad represents the ideal; Anfortas and Parzival represent the actual. Trevrizent tells Parzival:

> "Sir, a king was there who was called and is still called Anfortas. You, and I too, poor though I be, should never cease to feel compassion for his grief of heart, which pride gave him as reward. His youth and power brought grief to all around him, and his desire for love beyond all restraints and bounds.
>
> "Such ways are not fitting for the Grail. There both knight and squire must guard against incontinence."[39]

Trevrizent continues later on:

> "When Frimutel, my father, lost his life, they chose his eldest son to succeed him as king and Lord of the Grail and the Grail's company. That was my brother Anfortas, who was worthy of crown and power. We were still small. Then my brother reached the age when his beard began to grow—the time when Love wages battle with youth. Here Love does not act quite honorably, one must say, for she presses her friend so hard. But if any Lord of the Grail craves a love other than the writing on the Grail allows him, he will suffer distress and grievous misery.
>
> "My lord and brother chose for himself a lady, of virtue, so he thought. Who she was does not matter. In her service he fought as one from whom cowardice has fled. Many a shield's rim was riddled for her by his good hand. With his adventures the sweet and valiant man won such fame that never in all the lands where chivalry held sway could any one question that his was the greatest of all. *Amor* was his battle cry. But that cry is not quite appropriate for a spirit of humility.
>
> "One day the king rode out alone—and sorely did his people rue it—in search of adventure, rejoicing in Love's assistance. Love's desire compelled him to it. With a poisoned spear he was wounded so in the jousting, your sweet uncle, that he never again was healed, pierced through the testicles."[40]

Wolfram treats Anfortas in a very compassionate way, not condemning him for being young and susceptible to temptation, but also not evading the truth that he broke the Precepts of the Order and suffered the consequences thereof. The line "the time when Love wages battle with youth" is quite marvelous. Anfortas is human, even though he is the Grail King. One of the aspects of tragedy, both with the Greeks and with Shakespeare, is that when a great one errs it affects not only his own life, but also the lives of many others. In the case of a king, the error affects his whole kingdom. We see this very vividly with Anfortas. Not only is he personally in great pain, but the whole community of the Grail suffers as well.

Wagner adopts this scenario of the cause of Anfortas's fall and changes it in details to fit his own design. In *Parzival* Anfortas is not jousting with Clinschor (Wagner's Klingsor). His opponent is a nameless heathen, and in Wolfram's world the word "heathen" was used in most cases to refer to Arabs and Muslims, or people from the East in general. Trevrizent tells Parzival: "'It was a heathen who fought him in that joust, born in Ethnise, where from Paradise the Tigris flows. This heathen was sure that his valor would win the Grail. Its name was engraved on his spear, and only for the sake of the Grail's power did he seek knightly deeds far off, roaming over sea and land. In this battle our joy was lost to us.'"[41]

We see a parallel here between this "heathen" and Wagner's Klingsor, for both are trying to win the Grail through combat with the Grail King. Wagner again took the basic premise from Wolfram and then condensed the characters into what was manageable and practical onstage. In *Parzival*, Anfortas's opponent is killed in this fight, and we have another example of Wolfram's acceptance of all people: "The heathen lay dead where he had left him. Let us make lament for him too—but sparingly."[42]

Anfortas is horribly wounded. The spearhead breaks from the shaft and remains embedded in his body: "'When the king returned to us so pale and all his strength ebbed away, a physician probed the wound until he found the iron spearhead and a splinter of the reed shaft, and removed them. I fell on my knees and prayed.'"[43]

At this point Trevrizent made a vow to renounce knighthood, meat, bread, and wine, and to follow a holy life serving God if God would help his brother. Wolfram makes various references throughout the rest of the narration to the horrid nature of the wound and how no doctor or books on medicine could cure it. When Trevrizent vowed to become a hermit, the Grail Order did not know who would succeed Anfortas as king, and so they implored the help of the Grail: "'Straightway, hoping for God's help, they carried the king to the Grail. When the king beheld the Grail, that brought him further anguish, since now he could not die. Death was not permitted him, seeing I had dedicated myself to a life of poverty, and the lordship of that noble race hung upon such weak strength.'"[44]

After trying many, many cures, none of which work, "'We fell on our knees in prayer before the Grail. All at once we saw written upon it that a knight should come, and if from him a question came, our sorrow would be ended, but if anyone, child or maid or man, should prompt him in any way to the question, his question would not help, but the wound would remain as before and pain more violently.'"[45]

Wagner adopted all of this, up to the question. Wagner has Parsifal heal Amfortas with the spear that caused the wound in the first place. Interestingly, the Grail knights in *Parzival* try to heal the wound with the spearhead itself. Since the wound had festered from the poison on the spear point and thus was hot, the knights tried putting the spearhead in the snow to make it cold and then inserting it into the wound to try to take the infection away, but even this did not work. The only thing that can heal Anfortas is the properly asked question.

Both Wolfram and Wagner see Anfortas's fall as coming through romantic and sexual temptation. Significantly, Wolfram specifies that the wound Anfortas received as a result of breaking the precept against sexual indulgence is a wound to the genitals. In addition to following the tradition of having the

Grail King wounded in this fashion, Wolfram has also given us a vivid and explicit example of the law of karma. Anfortas was the Grail Lord, and part of his responsibility was to be an example of the spiritual practice and aspiration of the Grail Order. All the Grail knights knew that the love of women was forbidden to the community at Munsalvaesche, and thus Anfortas's taking a lover and fighting in the name of *amor* was a direct violation of the spiritual rule that he was expected to uphold and represent. The consequences matched the transgression exactly, both literally and symbolically.

Wagner is not as explicit about the wound as Wolfram is, but the overall symbolism is the same. Titurel grew old and bestowed upon his son Amfortas the kingship of the Grail. With brashness and pride Amfortas set out to subdue the sorcery of Klingsor, but he was ensnared by the trap Klingsor had set for him. Sexual desire was the element that Klingsor had not been able to overcome, and sexual desire was the trap he set for the knights of the Grail when they rode out into the world. Wagner, like Wolfram, uses the idea of the Waste Land symbolically. In the desert—that is, the Waste Land—Klingsor creates his magic garden:

> He transformed the desert into a magic garden
> in which bloomed women of infernal beauty;
> there he awaits the knights of the Grail
> to lure them to sinful joys and hell's damnation.[46]

The Waste Land here is the mind and spirit of the spiritual seeker who has not yet cleansed the karma of sensual desire, and who is thus still open to sexual temptation. Klingsor's castle and magic garden also parallel one of the common features of the Grail romances, that of the Castle of Maidens, or in Wolfram the Castle of Wonders, wherein many maidens are held captive. This magic castle in the romances represents both a temptation to the Grail seeker and the inverse of the Grail Castle itself. The Grail Castle on this level represents the mind of enlightenment, harboring and protecting the Grail, the symbol of spiritual wisdom. The Castle of Maidens is the inverse of this, the worldly mind harboring and indulging desire and attachment to the realm of impermanence, the world of delusion. It is in this "waste land" that Klingsor sets his trap.

Wagner does not place the wound specifically in the genitals, but it is sexual temptation through the beautiful aspect of Kundry by which Amfortas falls. Gurnemanz tells the squires:

> Hard by the keep our hero was drawn away:
> a woman of fearsome beauty bewitched him;
> in her arms he lay intoxicated,
> letting fall the Spear.
> A deathly cry! I rushed in:
> Klingsor, laughing, was vanishing from there,
> having stolen the holy Spear.
> Fighting, I guarded the king's flight;
> but a wound burned him in the side;
> this wound it is which never will heal.[47]

As I mentioned before, in the *Queste* and Malory Galahad represents the ideal, and thus he never falls prey to any of the temptations which confront him. He upholds the ideal of chivalry and spiritual quest in all his deeds, and he succeeds supremely in healing the Fisher King and in finding and comprehending the Grail. Amfortas is not perfect, and he is not strong enough in his training to recognize either the error of pride when it seizes him or the temptation of sensual desire when it arises in front of him. Thus he falls prey to both.

Where did Wagner get the idea of healing Amfortas with the same spear that caused the wound? There are two sources. As we saw in the last chapter, Galahad takes the blood of the spear that Balin had used to wound King Pellam and by anointing Pellam's legs and body with the blood heals him. The spear in this case was the spear of Longinus. Wagner also sees the Spear as the spear of Longinus, but the healing is done specifically by touch-

ing the point of the Spear to the wound itself. As Parsifal touches
Amfortas's side with the Spear, he says:

> One weapon only serves:
> only the spear which gave the wound heals the wound.[48]

The idea of the spear that caused the wound being the only
object that can heal the wound comes from the story of Achilles
and Telephus (Greek Telephos). Wagner had sketched a drama
about Achilles in 1849 and was thus familiar with the legend.

Telephus was the son of Hercules and Auge, the unmarried
daughter of King Tegea. When Telephus was born, Auge was
forced to hide her child in the sacred wood of Athena. When the
goddess consequently caused a famine to beset the land, King
Tegea exposed the fact that Auge had borne a child and sold her
as a slave. She ended up in Mysia, where she eventually married
King Teuthras.

Telephus was found and rescued by shepherds. When he
came of age, he traveled, on the advice of an oracle, to Mysia.
There he almost made the mistake of Oedipus—marrying his
own mother. But he married a daughter of King Priam of Troy,
and when King Teuthras died, Telephus succeeded him on the
throne. He thus became an ally of the Trojans.

The Greeks, on their way to Troy but lacking a leader who could
show them the way, attacked Mysia, but Telephus's army repulsed
them. However, in the fighting Telephus was wounded in the thigh
by the spear of Achilles. This spear had been given by the centaur
Chiron to Peleus, the father of Achilles. The shaft had been cut
from an ash tree on Mount Pelion, and only Achilles could wield
it. When the Greeks withdrew from Mysia, the wound of Telephus
would not heal, and he remained in fierce agony.

Agamemnon, the leader of the Greeks, had been told by an
oracle that the Greeks could never capture Troy without the aid of
Telephus. Telephus himself had been told by the oracle of Apollo
that he would be cured when the one who had wounded him
turned physician. Telephus traveled to Argos and begged the help

of Achilles. Achilles scraped the rust off the head of his spear and with it healed Telephus's wound. Once healed, Telephus was invited by the Greeks to join them against Troy, but he, being married to one of Priam's daughters, could not join the campaign himself. However, in return for being healed, he gave the Greeks directions to Troy and told them how it could be captured.

We have here a number of parallels to the Grail stories. Telephus is wounded through the thigh, just as are the Grail Kings. His wound will not heal, and he is in great agony. The rust of the spear corresponds to the blood of the spear in the *Queste* and Malory. And it is Achilles who inspired Wagner's idea of both wound inflictor and physician. In this case it was not the rust itself that healed Telephus. It was only Achilles, who inflicted the wound, who could also heal it. Wagner took this idea and applied it to the Spear.

On the agricultural level of the old fertility rites, Achilles takes the part of the Doctor, the one who brings the wounded (or dead) spirit of Vegetation back to health (or life). In this respect he also corresponds to the Grail hero. On the spiritual level, Achilles represents what the Spear represents in *Parsifal*, the two-edged sword of volitional action. In having human bodies, we have the opportunity to use our body, speech, and mind either to cleanse karma or to make more of it. No matter how far we may seem to have strayed from the spiritual path, we can always turn in the direction of the Eternal, of God, and anything that we have used for harm can also be used for kindness and good. It is our intention and commitment that matter. We can always heal the wound that we ourselves have caused. Just as Achilles first wounds Telephus and then "turns physician," so can we, who have caused harm to both ourselves and others, turn physician and heal that harm. In this regard Klingsor represents selfish karmic action and Parsifal, selfless enlightened action. The Spear in the hands of Klingsor causes suffering. The same Spear in the hands of Parsifal heals that suffering and brings redemption, both for the individual and the whole world.

We now come to the character of Clinschor/Klingsor.

In Chrétien, the Loathly Damsel tells Arthur's court of the

Castle Orgulous, with its 566 knights of fame and their lady-loves. She says that any knight seeking combat and feats of chivalry will find them there. She then tells of Montescleire, where a damsel is besieged. Gawain vows to go to Montescleire, and Giflet goes to Castle Orgulous. In *Peredur* the black woman gives the same message, except that instead of Castle Orgulous she calls the castle Castell Syberw, which in Welsh means "proud castle." She even mentions the exact same number of knights and ladies, 566. She also mentions a damsel in a besieged castle who needs rescuing, but she gives the place no name. Gwalchmei (the Welsh Gawain) again chooses to rescue the damsel.

Wolfram treats this part of the story in his own way. After chastising Parzival for not asking the question, Cundrie announces to Arthur's court that a great adventure is to be had at the Castle of Wonders, where four queens and four hundred maidens dwell. She says that fame and great reward are to be found there, but she says no more about it. There is no mention of Montescleire, and no knight volunteers to go there, for as soon as Cundrie leaves a knight comes to the court challenging Gawan to a fight to avenge an earlier wrong, and all the focus turns to the accusation against Gawan. Parzival and Gawan part, Parzival to begin his search for the Grail Castle and Gawan to answer the accusation.

In the course of the events that follow, Gawan also sets out to seek the Grail,[49] but his adventures lead him to meet Orgeluse, the duchess of Logrois. Her land was near Clinschor's wood, and Gawan learns that the four queens and four hundred maidens are being held captive by great enchantment in the Castle of Wonders. This castle belongs to Clinschor, and it is his magic that controls the castle and the lands around it. Orgulous is no longer the name of the castle, but the name of the duchess.

This is an interesting use of the French. Burton Raffel translates "Castle Orgulous" as "Castle Pride," which would equate with the Welch name in *Peredur*. *Orgueil* in French means "pride," and *orgueilleuse* refers to a proud or arrogant woman. Wolfram's Orgeluse, when we first meet her, more than lives up to her name in the way that she treats (or mistreats) Gawan. However, after Gawan has shown himself to be worthy, she changes her behavior and eventually the two marry. In *Perceval* she is not named but is called the Proud Beauty of Logres. Since Chrétien did not live to finish the tale, we don't know if he ever intended Gawain to end up marrying her.

Gawan undertakes the adventure of the Castle of Wonders, even though a kind ferryman and his family, who gave him shelter one night and told him of the enchantment, try to dissuade him, fearing for his life. He is told that if he does survive he will become lord of the castle and the captives will be set free, but that no adventure he has ever had before will compare with this one. One of the captive queens is Arnive, the mother of Arthur, who in Chrétien is named Ygerne, and in Malory Igraine. When Gawan tells the ferryman that he is resolved to undertake the quest, the ferryman says to him, "Now arm yourself against great peril."[50]

Gawan enters the castle and the magic begins. He encounters the *lit marveile*, the Wonder Bed: anyone who lies upon it must first endure the bed's crashing violently into the walls of the castle, and then survive being attacked first by five hundred slings hurling stones, and after that by five hundred crossbows firing arrows. The ferryman had told Gawan that "when you think your troubles have come to an end, then you will really be just beginning to fight."[51]

Gawan survives the first three perils, and then a ferocious and starved lion the size of a horse enters the room and attacks Gawan. Gawan manages to kill it after a protracted battle, but he is so exhausted at the end that he collapses on the body of the dead lion. Queen Arnive and the maidens have been secretly watching the fight, and when it is over they do not know if Gawan is alive or dead. The only way that the enchantment can be broken is if he survives. Two of the maidens enter the room to see if there is any hope and find Gawan unconscious but still breathing. Gawan is then brought to a room where Arnive, highly skilled in healing, treats him and saves him from dying, for he has many wounds.

His survival breaks the spell, the women are freed, and Gawan becomes lord of the castle and its lands.

Later Orgeluse tells Gawan that it was she whom Anfortas had served and fought for. King Gramoflanz had killed her husband Cidegast and had wooed Orgeluse for himself. But she would not have him and instead plotted his death. She tells Gawan that she enlisted the services of Anfortas in order to avenge herself against Gramoflanz, but before Anfortas could find Gramoflanz, he was wounded in battle against the heathen knight. Orgeluse tells Gawan that she has suffered more because of what happened to Anfortas than she had at the death of Cidegast.

Gawan has broken the spell of Clinschor, but he still desires to know more about the sorcerer. It is Queen Arnive who tells him the story. Clinschor had been the duke of Capua and a vassal of the king of Sicily, Ibert. King Ibert had a very beautiful wife named Iblis, and she and Clinschor had an affair. King Ibert caught them in bed together and in punishment castrated Clinschor. Out of revenge and shame Clinschor traveled to the city of Persida in Persia, where he learned magic arts, and now he uses those arts for harm and ill. Arnive goes on to tell Gawan that Clinschor is a man of his word, and that because Gawan survived the trials of the castle, Clinschor will leave everyone alone. Clinschor never actually appears in the story; we only hear about him. But we can see that Wagner adopted the basic premise of Clinschor's castration as the basis for his practice of magic, and that the castration was a result of sexual incontinence. Wagner reworked these elements into his own version of the story, but the basic premise was taken from Wolfram.

Clinschor does not exist as a character in *Perceval*. Although Wolfram is consistent in calling the castle the Castle of Wonders, both when Cundrie first announces it at Arthur's court and again when Gawan arrives there, Chrétien is not. The Loathly Damsel calls it Castle Pride. But when Gawain, upon arriving at the castle, asks what its name is, he is told it is called The Rock of Champguin. (Gawain never does go to Montescleire.) *Champguin* comes from *champ*, meaning "field," and *guin*, meaning "white." This is the same *guin* as in Guinevere, which can be translated variously as "white phantom," "white apparition," or "white shadow." The meaning of Guinevere's name in this context is "the light that shines from the Otherworld." In Celtic culture "white field" referred to the land of the dead. Thus in *Perceval* this castle is in the land of the dead, and that is why we see the character of Ygerne, Arthur's mother, who has long been dead on earth. In *Perceval* Gawain survives the trials, just as Gawan does in *Parzival*. On one level this adventure can be seen as another example of the hero's braving the perils of a journey to the Otherworld, where failure would mean death. On another level we see the archetype of the "Castle of Maidens" as an inverse reflection of the Grail Castle. In the Castle of Maidens it is women who must be released from enchantment by the hero, and this Gawan does. In the Grail Castle it is men, a wounded king and his company of knights, who must be released from their enchantment, symbolized by the wound that will not heal, and this Parzival does.

It is part of Wagner's ingenious condensing that he has one hero, Parsifal, releasing both the Castle of Maidens (Klingsor's castle with Kundry and the flower maidens), and the Grail Castle of Monsalvat. Wagner, in his own unique way, incorporates the archetype of the Castle of Maidens as the inverse of the Grail Castle, but he does so by using Wolfram's idea of Clinschor and his enchanted Castle of Wonders, not Chrétien's castle in the land of the dead.

At this point I will take a moment to relate briefly a very poignant episode in *Parzival*. I mentioned earlier that well before Frazer published *The Golden Bough*, both Wagner and Wolfram understood the tradition of sacred kingship. During the time that Orgeluse is still testing Gawan, she asks him to kill Gramoflanz in order to avenge Cidegast's death. Orgeluse takes Gawan to a section of Clinschor's forest where tamarisk and prisin trees grow. Orgeluse points out a particular tree and says to Gawan, "Sir, that tree is guarded by a man who robbed me of my joy. If you bring me a branch from it, never will a knight have received such a rich reward for love's service."[52] At great risk Gawan and his horse must cross the Perilous Ford, a ravine with a rushing stream at its bottom, to get to the tree. Gawan and his horse only barely make it, and Gawan breaks off a branch, which challenges the king. (In Chrétien this ravine is also called the Perilous Ford, but there is no mention of breaking a branch.) King Gramoflanz appears, and thus begins one of the best episodes in the poem. Eventually, through the chivalry of both Gawan and Gramoflanz, along with the help of Arthur, Gawan and Gramoflanz do not fight, but reconcile and become friends. (It is during this episode that Chrétien's *Perceval* ends uncompleted.) Gawan helps Gramoflanz marry the woman he loves, and Gawan himself marries Orgeluse. What is so striking about this event is that it is an *exact* parallel to the situation in the grove of Nemi in *The Golden Bough*. Here we have a tree guarded by a king, and the one coming to challenge this king does so by breaking off a bough of that tree. We can see here a vivid example of the tradition of sacred kingship enduring throughout the centuries and appearing in the Grail romances. That Wolfram included the particular detail of the bough as part of this adventure, where Chrétien had not, is another indication that Wolfram understood much more of the myths and their symbols than the other romance writers of that time.

One of the most interesting characters in the Grail legends is that of the Loathly Damsel. Sometimes she is named, sometimes only described, but in spite of her hideous appearance she is very wise and is able to tell the knights many things that they do not know themselves. Some of her knowledge comes from her wide traveling, but at other times it's as though she is clairvoyant, knowing things that she could not have witnessed herself. This is never fully explained, and an enticing mystery surrounding this character remains throughout the stories.

The Loathly Damsel is actually a common character in world mythology, and in keeping with the tradition of fertility ceremonies and Mystery religions, her symbolism is both agricultural and spiritual. On the simplest level she represents the land itself. Her hideous appearance represents the land in winter, and her transformation into a beautiful woman represents the blooming of spring and summer and the land's return to life. But of course there is much more to her than this.

On the spiritual level she has various guises and meanings. Joseph Campbell writes: "This figure of the Loathly Damsel is comparable, and perhaps related, to that Zoroastrian 'Spirit of the Way' who meets the soul at death on the Chinvat Bridge to the Persian yonder world. Those of wicked life see her ugly; those of unsullied virtue, most fair."[53] In this context she appears in hideous form to Perceval, Peredur, and Parzival to denounce them for not asking the question because she is reflecting back to them their lack of virtue in their failure to heal the Fisher King. Speaking of Parzival's failure to comprehend the Grail and the suffering of Anfortas, Campbell writes:

> However, Parzival's mind on that occasion was on himself and his social reputation. The Round Table stands in Wolfram's work for the social order of the period of which it was the summit and consummation. The young knight's concern for his reputation as one worthy of that circle was his motive for holding his tongue when his own better nature was actually pressing him to speak; and in the light of his conscious notion of himself as a knight worthy of the name, just hailed as the greatest in the world, one can understand his shock and resentment at the sharp judgments of the Loathly Damsel and Sigune. However, those two were the messengers of a deeper sphere of values and possibilities than was yet known, or even sensed, by his socially conscious mind; they were of the sphere not of the Round Table but of the Castle of the Grail, which had not been a feature of the normal daylight world, visible to all, but dreamlike, visionary, mythic—and yet to the questing knight not an unsubstantial mirage.[54]

In both *Peredur* and *Perlesvaus* it is revealed that the bearer of the salver and the dish respectively is identical with the Loathly Damsel who appears at Arthur's court and castigates the hero for his failure to ask the question. Loomis draws a parallel between the Grail Bearer, who is also the Loathly Damsel, with Ériu, the Sovranty of Ireland. She was the damsel in the mansion of Lug who served the cup to Conn:

> The most notable trait of the Sovranty of Ireland, likewise, was her transformation from extreme ugliness to radiant beauty. Several Irish tales are concerned with her metamorphosis, and some later retellings, like the *Wife of Bath's Tale*, are attached to the Arthurian cycle. Celtic scholars recognize that this allegorical figure originated as a personification of the land of Ireland itself, and under the name of Ériu (Ireland) she was thus described: 'One time she is a broad-faced beautiful queen [note the crown which the Sovranty of Ireland wears in *Phantom's Frenzy*] and another time a horrible fierce-faced sorceress, a sharp whitey-grey bloated thick-lipped pale-eyed battle-fiend.[55]

Loomis theorizes that although Chrétien does not identify either the Grail Bearer or the Loathly Damsel, the unity of the two would explain how the Loathly Damsel knew about Perceval's failure to ask the question, something she could only have known if she had been there.

Wagner also came to accept this unity. In his letter to Mathilde of August 1860 (the same letter in which he says that Savitri of *Die Sieger* is the rebirth of Elsa), he writes: "Did I not tell you once before that the fabulously wild messenger of the grail is to be one and the same person as the enchantress of the second act. Since this dawned on me, almost everything else about the subject has become clear to me."[56] Wagner uses this aspect of Kundry in his own way, which we will consider in detail in the next chapter, but we can still see the ugly/beautiful combination in his Kundry just as we see it in the various characters of mythology.

Another variation on this theme is a story with a number of different versions where the hero must marry a hideously ugly woman. There is a version of this story where Gawain must do this for the sake of Arthur, and when he and his new bride are alone for the first time she becomes wondrously beautiful. She tells him that his nobility in marrying her has broken part of the spell, and that she can now be beautiful for twelve of each twenty-four hours. She asks him which part of the day he would like her to be beautiful, the part of the day where the two are in public together, or the part where they are alone. He tells her that he would wish whatever part of the day she could most bear. She then embraces him in tears and tells him that his nobleness and generosity have broken the spell completely, and now she can be beautiful all the time. Other versions of this story often entail a monstrously ugly woman who has a treasure of some kind, and in order to receive this treasure, a man must give her a kiss. Most are unable to do it, but the hero of the story gladly and without hesitation gives her a big hug and kiss, and she immediately transforms into a beautiful woman. We all remember the fairy tale of the frog prince and the maiden. Here it is the ability and willingness to see through outward appearances alone to the true value within that allows the hero of the tale to accomplish the transformation.

On a deeper level even than the above stories is the simple religious truth of the dual nature of all impermanent forms. By nature some of the forms of the world that appear to us will be pleasing, and some will be repulsive. This is all part of the nature of maya. Inherent in the above stories is a grasping onto that which is pleasing. Something is to be gained from "braving" the ugliness of form. Even the simple winter/spring analogy implies waiting through the darkness and cold of winter to get to the warmth and light of spring and summer. There is still an attachment to outward form. We push away what we don't like and grasp onto what we do like. In meditation specifically and spiritual training in general, we learn to sit still within the conditions of the world, neither pushing away what we don't like nor grasping for what we do like. This ability to sit still amidst the constantly changing forms and appearances of illusion was a major part of the Buddha's enlightenment. The Tempter, Mara, came at the Buddha with everything he had, but no matter what terrifyingly horrible forms appeared, or what enchantingly beautiful forms tried to entice him, the Buddha sat still, neither grasping nor pushing away. The Buddha realized that all of these diverse forms were nothing but projections of his own mind and in themselves had no reality. At this point Mara's "army" disappeared, and all the weapons that had been hurled at the Buddha turned into flowers that fell at his feet.

In *Parzival* Cundrie and the Grail Bearer are not the same person, but Cundrie's symbolism is important nonetheless. Wolfram describes her as being very learned in all languages, including Arabic, as well as in dialectic, geometry, and astronomy. The harness and bridle of her mule are very rich and costly, her clothes of the finest cloth and fashion: "Over her hat swung a braid of her hair, so long that it touched the mule. It was black and hard, not pretty, and soft as the bristles of a pig. She had a nose like a dog's, and two boar's teeth stuck out from her mouth, each a span in length. Both eyebrows were braided and the braids drawn up to the ribbon that held her hair. . . . Cundrie had ears like a bear's, and no lover could desire a face like hers, hairy and rough."[57]

As is the case with other authors, the animal features are multiple, but the main image that we get from Wolfram's description is of a pig or wild boar. There is an Irish legend of Oisin, one of the sons of Finn Mac Cumhail, in which Oisin shoots more game in the forest than he can bring home, and a young woman with a pig's head offers to help him. The load is so heavy that after a while both sit down to rest, and the young woman is so hot that she opens her dress to let in the cool air. Oisin looks at her and sees the most beautiful female form he has ever laid eyes on. He asks her how she came to have the head of a pig, and she tells him that her father, the king of the Land of Youth, put her under a druidic spell. The Druid of the Land of Youth told her that if one of the sons of Finn Mac Cumhail would marry her, the spell would be broken. Oisin marries her, and her face again becomes as beautiful as it was before the spell was cast.

In mythologies around the world that feature a great hero, there is always the awakening of the hero to his true purpose in life. In the case of the Buddha, for example, that moment comes when Prince Siddhartha, the Buddha-to-be, goes outside the protective palace his father has built for him and sees the world as it really is. This is symbolized by Siddhartha's seeing the figures representing old age, disease, and death, the world of impermanence and suffering. Then, after he sees a wandering monk, he aspires to be a monk and find the cause and the cessation of all suffering.

Parzival's awakening comes in two stages. The first is when he sees the knights of King Arthur's court riding by. They are so radiant that he thinks they are gods. They awaken him to the first part of his purpose: to become a knight of King Arthur's court. But this is not enough, for the quest of the Grail still lies ahead. As Parzival shows in his first visit to the Grail Castle, he is still unawakened to the true spiritual path. Thus a second awakening is necessary, and this comes through the character of Cundrie. Campbell writes:

> The messenger, the summoner to this more inward quest is not, like the angel of the first task, a normal figure of the light world: in the case of Parzival, not a shining knight but an apparition with the muzzle of a boar, the boar of the wound of Adonis, the same pig-faced Daughter of the King of the Land of Youth who in the fairytale appeared to Oisin. And the adventure itself, in accord with the character of its announcer, required a passage beyond the known bounds and forms of time, space, and causality to a domain of vision, where time and eternity were at one: in Parzival's case, the Grail Castle, and in Gawain's—announced at the same weird hour by the same weird sister of night—the Château Merveil [Castle of Wonders].[58]

It is Cundrie who awakens Parzival to his true spiritual purpose and quest, even though he doesn't fully understand this at the time.

The wording that Campbell uses in the above passage is very interesting on a number of points. He uses the same day/night symbolism that we saw in the relationship of *Tristan und Isolde* to Schopenhauer's idea of the noumenon and phenomenon. We can remember that the outer world of time, space, and causality, Schopenhauer's world of representation or phenomenon, was symbolized in *Tristan* as day, while the inner world of the noumenon was symbolized by night. Thus Parzival's first awakening comes from characters representing light and the world of daylight, the brightly shining knights in armor. This is his awakening to the outward world of form, his birth into the world. But this is not enough, for we are not born into the world just to experience its transience. We are born into this world in order to find its true source, enlightenment, symbolized by the Grail. The search for this Grail is an inner search, leading into the depths of our own mind and consciousness, and this is symbolized by night, a withdrawal from the outward world of form into the visionary world beyond time, space, and causality, Schopenhauer's noumenon. The summoner to this inward quest is not of bright, happy form but of dark, foreboding form, jolting us out of our complacency and making us aware, as Cundrie does Parzival, that there is far, far more for us than the outward world of appearances, and that it is our duty not to settle for worldly fame and pleasure, but to renounce these in return for the spiritual path. It is fitting that Cundrie's announcement of this comes in front of Arthur and all the knights, where Parzival is enjoying fame and glory. Parzival must leave Arthur's company and strike out on his own if he is to find the spiritual treasure. Parzival's realization of his failure in the Grail Castle and his vow to find that castle again is the same as Dante's recognition of the Dark Wood, and Parzival's willingness to undertake the quest of the Grail is Dante's willingness to travel even into hell in order to find the light of God. It is the willingness to enter into the deepest recesses of our own psyches in order to find in that temporary darkness the light of truth.

Campbell also uses an interesting choice of words to describe Cundrie: "announced at the same weird hour by the same weird sister of night." Shakespeare used the words "weird sisters" to describe the three witches in *Macbeth*. In both Shakespeare and Campbell, "weird" does not mean "strange." "Weird" comes from the Old English *wyrd*, which means "fate." *Wyrd* can be traced in its origin to the Scandanavian *volva*, or *vala*, which in German becomes *wala*. "Wache, Wala! Wala, erwach!" calls Wotan to Erda at the beginning of Act III, Scene 1 of *Siegfried*, commanding her to wake and rise from her sleep and grant to him her wisdom. He calls her "Wala." This word, like *volva*, means "seeress," that is, a woman who can see the future. When Macbeth calls to the weird sisters in the forest, he is calling to them as those who can see not only the outward events of the future, but also the innermost recesses of his mind, for in *Macbeth* the witches are not just outward characters—they are representations of the phantoms and desires in Macbeth's own psyche. Campbell's choice of words places Cundrie in the same light. She is not only a character who appears before Arthur's court who can tell the knights many things, she is also the "weird sister of night," an apparition from Parzival's own mind, a manifestation of the inner desire for enlightenment. Cundrie, the Grail Messenger, assumes a wrathful form because Parzival must be shaken loose from his attachment to the outer world of fame, glory, and service to the social order. He must be turned inward to seek the Grail. Once he has found that, he can then serve both the Grail and the social order simultaneously, as he does at the end of *Parzival*.

Wolfram calls Cundrie *la sorcière*, not because she practices sorcery or is a witch, but because she has spiritual wisdom. Wagner's Kundry is a different character, unique in various ways to Wagner's own individual creativity. But there are several aspects of Cundrie that Kundry inherits. Just as Cundrie helps the Grail Order and indeed is their messenger, so too does Kundry help, bringing balsam for Amfortas's wound and, as Gurnemanz tells the squires in Act I, doing good deeds for the benefit of the Grail Brotherhood. He even refers to her as a message bearer. Like Cundrie, Kundry knows many things and travels to many distant lands; she does not spend all her time at Monsalvat. More

important than details such as these is Kundry's role in awakening
Parsifal to his spiritual purpose. Gurnemanz had begun the initial
awakening in the scene with the swan, but Kundry has two very
important moments in Parsifal's journey to wisdom. The first is
the kiss in Act II, where through that kiss Parsifal not only feels
the wound of Amfortas, but also perceives its origin and cause.
Parsifal had first felt Amfortas's pain at the end of Act I when he
witnessed the Grail ceremony. Hearing Amfortas's cry of agony at
the end of the ceremony, Parsifal clutched his own heart. At that
point he did not understand what he had seen, but he had experienced the pain. With Kundry's kiss, he begins to understand the
source of the wound and how it can be redeemed. In Wagner's
scheme this cannot happen without Kundry.

The second awakening comes in Act III, after Parsifal has returned to Monsalvat. When Gurnemanz tells Parsifal of Titurel's
death, Parsifal feels a great grief for all the suffering he has felt
and witnessed, and for a moment he doubts that he can fulfill his
role as redeemer.

> And it is I, I,
> who caused all this woe!
> Ah! What transgression,
> what burden of guilt
> must my foolish head
> have borne from eternity,
> since no repentance, no atonement
> can free me of my blindness;
> though I was appointed for deliverance,
> the last path of deliverance escapes me,
> lost as I am in hopeless error![59]

Parsifal is about to faint, but Kundry and Gurnemanz take
him to the holy spring, where Kundry washes his feet and
Gurnemanz anoints his head. The stage directions read in part,
"Kundry bathes Parsifal's feet with humble zeal. Parsifal watches
her in silent wonder." When the washing is over and Parsifal

knows it is time for him to heal Amfortas and perform the act of redemption, he says, "My first office I thus perform,"[60] and takes water from the spring and baptizes Kundry. In a subtle way, it is Kundry who awakens Parsifal to this final level of his purpose, first by the humbleness and sincerity of her devotion, and then by her baptism. Parsifal has transcended the final doubt, and again it is Kundry who provides the initial spark.

Although Wagner does not incorporate the question test specifically into his music drama, he does use it in a subtle way. When in Act I Parsifal first witnesses the Grail ceremony, he is awed, mesmerized, and so profoundly moved that he cannot speak. When Gurnemanz asks Parsifal if he knows what he has just seen, he cannot answer the old knight, and Gurnemanz thinks that Parsifal is just stupid. Gurnemanz throws him out, saying, "Just seek—foolish gander—a goose!"[61] And in the passage quoted above, where Parsifal has just learned of Titurel's death, he blames himself for having caused all the woe, and we see in Wagner's lines a reflection of the old romances where the hero has failed to redeem the Fisher King. We also see that like Parzival, Parsifal is not ready to be the redeemer when he first visits the Grail Castle. He must undergo a great deal of difficult training before the redemption can be accomplished.

While Wagner's conception of the Grail is not the same as Wolfram's, there are still a number of elements that Wagner borrowed from Wolfram. Wagner saw the Grail as the cup of the Last Supper, which also caught the blood of Christ while he was on the cross, and the spear that wounds Amfortas as the spear of Longinus. Thus the Spear and Grail for Wagner are Christian relics, whereas for Wolfram they are not. However, there are a couple of Christian connections to the Grail in *Parzival*: one, that no unbaptized person can see the Grail, and two, the Grail in its form of a powerful stone was brought to earth by the neutral angels who were sent to earth by God. Wolfram tells us that a heathen, Flegetanis, who was descended from Solomon and was an expert at reading the stars, first told humanity about the

Grail in a manuscript written in Arabic that Kyot had found in Toledo, Spain. Kyot, because he was baptized, was able to learn Arabic and to decipher the manuscript of Flegetanis and give its knowledge to Christendom, for "no heathen art could be of use in revealing the nature of the Grail and how its mysteries were discovered."[62] Wolfram then tells us:

> Flegetanis the heathen saw with his own eyes in the constellations things he was shy to talk about, hidden mysteries. He said there was a thing called the Grail whose name he had read clearly in the constellations. "A host of angels left it on the earth and then flew away up over the stars. Was it their innocence that drew them away? Since then baptized men have had the task of guarding it, and with such chaste discipline that those who are called to the service of the Grail are always noble men." Thus wrote Flegetanis of these things.[63]

Wagner eliminates Joseph of Arimathea and has angels from heaven bring the Cup and Spear to earth, thus borrowing part of Wolfram's idea and then expanding on it. Gurnemanz tells the squires in Act I:

> Titurel, the pious king,
> knew Klingsor well.
> There came a mighty heathen horde to threat
> our realm of Christian faith—our stronghold;
> but help arrived one sacred, solemn night.
> Down came our Saviour's heavenly heralds;
> the cup once used at that last holy supper,
> that noble cup, that consecrated vessel,
> wherein was caught His blood from off the cross;
> thereto the holy lance which shed that blood.
> These precious proofs of Love's great healing power
> were given by angels to our ruler's care.
> He gave these holy things a holy place.[64]

Wagner does not mention anything about neutral angels. In his conception the angels who bring the Grail and Spear to earth are part of the heavenly host.

After Gawan succeeds in freeing the Castle of Wonders from the spell of Clinschor, he reconciles with King Gramoflanz in front of Arthur and his knights, who have traveled to this place in order to aid Gawan. Parzival is among the company. Into this company rides a veiled woman on a splendid horse. She is richly attired, and her garments bear many golden-wrought turtle-doves, the emblem of the Grail knights. She pays courtesy to Arthur and Guinevere, then dismounts and goes to where Parzival is sitting. She pulls aside her veil, and all assembled recognize her as Cundrie. She then publicly prophesies that Parzival will heal Anfortas and become the new Grail King.

> "Blessed are you in your high lot, O crown of man's salvation!—
> The inscription has been read: you shall be Lord of the Grail.
> Condwiramurs, your wife, and your son Loherangrin have been
> named therein along with you. . . . your truthful lips shall now
> address greeting to that noble and sweet man, and that now the
> question from your mouth shall make King Anfortas well again
> and avert from him his sighs and great misery."[65]

This is a reversal of the earlier scene where Cundrie denounced Parzival in front of Arthur's court. In her role of seeress and Grail Messenger she has come to proclaim Parzival as the healer and redeemer and to lead him to Munsalvaesche. She tells him that he must choose a companion, and he chooses his half brother Feirefiz. The two of them follow Cundrie on the ride to the Grail Castle, and it is only through Cundrie's guidance that Parzival can find the castle a second time. She does not come for him until he is ready.

Wagner, in a subtle way, adopts this aspect of Cundrie for his Kundry, though there is a difference. As we saw in chapter 3, Parsifal asks Kundry in Act II how to find Amfortas, but she will not tell him. This still implies that Kundry knows the way, which she does.

Wagner also borrows from Wolfram the idea of the inscription on the Grail, though he again treats it in his own way. Trevrizent tells Parzival in Book IX,

"Hear how those called to the Grail are made known. On the stone, around the edge, appear letters inscribed, giving the name and lineage of each one, maid or boy, who is to take this blessed journey. No one needs to rub out the inscription, for once he has read the name, it fades away before his eyes. All those now grown to maturity came there as children. Blessed is the mother who bore a child destined to do service there. Poor and rich alike rejoice if their child is summoned to join this company. They are brought there from many lands."[66]

Then a while later Trevrizent tells Parzival that when all the cures for Anfortas's wound failed,

"We fell on our knees in prayer before the Grail. All at once we saw written upon it that a knight should come, and if from him a question came, our sorrow would be ended."[67]

Wagner adopts this scene, and then transforms it to fit his own scheme. Gurnemanz tells the squires in Act I:

Before the looted sanctuary
Amfortas lay in fervent prayer,
anxiously imploring some sign of salvation:
a blessed radiance emanated from the Grail;
a holy vision
clearly spoke to him
this message in words of fire:
"Enlightened through compassion,
the innocent fool;
wait for him,
the appointed one.[68]

Wagner also takes from Wolfram Amfortas's wish to die. Wolfram begins Book XVI with the following paragraph:

Anfortas and his people were still enduring the pain of grief. Their fidelity caused him to continue in his suffering. Often he begged them for death, and death would surely have come to him, except that they frequently had him view the Grail and the Grail's power.[69]

Wolfram tells us:

They *would* have released him from his misery, had it not been for the comforting comfort which Trevrizent had previously pronounced and which he had seen in writing on the Grail. They were awaiting the second coming of the man before whom all his joy had vanished previously and the hour of succor that would come with the question from his mouth.[70]

When Cundrie leads Parzival and Feirefiz to the Grail Castle, they are taken to Anfortas, who says to Parzival:

"I have bided in misery for you to come and make me glad. You left me before in such a way that, if you are sincere about helping me, you must regret. If ever praise was spoken of you, then prevail upon the knights and maidens here to give me death and let my agony end! If your name is Parzival, keep me from the sight of the Grail for seven nights and eight days, and then all my lamentations will cease. I do not dare give you any further hint."[71]

But Parzival does not allow him to die. Instead he bows three times in the direction of the Grail and then says to Anfortas, "Uncle, what is it that troubles you?"[72] Then, Wolfram writes, "He, Who for Saint Sylvester's sake brought a bullock back to life from the dead, and Who bade Lazarus arise, the Same gave help that Anfortas was healed and made well again."[73]

Parzival is then named Lord of the Grail, according to the writing on the Grail, and Anfortas remains as a knight of the Grail, but not as its Lord: "The noble and beautiful Anfortas was manly with pure heart. According to his rule, he rode many a joust for the Grail's sake, but he did not fight for women."[74]

Wagner gives us a very similar scene in Act III, albeit with different details. Titurel has died, and his coffin is borne into the hall by one group of knights while Amfortas on his litter is borne in by another group. We learn that Titurel has died of old age because he was denied sight of the Grail, and that it was Amfortas who withheld this sight because he had not performed the Grail ceremony in all these years. The knights ask Amfortas to perform the ceremony one more time, but he cannot do it. He implores Titurel in heaven to plead for him and grant him death. The knights then demand that he perform the ceremony one more time, but Amfortas still refuses.

No more! Ha!
Death comes, for I feel him approaching!
And yet you would summon me back to life?
Insanity!
Who would force me to live now,
when death is all I am seeking?
(He tears open his garment.)
Here am I! My open wound is here!
Here is the poison! Here flows my blood!
Out with your weapons!
Bury your swords here, deep, deep—to the hilt!
Up! You heroes!
Slay both at once: sinner and his sin.
Perhaps the Grail will shine then for you!

Parsifal then steps forward with the Spear and touches the side of Amfortas.

One weapon only serves:
only the spear which gave the wound heals the wound.
Be whole, forgiven, and absolved!
For I must now perform your charge!
And blessed be your suff'ring,
which gave the power of love
and strength of purity to him—
the timid fool!
The sacred spear—I bring it back to you!
Oh! Wondrous joy beyond compare!
The spear that touched the wound and healed it
is flowing now with blood most holy
which seeks to rejoin its kindred fountain
that wells within the holy vessel.
Nevermore let the cup be hid!
Uncover the Grail! Open the shrine![75]

We see the Bleeding Lance joined with the Grail, which holds
the blood of Christ. Parsifal performs the ceremony again and
gives renewed spiritual life to the Grail Brotherhood and the
land of Monsalvat. Amfortas is healed, and Parsifal becomes the
new Grail King. We also see Amfortas begging his knights for
death, but they will not kill him: "One weapon only serves."

It is interesting also to see the similarity of part of this scene
with the second scene of Act III in *Tristan und Isolde*, where
Tristan is lying on a couch (Amfortas's litter), and just as Amfortas tears open his garment, so does Tristan tear off his bandages,
revealing his flowing blood. Of course the endings are different,
but we can remember Wagner saying that the wound of Amfortas is Tristan's wound "inconceivably intensified."[76]

When Amfortas tears open his garment, he says, "My open
wound is here! Here is the poison." Here the poison is metaphorical, not actual as it was with the wound of Anfortas. The spear
of the heathen knight that had wounded Anfortas *was* anointed
with poison, but it was certainly not the spear of Longinus. With
Wagner, the poison of Amfortas's wound represents the corrup-

tion of sin, to put it in Christian terms. It represents Amfortas's corrupted blood, as opposed to the pure blood of Christ, which represents sinless action. When speaking in terms like these, which can be dangerous if misunderstood, it is very important to keep in mind how Wagner uses religious symbolism, especially in *Parsifal*. He wrote at the beginning of *Religion and Art*: "One could say that at the point where religion becomes artificial it is for art to preserve the essence of religion by grasping the symbolic value of its mythic symbols, which the former would have us believe in their literal sense, so that the deep, hidden truth in them might be revealed by their ideal representation."[77] Barry Millington says of this passage: "The value of religion, therefore, was to be found not in a fundamental acceptance of its tenets, but in a presentation in symbolic form of its universal spiritual truths."[78]

This is exactly what *Parsifal* does. It presents in symbolic form the universal truths of religion. It will be very important to keep this in mind as we continue to discuss *Parsifal*, especially in the next chapter.

This is not to say that we should not take the teachings of religion literally. We do, however, need to know *how* to take those teachings literally. Religious teaching very often has a literal level and a symbolic level, and both need to be understood properly. Witness the following account of the Last Supper:

> And as they were eating, Jesus took bread, and blessed it, and brake it, and gave it to the disciples, and said, Take, eat; this is my body. And he took the cup, and gave thanks, and gave it to them, saying, Drink ye all of it; For this is my blood of the new testament, which is shed for many for the remission of sins.[79]

There was a practice in the early fertility ceremonies where the body of the sacred king, either in human form or in symbolic animal form, was actually eaten and the blood actually drunk by the community. Obviously, the bread and the wine of Jesus are symbolic, and he is not telling his disciples to eat him literally or to drink his actual blood, as would have been done in the pagan ceremonies. Here, as we saw in the last chapter, Christianity is taking from the pagan religions certain practices and their symbols into the body of its own teaching and then transforming them onto a higher level for the purpose of attaining true spiritual understanding. And yet there *is* a literal level to what Jesus is telling his disciples. This literal level, however, cannot be understood by the intellect alone—only by the mind of meditation, which sees in the communion of bread and wine shared with the master the actual communion between God and man, the meeting of spirit with spirit, like two arrows meeting in midair. This communion between man and God is acted out in human form, for that is the form we have. And human form does not stand against spirit, and spirit does not stand against human form. It is not the case that one is pure and the other impure. Both are enlightened, both are pure, and in this true communion there is salvation. Spirit flows into spirit. This is the meaning of the pure blood of Christ in *Parsifal*.

Wolfram specifically calls the knights of the Grail Templars, whereas Wagner calls them *die Ritter des Grales*. He also uses the term *Ritterschaft*, or brotherhood of knights. The actual Knights Templar was an order founded in 1119 in Jerusalem following the First Crusade in 1099. By Wolfram's time they had become very powerful and influential, and they had a code that Wolfram adopted for his knights of the Grail. The king of Jerusalem was allowed to marry and have children, just as was the Grail King, but the Templars themselves took a vow of celibacy, just as do Wolfram's knights. However, Wolfram gives his Grail knights the emblem of a turtledove, which was not the historical emblem. We can see Wolfram's knights as a reflection of the historical Templars, but still fictional as concerns *Parzival* itself. Wagner's *Ritter des Grales* are based on Wolfram's, but as usual he has made them his own creation.

There is an interesting detail in Wolfram that relates specifically to the *Ring*. When Parzival first sets out for Arthur's court, he meets a knight on the road. They fight, and Parzival kills the knight using his darts (arrows), as Parzival has not yet learned how to joust. Speaking of the young Parzival, Wolfram writes,

"He who never knew the sweat of fear now saw a knight riding toward him."[80] Here we have, in Wolfram's description of the
young Parzival, Wagner's young Siegfried.

There is one final aspect of *Parzival* that relates directly to our
interpretation of the *Ring* and *Parsifal* as one work. This is the
Buddhist teaching of the Middle Way. The Middle Way is not only
the middle path between opposing opposites, it is also the third
position *beyond* the opposites, the spiritual seat that recognizes attachment to opposites as the world of illusion, the world of maya.
When one has gone beyond the opposites, one sees the world as it
actually is, free of the veil of illusion. This idea of going beyond the
opposites was intrinsic not only to Wolfram's vision of spiritual
wisdom in *Parzival*, but also to the name "Parzival" itself.

Wagner's own etymology for his name Parsifal was "pure (or
innocent) fool." Wagner thought the name came from two Arabic
words, *fal* and *parsi*. Scholars no longer accept this and believe
that Wagner's source, Joseph Görres's edition of *Lohengrin*, was
in error. Chrétien did not attempt any etymology, simply using
the name Perceval. Some have tried "pierce valley" for Perceval,
but this by itself doesn't make much sense. Wolfram does use a
specific etymology for Parzival. When Parzival first encounters
Sigune, he does not know his name, for he has been called *bon
fils*, *cher fils*, and *beau fils* by his mother and others at home.
Sigune then recognizes him and says, "In truth, your name is
Parzival, which signifies '*right through the middle.*' Such a furrow did great love plow in your mother's heart with the plow of
her faithfulness."[81] Mustard and Passage write of this line: "On
the basis of the Old French form of the name *Perceval* Wolfram
etymologizes: *perce à val!* = 'pierce through!' A subsequent poet,
Heinrich von der Türlin, will explain in his poem *Diu Krone*
that *val* means both 'valley' and 'furrow,' an interpretation which
clarifies Wolfram's next sentence here. Chrétien offers no etymology at all in *Li Contes del Graal*."[82]

We can see one meaning of his name in the use of "furrow,"
where Herzeloyde's love for Parzival has "plowed a furrow of
love" in both her heart and his. This love stays with Parzival

throughout his adventures, acting as a kind of guardian angel, keeping him from death and harm until he has accomplished his mission of finding the Grail.

Campbell interprets the name in the sense of the Buddha's Middle Way.

> [Wolfram's] aim for life was neither rapture aloft, quit of the flesh, nor rapture below, quit of the light, but—as the symbol on his [Wolfram's] shield and flag, horse and helm makes known— the way between. His own fanciful interpretation of his hero Par-zival's name, *perce à val*, "pierce through the middle," gives the first clue to his ideal, which is, namely, of a realization here on earth, through human, natural means (in the sinning and virtu-ous, black and white, yet nobly courageous self-determined de-velopment of a no more than human life) of the mystery of the Word Made Flesh: the *logos* deeper than logic, wherein dark and light, all pairs of opposites—yet not as opposites—take part.[83]

We can see examples of this Middle Way in the advice that Parzival receives from his two teachers, Gurnemanz and Trevri-zent. When Parzival first comes to Gurnemanz as an inexpe-rienced youth, Gurnemanz gives him many words of advice. We saw earlier that he had told Parzival, "Do not ask too many questions." He did not say, "Never ask a question." He also tells Parzival at this same time, "Be both poor and rich appropriately: if a lord squanders, that is not lord-like; if he hoards treasure too much, that is dishonor also. Make your rule the true mean."[84]

Later Trevrizent says to Parzival, "And you must not grieve too much. You should in right measure grieve and abstain from grief."[85] The closing message of the poem reflects this Middle Way very profoundly: "A life so concluded that God is not robbed of the soul through fault of the body, and which can obtain the world's favor with dignity, *that* is a worthy work."[86]

We saw in chapter 4 that the *Queste del Saint Graal* was writ-ten by a cloistered Cistercian monk. In his work he emphasized the renunciation of the world and strict celibacy on the part of the Grail hero in order for him to achieve the Grail. In both the *Queste* and in Malory, when Galahad's year as Grail King is over, he and the Grail are taken up into heaven, the Grail never more to shine its light in the world, because the world, in the author's mind, was no longer worthy of this light. In *Parzival*, Wolfram sees the way to the Grail as being *within* the world, where the Grail hero fulfills his duties both to society and to the Grail community. It is true that Parzival must at one stage leave the worldly aspects of life behind in order to enter and succeed in the spiritual quest, but he returns to the world when that quest is fulfilled. He had to leave Condwiramurs for five years, but when he is made the new Grail King, she joins him at Munsalvaesche along with Loherangrin, and they live together as a family, serving the Grail. Parzival's other child, Kardeiz, remains at the former home of Parzival and Condwiramurs, governing the lands there. Thus both religious and worldly obligations are served equally. Parzival, like Wagner's Parsifal, remains in the world to serve others. He does not, like Galahad, leave the world behind because it is no longer worthy. This is a very important aspect of true compassion. One never considers the world unworthy of spiritual help. This would be to judge it and to deny its Buddha-nature. The Buddha himself left the world in order to find enlightenment, but once he did, he returned to the world to teach, never withholding from it his compassion and wisdom.

It is a very important part of Wolfram's spiritual vision that man and God meet, that the grace of God and the individual effort of each human being both play a part in salvation. When, after he has healed Anfortas, Parzival goes to see Trevrizent to tell him of the healing and to thank him for his counsel at a critical time in the spiritual journey, Trevrizent says, "God is man and also His Father's Word, God is Father and Son, His Spirit can lend great aid."[87] The true path to the Grail is the true home of the Grail: the middle path where God and man meet, where grace and effort meet, where worldly duties and spiritual duties meet, where worldly pleasures and spiritual pleasures meet, where all the opposites meet and are then transcended. This is the true meaning of the Buddha's Middle Way: the third position beyond the opposites.

At the very end of Wagner's *Parsifal*, when the Grail ceremony has been performed, a white dove descends from the dome and hovers over Parsifal's head. The immediate reference is, of course, the baptism of Jesus by John:

> And Jesus, when he was baptized, went up straightway out of the water; and, lo, the heavens were opened unto him, and he saw the Spirit of God descending like a dove, and lighting upon him: And lo a voice from heaven, saying, This is my beloved Son, in whom I am well pleased.[88]

There is also a passage from Wolfram that becomes part of Wagner's final scene. When Trevrizent is telling Parzival about the Grail he says:

> "This very day there comes to it a message wherein lies its greatest power. Today is Good Friday, and they await there a dove, winging down from Heaven. It brings a small white wafer, and leaves it on the stone. Then, shining white, the dove soars up to Heaven again. Always on Good Friday it brings to the stone what I have just told you, and from that the stone derives whatever good fragrances of drink and food there are on earth, like to the perfection of Paradise."[89]

Wagner's dove can be seen as both the Spirit of God and as Wolfram's dove bringing power to the Grail.

Lohengrin

The story of Lohengrin (Loherangrin in Wolfram) is told at the end of *Parzival*. Elsa is not named specifically; she is referred to simply as the princess of Brabant. Loherangrin calls her "My Lady Duchess": "From Munsalvaesche was sent he whom the swan brought and whom God had chosen for her. [Loherangrin says to her,] 'My Lady Duchess, if I am to be the lord of this country, I must give up its equal. Now hear what I am about to ask of you. Never ask me who I am; then I shall be able to remain with you. But if I am subjected to your question you will lose my love.'"[90]

She gives him her pledge, and they marry and have children. Loherangrin becomes famous for his deeds of chivalry, but eventually, "because of love," she breaks the pledge and asks him the question, driving him away. Wolfram says, "He left much against his will."[91]

Wolfram explains why the question of Loherangrin's origin must not be asked.

> Upon the Grail it was now found written that any templar whom God's hand appointed master over foreign people should forbid the asking of his name or race, and that he should help them to their rights. If the question is asked of him they shall have his help no longer. Because the sweet Anfortas was so long in bitter torment and went so long without the question, questioning is forever displeasing to them. All keepers of the Grail want no questions asked about them.[92]

There is certainly more to Wagner's conception of the question in *Lohengrin* than is mentioned here, but this is the basis for Lohengrin's not wanting Elsa to ask about his origin.

~

We have now completed our discussion of the tradition and mythology of the Grail, and of the different versions of its legend. We are ready to examine in detail the final interpretation of the *Ring* and *Parsifal* as one five-opera cycle.

CHAPTER 6

The Separation and Reunion of the Spear and Grail

The separation of the Spear and Grail does not happen just prior to the start of *Parsifal*. The separation comes at the start of the *Ring*.

Even though Wagner originally meant the opening orchestral passages of *Das Rheingold* to portray the beginning of the world emerging out of primordial darkness (which they do very well), the actual events of the story that becomes the *Ring* begin prior to Alberich's appearance on the Rhine in Scene 1. As we are told by the First Norn in the Prelude of *Götterdämmerung*, everything starts with Wotan breaking a branch from the World Ash-tree and fashioning that branch into a spear that he uses to rule the world.

> At the World Ash-tree
> once I wove,
> when fair and green
> there grew from its branches
> verdant and shady leaves.
> Those cooling shadows
> sheltered a spring;
> wisdom's voice
> I heard in its waves;
> I sang my holy song.
> A valiant god

came to drink at the spring;
    and the price he had to pay
was the loss of an eye.
    From the World Ash-tree
mighty Wotan broke a branch;
    and his spear was shaped
from that branch he tore from the tree.

As year succeeded year,
the wound slowly weakened the tree;
dry, leafless, and barren—
death seized on the tree;
    whispering waters
    then failed in the spring:
    grief and sorrow
    stole through my song.

Prior to Wotan's appearance, the World Ash-tree bloomed "fair and green," and the spring of wisdom ran with water. The three Norns wove the rope of fate, and even though Wagner does not specify this, we can use our imaginations to see also the three Rhinemaidens representing the elemental forces of nature, and of course Erda, the Earth-mother, asleep and dreaming the world.

Into this world of women and original innocence comes a male sky god bent on conquest and power. He commits an act of violence against nature and uses this act to give himself power over the world. The Wheel of Karma has started to turn.

We can see several important symbols here that relate to Grail mythology. First are the symbols of the Dolorous Stroke and the Waste Land. Wotan breaks a branch off the tree, and immediately it begins to wither and die, and the spring to dry up. The tree becomes leafless and barren, the waters cease to flow. The Dolorous Stroke has plunged the world into a waste land, both in terms of nature and in terms of spiritual understanding, for it is the spring of wisdom that has run dry. Wagner even refers to the "wound" slowly weakening the tree. As we shall see, Amfortas receives a reciprocal wound by a blow from the branch of that very tree.

We also see a version of Genesis, a portrayal in symbolic form of the original Fall. Through an act of greed and violence the original "Garden of Eden" has been spoiled, raped, and the world falls into a cycle of fear, greed, hate, violence, despair, and eventual destruction. The world is in need of a savior, a great hero who will perform the act of atonement for the original sin, who will redeem the world from its present state of chaos, and who will restore the world, both naturally and spiritually, to its original pure state.

In Buddhist terms this scene symbolizes the way in which the Wheel of Karma was first set in motion. Although the Buddha himself never tried to explain an "ultimate beginning," and even said that such a beginning, at least in intellectual terms, was not fathomable, Buddhism does teach that we can find the beginning of our own individual karmic stream. That is, we can find out what started the ball rolling in our own particular case. In seeing what it was that started the turning of the Wheel of Karma, we can see how to stop it, and how to turn instead the Wheel of the Dharma, the Wheel of Truth. By ceasing to turn the Wheel of Karma and turning instead the Wheel of the Dharma, we can cleanse the karma from our own karmic stream and find the way to enlightenment. By finding the way to enlightenment for ourselves, we help the whole world find that way. In the context of Buddhism, the great savior and hero who found the way was the Buddha. In Christianity this hero/savior was Christ. In Wagner this hero/redeemer is Siegfried, reborn as Parsifal.

Wotan's act of violence and theft against the World Ash-tree is only one half of the separation of the Spear and Grail. The other half is performed by Alberich.

We have mentioned before that Wotan and Alberich are reflections of each other, and that this reflection continues from Wotan-Alberich to Amfortas-Klingsor. Alberich is *Schwarz-Alberich*, "black Alberich," and Wotan is *Licht-Alberich*, or "light Alberich."[1] Here the "black" refers to the earth, Alberich the dwarf coming from the darkness of caverns and mists beneath the earth. The "light" refers to the sky and sun, where Wotan dwells in the realm of the gods. Both Wotan and Alberich desire world power. Both, in their own ways, renounce love in order to acquire that power. And both commit an act of violence and theft against nature, fashioning the stolen objects of nature into objects of power. With Wotan this object is the broken branch of the World Ash-tree formed into a spear. With Alberich it is the theft of the Rhinegold and the fashioning of this gold into a ring of power. At the end of Scene 1 of *Das Rheingold* both the Spear and the Grail have been torn away from their original places in nature, which is the original Temple. Spear and Grail have thus been separated, and the world has become a waste land. Redemption will not be found until the Spear and Grail are once again united and the karma of the thefts and violence finally cleansed.

At this point one can rightfully ask, "What is the basis for equating the Rhinegold with the Holy Grail?"

Wagner completed the scoring of *Lohengrin* in April 1848. He then wrote a prose piece called *The Nibelungen Myth as Sketch for a Drama*, from which he fashioned the original libretto to *Siegfrieds Tod* (Siegfried's Death). This was finished in time for Wagner to read it to a group of friends that December. In February 1849 he wrote the essay *The Wibelungs: World-History as Told Through Myth.*[2] This essay of approximately 13,000 words is Wagner's attempt to put his research into Teutonic myth and German history together with his own ideas concerning Friedrich Barbarossa (1122–1190), about whom Wagner had planned an opera in 1846. Friedrich was Holy Roman Emperor from 1152 to 1190, as well as king of Germany during those same years and king of Italy from 1155 to 1190. It was the Italians who gave him the nickname Barbarossa, or Redbeard. Friedrich died while leading an army to the Holy Land during the Third Crusade. He did not die in combat; he drowned trying to swim across a river.

Many of the historical conclusions that Wagner draws in the *Wibelungen* essay can never be taken seriously as history, and much of what he says about Friedrich is more myth than historical fact. But if we examine the essay closely we can, amidst the convoluted writing and unsupportable ideas about Friedrich and world rule, find moments of genuine insight into Wagner's original inspiration and design concerning the *Ring* and the Holy Grail. In 1849 Wagner was by no means clear in his mind about all these concepts, and a great deal was still undeveloped. However, we can see in his thoughts of 1849 embryonic ideas that over the next thirty-three years fully bloomed into what we have now as the *Ring* and *Parsifal*. And a number of these ideas lead us directly to our interpretation of the *Ring* and *Parsifal* as one work.

Because Wagner's unedited prose in the *Wibelungen* essay is often difficult, I will simplify and sum up the relevant ideas and put them into my own words, rather than try to explain these ideas by using Wagner's own quotations. The translation I have used is that by William Ashton Ellis, published in 1898.

Wagner believed that during the era of the Great Deluge, the cradle of civilization was in the highest mountains of India, what we know as the Himalayas. He believed that this area was the ancestral seat of all religions, and that this civilization was ruled by a line of great priest-kings. He held that when the waters receded, a great migration over the rest of the earth began. As time went on and civilization spread throughout the world, the peoples of various races and cultures retained in their collective consciousness a memory of this original home and believed that there had been an original great ruler, the "Stem-father," who was descended from the gods. These people believed that their own race and culture were descended from this divine king.

Wagner believed that people migrating from this original kingdom eventually reached Europe, and that the German branch of this migration retained its connection to the original race through the lineage of the Franks. Wagner used the word *Wibelingen*, or *Wibelungen*, to identify the connection of the Frankish Merovingians to the original peoples from Asia. Along with this connection, in Wagner's mind, came the right to rule. Wagner further believed that the myths and sagas of a particular culture retained not only a memory of ancient events, but also the spiritual heritage of that culture, and that a particular people could trace its origin through its myths and sagas.

Through a very long and complex analysis, with which we do not have to concern ourselves, Wagner places Friedrich Barbarossa in line with the original rulers from India, in terms of both blood lineage and spiritual succession. Wagner then speaks of a legend that told of a distant land in "farthest India" where a divine Priest-King ruled through the power of a "wonder-working relic called the Holy Grail." According to this legend, the Keeper of the Grail had once brought this relic to the West, but when the West proved unworthy of this spiritual light, the Keeper returned with the Grail to the mountains of India. According to Wagner, Barbarossa was on his way to India in search of this Grail when he died in the river after defeating the Saracens.

Historically, Barbarossa was on his way to the Holy Land with an army in 1190. Barbarossa did indeed win an initial confrontation with the Saracens, but he had by no means reached Jerusalem, and he died trying to swim across a river rather than travel over a steep mountain pass. He was not on his way to India. Wagner was dealing far more with myth than with history, and we do not need to concern ourselves with Barbarossa. Wagner himself abandoned his Barbarossa project and completed instead what turned out to be the *Ring* and *Parsifal*. But there is a portion of the *Wibelungen* essay that does concern us. This is the relationship between the Nibelungen Hoard and the Holy Grail.

The word *Nibelung* is problematic even in the sagas. There is no firm consistency as to what the word refers to when it is mentioned in connection to the Hoard. In the Norse *Volsunga Saga*, Nibelung is the son of Hogni, who is the brother of Gunnar. Hogni becomes Hagen in the German *Nibelungenlied*, and Gunnar becomes Gunther. Nibelung as a character plays no great part other than to help Gudrun slay Atli. Gudrun becomes Kriemhilde in the *Nibelungenlied*, and Gutrune in Wagner. Atli refers to the historical Attila, who is Etzel in the German epic.

In the *Nibelungenlied* there are two Nibelung princes who

rule the Nibelungs, a people consisting of humans, dwarfs, and giants. These two princes are Schilbung and Nibelung. Sifrid (Siegfried) kills both of them, thus inheriting their jewels, gold, a magic cloak, and a great sword called Balmung, all of which together are known as the Nibelung treasure. (In this work Sifrid kills a dragon, but it is not connected with the gold.) Alberich is a dwarf who was in the service of the two princes, but with their (and his) defeat at the hands of Sifrid, he becomes Sifrid's servant and is put in charge of guarding the treasure. Later in the work there is further confusion when Sifrid marries into the Burgundian clan. Because he had conquered the Nibelungs, he was referred to as "hero of the Nibelungs." The Burgundians are now sometimes referred to as Nibelungs, and the two names become at times confused.

The word *Nibelung* itself comes from *nebel*, which meant "mist" or "fog." There is also the word *Niflheim*, which in the Teutonic mythology of creation referred to an area of shadows and clouds north of the great void. This area existed before the creation of earth and sky. Niflheim later became associated with the goddess Hel and the land of the dead.

In the *Wibelungen* essay, Wagner states what he believes to be the true meaning of the word *Nibelung* and how it is connected to the Hoard. He takes the word *Niflheim* and combines it with *Nebel* or *Nibel* to get *Nibelheim*, the "Home of Haze." He equates this word with the subterranean realm of Night Spirits, which he terms *Schwarzalben*. Opposed to these are the Spirits of Light, *Lichtalben*, who dwell in the heavens. The Nibelungen are the children of Night and Death, who burrow into the earth and live in its dark caverns and crevices. They find the ore deep in the earth, and through their skills as smiths they fashion this ore into weapons and trinkets, creating the Nibelungen Hoard.

This is, however, just the physical level of the term and idea of the Hoard. There are also mythological and spiritual levels.

Wagner believed that what he called the "Nibelungen-myth" rose out of man's first attempts to perceive and comprehend the forces of nature around him. The most important natural phenomenon was the rising of the sun. The sun gave warmth, sight, and life to nature. Nightfall brought cold, blindness, and, consequently, fear. Thus the earliest and simplest form of the myth was the celebration of the rising of the sun and the conquest of the forces of darkness. In this context, Siegfried is the Sun god, or God of Light, who slays the monster (or dragon) of Chaotic Night. But just as the sun sets each day, and night conquers day, so must the Sun god himself be slain, and thus his victory also carries with it the necessity and inevitability of defeat and death.

As the myth evolves, the dragon becomes the representation of the forces of darkness as well as a guardian of the treasures of the earth. Thus Siegfried killing the dragon is the God of Light who vanquishes the Night, and who also inherits the treasure the dragon was guarding, the Nibelungen Hoard. This gives him, for a time, great powers. But all the while the heir of the dragon plots to win back the Hoard, just as night must again conquer day. Thus there is a "curse" on the gold, for whoever slays the dragon and for a while possesses the Hoard must also die because he in turn is the possessor of that Hoard. The cycle of day and night becomes a symbol of the constant and ever-renewing cycle of birth and death.

Wagner then takes the symbolism a step further and attempts to reconcile the confusion in the sagas as to the identification of the Nibelungs. According to Wagner's idea, the Hoard becomes the source of all worldly might, and an inevitable struggle develops among the races and kingdoms of the earth to possess this Hoard and its attendant power. Whoever owns the treasure and rules by the power of the Hoard at any one time becomes known as a Nibelung.

At this stage the Hoard represents not only earthly power, but also the right to this power. In what Wagner called "the ascent of the ideal content of the Hoard into the Holy Grail," this Hoard over time lost more and more of its material worth and in the process yielded to a higher spiritual content. The struggle to possess and control the Hoard gave way to the quest for the Holy

Grail, and the Grail became what Wagner called "the Ideal representative of the Nibelungen-Hoard." This "ascent" is a transfiguration of consciousness whereby the initial desire for worldly wealth and power becomes transformed into desire for spiritual knowledge and understanding. This correlates with the conclusion reached in chapter 3 concerning *arete* and Greek tragedy: When the desire to assert one's own will over the world is transformed into the desire to merge the individual will with the will of the divine, the energy and effort of *arete* (the will to greatness) are channeled away from glorification of the individual and into spiritual quest. Wagner believed that this transfiguration had happened in the character of Friedrich Barbarossa, and that when he died he was on his way to India to reclaim the lost relic. Wagner ends his essay with a reference to the legend that Barbarossa sits to this day asleep in the interior of the Kyffhäuser hills in Thuringia, awaiting the time when his people will need him most, and he will awaken and lead them to victory against their enemies: "There in the Kyffhäuser he sits, the old 'Redbeard Friedrich,' all around him the treasures of the Nibelungen, by his side the sharp sword that one-time slew the dreaded Dragon."

It is interesting to note that an exactly parallel legend exists about King Arthur. According to this legend, Arthur right now is asleep in a cave underneath Glastonbury Tor, awaiting the day when the people of Britain will need him most, and he will awaken and ride out with his knights to protect them from their impending disaster. Mythologically, if not historically, Barbarossa has become equated with both Siegfried and King Arthur.

Robert Gutman, in his introduction to William Morris's translation of the *Volsunga Saga*, has summed all of this up very well.

> *The Wibelungs* identifies Frederick Barbarossa as the reborn sun god, Siegfried; the Nibelungen hoard mysteriously ascends, is transmuted in the process of time into the Holy Grail, and becomes the object of the emperor's last journey to the East. Despite the turgid prose, a reader with knowledge of the completed

cycle of Wagner's masterworks is thrilled to perceive in this essay what the struggling young genius could himself only dimly
apprehend, the unparalleled path that lay before him from *Rhinegold* to *Parsifal*, a road that was to lead from the theft of the
treasure in the river's depths to the reunion of spear and grail in
the temple of Monsalvat.[3]

Gutman is not alone in his perception of the connection between the *Ring* and *Parsifal*. There were those in Wagner's own
time who intuited part of it, though certainly not to the extent
that we have been discussing in this present book. Bernard
Förster, for example, a schoolteacher who married Nietzsche's
sister Elisabeth in 1885, wrote a pamphlet on *Parsifal* after the
1882 premier. Cosima recorded in her diary on January 17, 1883,
"Today he [Wagner] reads B. Förster's little pamphlet, critical of
certain things . . . but also pleased with some others, e.g., that the
stronghold of Valhalla has turned into the Temple of the Grail."[4]

Wagner himself had many notions of the connection. Two
examples are poignant. On February 19, 1878, Cosima wrote of a
moment when the two of them were alone:

> "Who is Titurel?" he asks me. I reflect. "Wotan," he says. "After
> his renunciation of the world he is granted salvation, the greatest
> of possessions is entrusted to his care, and now he is guarding
> it like a mortal god"—a lovely thought! I say that Wotan's name
> ought to be reflected in the name Titurel, and he replies, "Titurel,
> the little Titus, Titus the symbol of royal standing and power,
> Wotan the God-King."[5]

I will discuss Wotan's renunciation further in a while, but it
is clear from Wagner's remarks to Cosima that he sees it as being enough to achieve salvation. In the context of the Buddhist
view of cleansing karma, renunciation is not, by itself, enough,
though it is a necessary first step. Remember also that we are
going beyond Schopenhauer here, and in Buddhism renouncing
the will is not the path to salvation. Therefore, in the view that I

am putting forth in this book, Wotan is reborn as Amfortas, not Titurel. I will discuss this more later on, but there is another entry in Cosima's diaries that is very interesting concerning Wagner's own sense of the connection between the *Ring* and *Parsifal* in which he came remarkably close to, though just short of, the view that I am taking here. Cosima wrote on April 29, 1879, three days after the orchestral sketch for *Parsifal* had been completed: "Over coffee he said to me that in fact Siegfried ought to have turned into Parsifal and redeemed Wotan, he should have come upon Wotan (instead of Amfortas) in the course of his wanderings—but there was no antecedent for it, and so it would have to remain as it was."[6]

The great irony of Wagner's statement, in light of our current interpretation, is that Siegfried does "turn into" Parsifal, and he does come upon and redeem Wotan—Wotan reborn as Amfortas.

Wagner's Sources for the *Ring*

Many parallels between Siegfried's story and the Arthurian and Grail legends can be found in Wagner's sources for the *Ring*. Three of these sources came from Iceland, and the extant manuscripts were written during the thirteenth century. Like the Grail stories written during the same period, the Icelandic works had their origins in tales and myths from a much earlier time, finally being written down after centuries of oral transmission. The first of these was the *Elder Edda*, or *Poetic Edda*, written by an unknown number of anonymous poets and said to have been collected originally by Saemund Sigfusson, who was born in Iceland in 1056 and died in 1133. Scholars now believe that the poems in the *Elder Edda* were created between the ninth and the thirteenth centuries, so Saemund could not have collected the exact version we have now, but his name is still associated with this famous work.

The *Elder Edda* consists of two parts. The first part deals with the mythology and cosmology of the Teutonic world, and the second part concerns the tales of heroes, specifically the story of the Volsungs and the Giukis. The Volsungs, descended from Odin, include Sigmund and his son Sigurd, the Norse Siegfried. Giuki was the father of Gunnar and Gudrun, who become Gunther and Gutrune in the *Ring*. Scholars believe that the authors of these poems were either Norwegians or Icelanders of Norwegian descent.

The second of Wagner's Icelandic sources was the *Prose Edda*, sometimes called the *Younger Edda*, written mostly by Snorri Sturluson, and completed after his death by an unknown author. Snorri, born also in Iceland, lived from 1178 to 1241. Writing in prose, he based his work very largely on the *Elder Edda*, intending his own work to be a manual for the *skalds*, or poets, of his time. He wanted to supply these poets with all the information they needed in regard to mythology, history of the heroic age, and poetic means. Part of his work expands and interprets what is in the *Elder Edda*, as well as his other sources. Although the origin of the word *Edda* itself is obscure, it is possible that it means "poetics," coming from the word *óthr*, meaning "spirit" or "reason."

The third of the Icelandic sources was the anonymous *Volsunga Saga*, which recounted the life of Sigurd and the events following his death. Written also in the thirteenth century in prose, this great work expands the story of Sigurd and the Giukis, filling in and expanding certain parts of the story that seem to be either missing from the *Eddas* or just not included in them. Scholars believe that the author may have worked from a more complete copy of the *Elder Edda* than we have now.

Written somewhat earlier, at the end of the twelfth century, was the Middle High German *Nibelungenlied*, which told of Sifrid's coming from the Netherlands to the Burgundians, his marriage to Kriemhilde, his death by the hand of Hagen, and the revenge that Kriemhilde took against her kinsmen on account of that death. A version of this story was well enough known by Wolfram's audiences that he makes various references to it and its main characters in *Parzival*. The context of the references, such as Rumolt's advice to King Gunther concerning the Huns, makes it clear that Wolfram expected his audiences to know the story in detail and to have it fresh in their minds. The poet who composed this work is now unknown.

A very early poem, written about 800 in old Low German, was the *Hildebrandslied*. Hildebrand, in the *Nibelungenlied*, is a vassal of Dietrich of Bern. Dietrich captures in single combat both Hagen and Gunther, and turns them over to Kriemhilde. She, in her hate and fury over the death of Sifrid, beheads both of them while they are bound and imprisoned. Believing that this is a shameful and unacceptable way to treat a king and his brother, Hildebrand kills Kriemhilde, and thus the race of the Nibelungs comes to an end, the others having all died in the last fateful battle. The *Hildebrandslied* is a poetic fragment that tells the story of Hildebrand's journey homeward through the land of the Huns after the great calamity. Hildebrand meets his son, Hadubrand, who does not recognize his father because Hildebrand had left home thirty years earlier when Hadubrand was just a boy. The son thinks his father's offering of peace is a trick, and the two fight. The conclusion of the poem is lost, but Wagner may have found part of his inspiration for the meeting of Siegfried and Wotan in this episode.

Wagner adopted various details of the early life of Siegfried from *Thidreks Saga af Bern*, a prose narrative from around 1260 written in Old Norse but that told the stories of German characters. Wagner certainly used other sources, including Aeschylus's *Oresteia* and *Prometheus Bound*, but the works that I have just mentioned are the ones from which he gathered most of his material.

The Teutonic mythology that Wagner used for the background of the *Ring* comes primarily from the two *Eddas*. The world of *Das Rheingold* comes largely from Snorri, while the idea of the Twilight of the Gods, the Norse *Ragnarök*, comes from the great *Elder Edda* poem *Voluspá*, "The Vala's Prophecy." This poem, regarded to have been spoken by a great *volva* or *vala*,[7] tells of the creation and destruction of the world and of its rebirth after the great holocaust. Wandering *volvas*, common in Scandinavia during the Viking era, were esteemed for their gift of prophecy and were often asked to predict both world events and family or individual fortunes. Even after the "official" conversion of the northern lands to Christianity, many of the old beliefs and practices continued, and the *volvas* remained highly respected.

The details of the human characters in the *Ring* come primarily from the *Volsunga Saga* and the *Nibelungenlied*. The great innovation that Wagner made in his use of this material was to link Siegfried's death with the end of the world. Nowhere in the myths or sagas does the death of the hero specifically initiate the fall of the gods. Having the flames from Siegfried's funeral pyre ignite Valhalla itself was entirely Wagner's invention.

Whereas the *Nibelungenlied* is Christianized and romanticized, the *Volsunga Saga* retains the atmosphere of the old pagan culture. The heroes of the *Nibelungenlied* are medieval knights living and fighting according to courtly chivalry. The influence of the French romances is very apparent when one reads this work, at least as we have it now. Not so with the *Volsunga Saga*. The world of this saga is pre-Christian and primeval, full of magic, shape-changing, and interactions among humans, gods, dwarfs, and spirits. It is this work that gave Wagner not only many of the actual events for the *Ring*, but also the wild and lawless landscape of *Die Walküre*, a world of violence, storms, wolves, and Valkyries. The appearance of Wotan as the Wanderer comes from the *Volsunga Saga*, especially the scene where Wotan appears at Sieglinde's wedding and thrusts Notung into the tree, declaring that only he for whom the sword is meant will be able to draw it out. This is one example of the parallels in the Teutonic legends to the stories of King Arthur, where swords set in stones can be drawn only by those for whom they are meant.

Another example is that of reforging a broken sword. We saw in chapters 4 and 5 that reforging a special sword was often one of the tasks of the Grail hero. In the *Volsunga Saga* Odin gives Sigmund the sword Gram by thrusting it into the oak tree Branstock, and only Sigmund, later the father of Sigurd, can draw it. But when Sigmund dies in battle, Odin again appears and causes

Gram to break. When the battle is over and Sigmund lies dying, his wife, Hjordis, pregnant with Sigurd, searches among the dead on the battlefield for Sigmund, and when she finds him, he gives her the broken pieces of the sword and tells her to keep them for their son. Though it is the smith Regin, not Sigurd, who eventually reforges Gram, the theme is again present.

In chapter 4 we learned that Finn MacCumhail, the Irish prototype of King Arthur, gained the wisdom of all things after he burned his thumb by touching a roasting salmon, and put his thumb into his mouth. In the *Volsunga Saga*, after Sigurd has killed the great *Worm* Fafnir, he cuts out Fafnir's heart. Regin tells Sigurd to roast the heart so that he, Regin, can eat it. Sigurd begins roasting the heart, but as it is cooking he touches it to see if it is done. He puts his finger into his mouth and immediately is able to understand the voices of all fowls. A woodpecker tells him that he should eat the heart himself, and then he would become the wisest of all men. A second bird warns him that Regin is false, and a third tells him to kill Regin (who is one of Fafnir's brothers), which he does. The birds also tell him of the Hoard and of the sleeping Brynhild.

Shape-changing and magic are found in both the Arthurian legends and the Teutonic sagas. In spite of the Christianization of the Arthurian romances, elements of the old pagan practices not only survive but are even central to the stories. Merlin is a wizard and a shaman, and magical powers are prominent with the women of Avalon: Vivian (Nimue), Morgana le Fay, and, in some versions, Morgause as well. Arthur himself is conceived through magic and shape-changing (as is Galahad, the foremost Christian knight): When Uther Pendragon falls in love with Igraine, the wife of Gorloise, king of Cornwall, Merlin uses his magic to turn Uther into the likeness of Gorloise, and Igraine sleeps with him thinking he is her husband. Gorloise is killed in battle against Uther's army while Uther and Igraine are together.

It is through magic that Elaine, daughter of the Grail King Pelles, is changed into the likeness of Guinevere. In this guise she sleeps with Lancelot and conceives Galahad. Morgana le Fay, the half-sister of Arthur, changes her appearance through magic and sleeps with Arthur, thus conceiving Mordred, who eventually destroys Camelot. This is Morgana's revenge for the death of her father, Gorloise.

Shape-changing and deception are also prominent in the Teutonic legends. In the *Volsunga Saga*, Sigmund, the son of Volsung (who is descended from Odin), has a sister, Signy, who is married to Siggeir. Siggeir and his men treacherously slay Volsung, and Sigmund escapes into the forest. Signy plans revenge against her husband, but her own sons are not strong enough for the task. She knows that only one of Volsung's line will be strong enough to help her brother, so she enlists the help of a witch-wife, and the two exchange semblances. In this guise Signy goes to Sigmund and sleeps with him. The child born from this union is Sinfjotli, and when he is old enough Signy sends him to Sigmund. Sigmund thinks the boy is Siggeir's but accepts the child because he was sent by Signy. For a long time the two live in the forest as werewolves, and when the time is right they change back into humans and avenge the death of Volsung. It is this part of the *Volsunga Saga* that forms the wolf background for the first act of *Die Walküre*.

In both the *Volsunga Saga* and the *Nibelungenlied*, Sigurd (Sifrid) wins Brynhild (Brünnhilde) for Gunnar (Gunther) through magic and deception. In the first, Sigurd and Gunnar exchange appearances using magic taught to them by Gunnar's mother, Grimhild. In the second, Sifrid uses the magic cloak he has taken from the Hoard to make himself invisible and thus helps Gunther perform the feats of strength that are required for him to win Brünnhilde as his wife.

In the *Volsunga Saga*, when Sigurd rides away from Brynhild's mountain after receiving her wisdom, his shield is emblazoned with the image of a dragon, "brown above and bright red below." King Arthur fought under the banner of the Red Dragon.

These are examples of mythological parallels between the Teutonic and Arthurian legends. But there are also historical parallels between the Teutonic sagas and the stories of Arthur and Camelot. Although the exact identification of the man Arthur cannot be determined for sure, we know that in 385 the Romans began withdrawing their legions from Britain in order to use them on the German frontier. By 411, if not sooner, all of the Roman legions were gone from Britain. This left the Britons alone to defend themselves against the Saxon invasions that were already under way. Sometime during the fifth century a great Briton "war duke," known in Latin as the *dux bellorum* and among the Britons as Pendragon,[8] rose up and, at least temporarily, kept the Saxon invasions in check. Most modern scholars believe that this man fought for many decades, from the later fifth century well into the sixth. Thus we can pinpoint Arthur's historical period, if not his exact identity.

The *Volsunga Saga* and the *Nibelungenlied*, as well as some of the poems and sections from the *Eddas*, have a specific historical basis, even though much of the content of these works has obviously been mythologized. These works tell of the terrible destruction and annihilation in 437 of the Burgundians by the Huns. The trauma of this catastrophe was so indelibly impressed in the memories of the Germanic peoples that it became the basis for their greatest literary epics. Over time the legends of the great mythological hero Siegfried became intertwined with the historical events of the Burgundian tragedy, and the sagas as we have them now were born.

For centuries there had been a migration of first Celtic and then Germanic tribes from eastern regions into the west. The Burgundians had moved from the area around the Baltic into the lands along the Rhine near the city of Worms, where they settled by the early fifth century. This inevitably brought confrontation with Rome, and in 435 they rose up against the Roman governor Aëtius. The Romans formed an alliance with the Huns, and in 437 the Huns attacked the Burgundians and annihilated them. It was the neighboring Franks who preserved the memory of this event, and this is the period that is referred to when people speak of the Germanic Heroic Age, or the Era of the Sagas.

Even though Attila was not present at this battle, legend eventually placed him there, and thus he appears as Atli in the *Volsunga Saga* and Etzel in the *Nibelungenlied*. Although Sigurd/Sifrid/Siegfried is mythological and not historical, a number of the other characters are based on real people. The most central is Gunnar/Gunther, who was the Burgundian king Gundahari, killed in 437. Dietrich is the Ostrogothic king Theodoric the Great of Verona. King Giuki, father of Gunnar, can be related to the Burgundian prince Gibica, the name from which Wagner derived the Gibichungs. There are others as well, some of whom relate to specific historical people, and some who are composites.

The year 437 places these events very close to the time of King Arthur. The Arthurian and Teutonic legends grew out of the same historical period and flowered literarily at exactly the same time, from the late twelfth century through the thirteenth century.

One final comment can be made about Wagner's sources. The old Germans believed in reincarnation, or rebirth. When the Germanic and Scandinavian lands were converted to Christianity, the missionaries tried to stamp out the old beliefs, but many of these old beliefs never completely died out, and were preserved in the literature. There are various references to reincarnation in the sagas, and I will mention one as an example. In the *Elder Edda* and the *Volsunga Saga*, Sigmund has a wife before Hjordis named Borghild. They have a son named Helgi who becomes a famous hero, and in the *Elder Edda* there is a long poem called "The Second Lay of Helgi Hundings-bane." Helgi marries Sigrun but is killed in battle by Sigrun's brother Dag. Helgi is buried in a great barrow and goes to Valhalla. Sigrun goes to the burial mound and converses with Helgi. She dies shortly afterward, and at the end of the poem there is a prose paragraph that reads:

> But a little while lived Sigrun, because of her sorrow and trouble. But in old time folk trowed that men should be born again, though their troth be now deemed but an old wife's doting. And

so, as folk say, Helgi and Sigrun were born again, and at that tide was he called Helgi the Scathe of Hadding, and she Kara the daughter of Halfdan; and she was a Valkyria, even as is said in the Lay of Kara.[9]

The Sins of the Fathers

The sins of the fathers shall be visited upon the children unto the third and fourth generation of them that hate me.

Exodus 20:5

The separation of the Spear and Grail, the setting in motion of the Wheel of Karma, affects the whole world, not just the individuals who commit the act itself. And until the karma is cleansed, future generations are affected as well. This is very dramatically illustrated in the *Ring*. Because both Wotan and Alberich have tried to force their will upon the world through the acquisition of power, life for everyone is filled with fear and violence. The times are barbaric, with humans living barely above the level of animals. Even Wotan, the king of the gods, descends to earth to live with his son in the forest, where the two of them roam like wolves. Wotan fathers children specifically for the purpose of furthering his plan to regain the ring. As soon as these children come into the world they are immediately presented with the conditions of violence, treachery, and hunger for power, conditions they themselves did not create. They must face them anyway and find their way in a world of darkness and suffering. The tragic events experienced by Siegmund and Sieglinde testify to the extent of the suffering caused by greed, hate, jealousy, and the willingness to harm others in order to satisfy one's own desire.

Here again Alberich mirrors Wotan. He too fathers a child, not out of love, but out of the desire to win back the ring. And so Hagen is brought into the world, inheriting, like Siegmund and Sieglinde, the consequences of his father's actions. He is old before his time, feared but not loved, existing only to perpetuate a crime committed before he was born. He is never as sympathetic a character as Siegmund or Sieglinde, but he shares their circumstance and burden in a world whose conditions he did not create, but whose consequences he must bear.

Siegfried represents another generation brought into this same world and bears the same burden his parents did. At this point we have an opportunity to examine the nature of karmic consequence as it continues over time, and how it is portrayed and symbolized in the *Ring* and *Parsifal*.

After who knows how many thousands of years of human history on this planet, no historical beginning of humanity can be traced. The circumstances of the world we live in now are certainly not the result of the actions of any one generation. They are the accumulated result of actions, both meritorious and non-meritorious, of countless generations. As new people come into the world, they inherit the condition of the world created by previous generations. How these new people behave in the world in the course of their lifetimes will determine how much old karma is cleansed or perpetuated and how much new karma is made or not made. This will in turn affect the condition of the world that the next generation inherits. If the old karma is simply perpetuated, that is, if the new generation behaves in essentially the same way as previous generations, not much will change. If a lot of the old karma is cleansed and *not* perpetuated, things can improve. If a large amount of non-meritorious new karma is created, they can get worse. Karma can accumulate and literally tumble down upon us generation after generation if we do not do something about it and about ourselves. Each generation is in the position of having to deal with the consequences of previous actions and of being responsible for the conditions that future generations will inherit.

The epigraph for this section pertains both to this idea and to rebirth. It pertains not only to the effect our previous actions have had on the world as we find it today, but also to the effect these actions have had, and will have, in the context of our own individual karmic stream.

Because we have had previous lives on earth, our actions in those lives are part of the accumulated karma affecting the world today. Thus, in a certain way and to a certain extent, it can be said that we *did* create the conditions we were born into, even though the actions of others certainly contributed too. Karma that we create in one life will have to be dealt with in another, and thus it is said in Buddhism that although we do not create, by ourselves, the conditions and circumstances of the whole world, we do create the conditions and circumstances of our own rebirths. And thus the idea of the sins of the fathers being passed on to the children for a number of generations refers not just to our literal children, but also to our own future lives. The "children" who inherit the "sins" are the beings of our future lives who will have to inherit whatever uncleansed karma we leave behind in this lifetime. Thus, in each lifetime we are in the position of the father, and what we do in this lifetime will affect not only our children and our grandchildren, but also our own future lives.

This is what is being portrayed in the *Ring* and *Parsifal* as one work, on each of the levels I have just discussed. The separation of the Spear and Grail, in all its aspects, is symbolic of what has caused the conditions of the world that we see around us today. It is also symbolic, as I mentioned before, of the original act that set the Wheel of Karma in motion for our own individual karmic stream. The reuniting of the Spear and Grail, in all its aspects, is symbolic of what can be done to help the circumstances of the world today. This reuniting is also symbolic of the path to salvation and the final cleansing of all the karma in our karmic stream. Thus we return to the original pure state, where the Spear and Grail once again occupy their ordained places in the resurrected Temple, the mind of enlightenment.

In Greek tragedy, each play had two parts, the *complexity* and the *catastrophe*. At any point during the first part of the play—the complexity—the tragic hero could still avert the tragic ending. He still had time to change his course of action and thus change the result. But there was always a crucial "point of no return," a point beyond which events had gone too far for the end to be averted. At this turning point the play entered the catastrophe, and the hero now had no other choice but to follow the tide of events to their inevitable tragic conclusion.

For Wotan, this point comes in Act II, Scene 1 of *Die Walküre*. Fricka punctures his argument that Siegmund is an agent of his own free will and should be allowed to triumph over Hunding. The scene ends with Wotan realizing that all his plans have come to nothing, and that he must destroy the sword he gave to his son and then watch him die. He sees at this point the futility of all his efforts to recapture the ring and cement his power over the world. He confesses to Brünnhilde at the start of Scene 2 after Fricka has left:

> I forged the fetters;
> now I'm bound.
> I, least free of all living!

Wotan's feeling "bound" is an ironic parallel to the binding of Alberich in *Das Rheingold*, when Wotan and Loge capture Alberich and Wotan later tears the ring off of Alberich's finger. It is also a recognition on Wotan's part that he is powerless to succeed in his ambition, and that now all he can do is renounce his attempts to control the outcome of events, and watch as the actions of others bring about the inevitable end. He says to Brünnhilde:

> Fade from my sight,
> honour and fame,
> glorious godhead's
> glittering shame!
> And fall in ruins,
> all I have raised!
> I leave all my work;
> but one thing I desire:
> the ending,
> that ending!

(He pauses in thought.)
And to that ending
works Alberich!
Now I grasp
all the secret sense
that filled the words of the Wala:
"When the dusky foe of love
gains in hatred a son,
the gods may know
their doom is near."

The tragedy has entered the catastrophe, and the end of the gods cannot be averted.

Wotan could have averted the tragedy during the complexity, specifically in Scene 4 of *Rheingold*, when he briefly possessed the ring. At that point he could have returned the ring to the Rhinemaidens; but he did not. In Scene 2, Loge had told Wotan about the Rhinemaidens mourning for their gold:

They turn, Wotan,
sadly to you,
for they hope that you will avenge them;
the gold—they pray
that you'll restore it,
to shine in the waters for ever.
So I promised
I'd tell you the story;
and that's what Loge has done.

But Wotan was thinking only of himself and his own ambition. He answered Loge:

Are you mad,
or simply malicious?
You know I am in need;
How can I help someone else?

Wotan gave no thought to how, by helping someone else, he might in fact help himself as well. He dismissed Loge's suggestion and in so doing ended up missing a magnificent opportunity to avoid the calamity.

Even after this he still has a chance to turn his own karmic stream around. In the great scene where Erda rises from the earth and warns him about the danger inherent in greed for the ring and its power, Wotan does listen to her. In this scene Erda represents the voice of the Eternal, the voice of the Buddha-nature, which is always speaking to us if we quiet our own minds and hearts enough to listen and hear it. At crucial points in our lives and spiritual development, this voice will speak to us urgently, not wanting us to take the wrong path or make the wrong decisions. This voice is an outpouring of great compassion, both for ourselves and for the world, but we must still be able and willing to listen to it. Unfortunately for Wotan, at this moment it is only his fear that is awakened, not his wisdom. He listens well enough to give up the ring, but not well enough to hear what she is *really* saying. He gives up the ring, but not the pursuit of the ring. This is his downfall. After he gave the ring to the giants and watched in horror as Fafner brutally killed Fasolt for it and for the gold, he could have worked for the good of the world, but instead he plotted through force and deception to win back the ring for himself. His actions perpetuate the original error of the breaking of the branch and the theft of the gold. He perpetuates the negative karma, and in doing so compounds it, over and over, until finally its cumulative effects can only be worked out in the form of catastrophic suffering. Erda says to him when he asks her to tell him more:

You heard my words;
you know enough:
brood in dread and fear!

Part of the tragedy of Wotan is that he *has* heard the voice of Erda; he has heard the teaching, and yet he willfully ignores it and continues to pursue his own greed and desire. This is how karma is made, and the law of karmic consequence is an inexorable law of the universe.

Brünnhilde is one of the children who inherit the sins of the father. Brünnhilde and her sisters were all brought into the world in order to serve Wotan's will. Brünnhilde is even known as "Wotan's will" and actually refers to herself as such in Act II, Scene 2, of *Die Walküre*. There is a very tender exchange between the two of them when Brünnhilde sees how unhappy Wotan is after Fricka has left. Brünnhilde asks Wotan to tell her what has happened. He sings to her very softly:

> If I should tell you,
> might I not lose
> the controlling power of my will?

Brünnhilde answers him just as softly:

> To Wotan's will you're speaking;
> you can say what you will;
> what am I
> if not your will alone?

Wotan then opens his heart to her, telling her how he had longed in his heart for power and had won himself the world, yet in doing so had acted wrongly, trusting in treaties "where evil lay," stealing the ring from Alberich and not returning it to the Rhinemaidens. He tells her that when he heard the warning of Erda,

> Then I lost all my joy in life;
> my only desire was to learn.
> So I made my way
> down into the depths;
> by love's enchantment
> I conquered the Wala,

humbled her silent pride,
till she told me all she knew.
Wisdom I won from her words;
the Wala demanded a pledge;
the wise Erda conceived
a daughter—Brünnhilde, you.

These are very tragic lines, for Wotan confesses that he has
done exactly what Alberich did. Wotan descended to the depths,
used "love's enchantment" for power, and conquered Erda, raping her, just as Alberich had attempted to do with the Rhinemaidens. Alberich's rape ended up being material, not sexual,
but the intention is the same. Wotan forces Erda to tell him her
wisdom, and he uses this knowledge to sire eight more Valkyrie
daughters whom he uses to shore up his power over the world,
all the time living in mortal dread of the end. He has made a hell
out of the world, for himself and for others alike. This is exactly
what the consequences of non-preceptual action are. When we
break the Precepts, the Commandments, especially if we will-
ingly harm others in the process, we create a hell. This is the law
of karmic consequence, and Wotan, like so many others, learns
this wisdom too late. By the time he realizes what he has done
and is willing to stop, it is too late, for karma has been set in motion that only a great deal of suffering, both on his part and on
the part of others, can cleanse.

Once Wotan has made the decision to allow Siegmund to
die, he recognizes that in Siegmund's death all his hopes and
plans have failed, and there is nothing more for him to do
except watch and wait for the end. At this point he begins
what Wagner called his renunciation of the will. But he does
not do it all at once. Even after his confession to Brünnhilde,
his will very quickly springs up in the form of terrible rage.
Brünnhilde at first refuses to obey him when he tells her that
she must fight for Hunding, for she knows that his true desire
is to have Siegmund live. Her refusal causes Wotan to erupt
in violent anger:

Rebellious child!
Do as I say!
What are you but the obedient,
blind slave of my will?

Here is Wotan considering his own child to be nothing but a
slave to his will. He continues:

When I told my sorrows,
sank I so low,
that I'm scorned, defied
by the child whom I raised?
Daughter, know you my wrath?
Your soul would be crushed
if you confronted
that fierce, furious rage!
Within my bosom
anger is hid,
that could lay waste
all of a world—
that world I once used to love:
woe to him whom it strikes!

He then orders her to carry out his command and not to
rouse his anger. He storms away and leaves Brünnhilde alone,
"shocked and stunned," and she finally realizes that she must
fight for Hunding and cause the death of Siegmund:

This hateful task
fills my heart with fear.
Woe, my Wälsung!
In deepest sorrow
this true one must falsely betray you!

This last line contains the truth of the world Wotan has created. We saw before that Erda represents the voice of the Eternal,

the voice of the Buddha-nature as it tries to speak to us. In the act of forcing and raping Erda, Wotan symbolically rapes the Buddha-nature, that is, acts in a manner so contrary to the Precepts that he turns the world inside out and upside down: truth becomes falsehood and falsehood becomes truth, and even actions stemming from love can result only in betrayal and sorrow. This is the true Waste Land; Wotan has indeed "laid waste all of a world."

Wagner wrote the poem of the *Ring* before he had read Schopenhauer, but he later came to see Wotan's renouncing of his will to be the archetypal Schopenhauerian act. After his first reading of *The World as Will and Representation*, Wagner sent a printed copy of the poem to Schopenhauer but never received an acknowledgment. He remained offended by this, even after he learned from mutual acquaintances that Schopenhauer had spoken well of the work. On March 29, 1878, Cosima recorded a very important discussion with her husband:

> As we return home through the palace gardens, he says: "It does not say much for Schopenhauer that he did not pay more attention to my *Ring des Nibelungen*. I know no other work in which the breaking of a will (and what a will, which delighted in the creation of a world!) is shown as being accomplished through the individual strength of a proud nature *without the intervention of a higher grace*, as it is in Wotan. Almost obliterated by the separation from Brünnhilde, this will rears up once again, bursts into flame in the meeting with Siegfried, flickers in the dispatching of Waltraute, until we see it entirely extinguished at the end in Valhalla."[10]

As we saw on page 196, Wagner believed that Wotan's final renunciation of the world and his will was enough to accomplish his salvation, and that he was reborn as Titurel and entrusted with the Holy Relics of the Spear and Grail. In the context of Buddhist teaching, renunciation is not, by itself, enough. It is the first step, but much more must be done than simply renouncing the world and one's pursuit of it. Thus, from this point of view,

Wotan does not achieve salvation in the fiery destruction of Valhalla. He must be reborn as Amfortas in order to attain final
emancipation. Wotan's renunciation and the wisdom he gains in
the course of the remainder of the *Ring* are enough to allow him
to be reborn as Amfortas and to obtain the wonderful opportunity it affords, but he still needs much more training. Karma
that is already made is not cleansed by renunciation alone; it is
cleansed through assiduous spiritual training and the willingness to take upon oneself, and accept, the consequences of all
previous actions. It is not enough simply to refrain from what is
wrong. One must also put into practice what is right.

Wotan's will flares up in more instances than the ones Wagner
mentions above. We have just seen that it flares up in anger at
Brünnhilde's initial refusal to obey him. It flares up again when
his favorite daughter *does* disobey him.

The *Todesverkündigung*, the "annunciation of death," is one of
the greatest scenes in all of drama. Among its many grandeurs,
Brünnhilde undergoes a transformation that changes the course
of the *Ring*. She mirrors the heroism of Siegmund and, in a subtle
but important way, the heroic act of Wotan's renunciation.

The Valkyries have come to be romanticized to the extent that we
envision them as heroic and beautiful maidens riding through the
sky on their flying horses as they bring the fallen heroes to Valhalla,
where these heroes will stand with the gods in their final battle
against the giants and the forces of chaos. The gods, representing
the forces of light and order in the universe, will succumb to the
forces of darkness, and all will plunge again into the primordial
night. But out of this darkness and chaos a new universe will be
reborn. The earth will rise anew, green and fertile, out of the sea, and
a new race of gods will appear on the old site of Asgard, resplendent
in their new glory. Balder, the god of light, will rise again from Hel's
kingdom and sit on the high throne, and a fresh era of peace and
wisdom will reign over the world.

This is what the mythology tells us about the end of the gods
and their regeneration, but this description does not reflect the
original image of the Valkyries.

The origin of the Valkyries can be found in early Celtic mythology. The Celts often envisioned the ghostly spirits of battle and of death as women who could take both human and animal form. Morrigu and Bobd are examples of battle spirits who could appear on a battlefield as birds of prey as well as in the form of women who could prophesy the results of war and its attendant slaughter and death. In both Celtic and early Germanic culture, men were said to have dreams and visions before a battle of hideous female creatures drunk on blood, riding on wolves or weaving on looms made of entrails and severed heads. These sinister and terrifying images reflected the premonitions of pain and death that many men would have before a battle. Out of these early visions grew the tradition of Valkyries, the choosers of the slain, who decided who would live and who would die, and who brought the dead to the fortress of Odin.

When we speak of Brünnhilde as a Valkyrie, we must keep in mind that although Wagner represents her in the form of a beautiful and sympathetic warrior maiden, she also carries with her the images of death and slaughter. She lives for death and joyfully carries her weapons into battle. We must not forget the true nature of this kind of battle. It was gruesome, barbaric, and hideously cruel.

It is Siegmund who sparks the first stage of her transformation. When she first appears to him and tells him that she has come to call him hence, he asks her who she is, "who so stern and beauteous appear?" She answers that only those doomed to die can see her, and that she has come to take him to Valhalla. He asks if Wotan rules alone there, and she tells him that the heroes and wish-maidens are there as well. Siegmund then asks if his father, Wälse, is there also, and it is plain that Siegmund does not know Wotan is his father. Brünnhilde simply answers, yes, his father is there too, waiting to greet his son. Then Siegmund asks if Sieglinde is called to Valhalla as well, and when Brünnhilde answers no, Siegmund sings perhaps his most heroic lines:

Then greet for me Walhall,
greet for me Wotan,

greet for me Wälse
and all the heroes;
greet all those fair
and lovely maidens.
To Walhall I will not go!

Siegmund rejects Valhalla and all its "loveless pleasures" if Sieglinde cannot go with him. Brünnhilde tells him that he has gazed upon a Valkyrie, and that he has no choice. Siegmund still refuses, believing he will not die as long as he has his father's sword. Only when Brünnhilde tells him that the god who bestowed the sword now takes back the spell does Siegmund realize he is doomed, yet still he will not go to Valhalla:

Yet though I die here,
I'll not go to Walhall:
hell may hold me instead!

This begins the transformation in Brünnhilde, for she cannot believe that anyone would forsake Valhalla for anything on earth:

So you would sacrifice
joy everlasting?
Is she all
in the world to you,
that maid who lies there
limp and afraid in your arms?
You'd leave Walhall for her?

Siegmund is awakening in Brünnhilde something she has never known: compassion and fellow-suffering. Brünnhilde had known a love between father and daughter, but outside of that relationship she had never experienced the suffering of another on a human level. This is what is happening to her now. She is losing her godhead and starting to become human. It is the innocent and uncorrupted love between two humans, brother and sister, husband and wife, that transforms the "heartless, cold, cruel maid" who has known only celebration in death, and awakens in her compassion and a reverence for life:

> I see the distress
> and grief in your heart,
> I feel all your suffering,
> share in your pain!
> Siegmund, I'll care for your wife;
> I'll shield her safely from harm.

But Siegmund will not allow anyone else to protect Sieglinde, and if he cannot defend her he will kill both her and himself. When he draws Notung and aims it at Sieglinde, Brünnhilde cries to him to stop, that she will fight for him after all, and he will win and live:

> The choice is mine;
> and fate is altered;
> you, Siegmund,
> take my blessing, and win!

In fighting for Siegmund and attempting to change the course of events, Brünnhilde rebels against Wotan, rejecting, like Siegmund, Valhalla and all that it stands for. Even if she believes that she is doing what Wotan really wanted all along, her defiance is still an act of rebellion, for she has gone against Wotan's will. In so doing she has turned away from her old self and opened the way to the new.

But Wotan's power in the world is greater than Brünnhilde's, and she fails in her attempt to save Siegmund. When Wotan sees her act of rebellion, his will, in the form of anger, rages up again, more terrifying than before. In the full throes of this anger, Wotan disinherits her. He takes away her godhead and makes her human:

No more will you ride from Walhall;
no more will you choose
heroes who fall;
or bring me the warriors
who guard my hall; . . .
You broke the bond of our love,
and from my sight, henceforth, Brünnhild is banned!

In banishing Brünnhilde from the realm of the gods and making her human, Wotan is completing the process Brünnhilde began herself when she first perceived and understood the love of Siegmund and Sieglinde. When Brünnhilde first steps out from behind her Valkyrie sisters, having realized that she cannot hide from Wotan's wrath and that to try to do so is dishonorable, she says to him, "Here am I, father; / now tell me my sentence!" Wotan replies:

I sentence you not:
you have brought your doom on yourself.
My will alone
woke you to life,
and against that will you have worked. . . .
Though once you were
all that I made you,
what you have become
you choose for yourself!
No more child of my will;
Valkyrie are you no longer;
Henceforth remain
what you chose to be!

By choosing, of her own free will, to fight for Siegmund against Hunding, Brünnhilde chose the human state over the Deva state, the state of the gods. She is not fully conscious of this until Wotan banishes her from Asgard, and thus she is terrified when she first hears Wotan's pronouncement of exile. She pleads to be allowed to remain with the gods, telling her father how moved she had been by Siegmund's resolve and how her actions reflected Wotan's true desire. But Wotan knows what has really happened, and that she can no longer serve his will:

> So you would attempt
> what I longed so dearly to do,
> but which cruel fate
> forbade me to achieve?
> So you thought
> that love could be captured so lightly,
> while burning woe
> broke my heart in two,
> and terrible grief
> awoke my rage;
> when, to save creation,
> the spring of love
> in my tortured heart I imprisoned?

These are magnificent lines, and they show the tragic wisdom that Wotan has gained at so great a price. He says to her, "You indulged your love; / now let it lead you." He knows that she must now learn what love truly is and the responsibility in life that it carries. In the last part of this great scene Brünnhilde prevails upon him one last time: to protect her sleep with a ring of fire so that only the bravest hero can penetrate the flames and awaken her to claim her as his own. This last wish Wotan grants:

> the weak will flee
> from Brünnhilde's rock!
> For one alone wins you as bride,
> one freer than I, the god!

Then Wotan performs his last act as Lord of Valhalla.

And sadly
the god must depart;
my kiss takes your godhead away!

Wotan kisses her on her eyes, and Brünnhilde falls into a deep sleep. When Siegfried awakens her on the rock, her transformation from Deva to human is complete.

It has often been perceived by commentators that in Wagner's scheme of the *Ring*, the human state is higher than the god state, and that by losing her godhead and seeming to fall from a higher state of existence to a lower one, Brünnhilde actually rose to a more exalted state when she became human. Certainly she went from being a servant of Wotan's will to a state where she has free will of her own. This was the reason for her banishment. Having tasted the elixir of free will, she could not remain in Valhalla as a *Wunschmaid*, and Wotan knew this. It is as a human that she has true free will, and in this way she is higher than the gods.

A similar idea is held in Buddhism. The Deva state may seem much more exalted than the human, and life in the heaven realms may be much more enjoyable in terms of fulfillment of sensual desires than life on earth, but Buddhism teaches that in terms of the opportunity for spiritual training and the realization of enlightenment, the human state is superior to that of the Devas. Narada Thera had said about the Devas: "These celestial beings too are subject to death as all mortals are. In some respects, such as their constitution, habitat, and food they excel humans, but do not as a rule transcend them in wisdom."[11] Buddhism holds that humans have a better opportunity for spiritual training largely *because* of the conditions on earth. The Devas, so happy in their sensual delight, do not have much of an impetus to train rigorously. Thus it is said that heaven, and the condition of heaven, is the most dangerous place of all, because there one can lose sight of the need for spiritual training. If one has a fortunate birth and spends that lifetime merely enjoying fleeting pleasures without generating further merit, who knows where that one will be reborn once the merit that caused the fortunate birth has run out? Both the Buddhist scriptures and the Bible tell of angels who fell from heaven into hell. Wagner's idea that the human state is a higher one than that of the gods very closely parallels Buddhist teaching.

As the fire leaps to encircle the sleeping Brünnhilde, Wotan looks back twice before dejectedly disappearing through the fire. His plans are in ruins. His son is dead and his favorite daughter is lost forever, all because of his own actions. The renunciation of love has come back to him in the most painful of ways, and as he walks away from the fiery rock, he too renounces Valhalla and all that it stands for. From this point onward he roams the world as the Wanderer, observing the ensuing events but taking no part in them. Wagner believed that this renunciation of the world was enough to accomplish redemption, but Buddhism goes a step further than this. Renouncing the errors of one's actions and ways is certainly a profound and necessary first step, and takes a great deal of courage, but by itself it is not enough. Stopping wrong action is the first step. Initiating right action is the all-important second step.

This is why Wotan's renunciation by itself is not enough. Simply refusing to act is not Buddhism, and it will not accomplish the work that needs to be done for salvation. Metaphorically speaking, the karmic stream has become polluted. In order to clean the stream, two basic steps are necessary. First, one must stop pouring more pollution into it. And second, one must clean out the pollution already there. This takes active participation in spiritual training, in right action, both physical and mental. Buddhist meditation is not passive. It is not non-action. It is the highest form of action.

As he wanders the world, watching and waiting, Wotan makes no effort to help the world, no effort to alleviate the world's suffering. He makes no effort to right any of the wrongs he has caused. He only waits for the end. Because Wotan takes only the step of renunciation and not the step of karmic cleansing, he must be reborn as Amfortas. But before that happens, his will flares up in grand fashion one more time.

Siegfried

I recall now having singled out the character of my Siegfried with this particular aim in mind, intending to put forward here the idea of a life free from pain; more than that, I believed I could express this idea even more clearly by presenting the whole of the Nibelung myth, and by showing how a whole world of injustice arises from the first injustice, a world which is destroyed in order—to teach us to recognize injustice, root it out and establish a just world in its place.

Wagner, letter to August Röckel, August 26, 1856

We have just seen how a whole world of injustice can arise from the first injustice, how the first turning of the Wheel of Karma can set in motion events that affect the whole world for generations to come. It is now time to examine Siegfried, and the idea of a life free from pain.

When Brünnhilde rebelled against the will of Wotan, there came into the world of the *Ring* an opportunity for redemption. A voice free from the curse of the ring had spoken, and a will free from the pain of the curse had risen up and taken action. With the birth of Siegfried, born free of the pain of that curse and with a will unfettered by the control of another, that redemption was at hand. The tragedy of Siegfried and Brünnhilde, and their failure to accomplish the act of that redemption, necessitated the births of the characters in *Parsifal*.

When Wotan tore the ring off of Alberich's finger in Scene 4 of *Das Rheingold*, Alberich placed a curse on the ring and anyone who possessed it. But Alberich did not need to curse the ring. The curse—the karmic consequence of non-preceptual action— is there already, inherent in the law of karma itself. When the various characters who plot to gain the ring suffer as a result of their plotting, it is not because of Alberich's curse. It is because the inexorable law of karma is taking its natural course.

Thus, anyone who is free of the desire for the ring and its power and who does not commit non-preceptual acts in order to acquire that power is free of the curse. When Brünnhilde perceived the true nature of the love between Siegmund and Sieglinde, she acted out of the full embracing of love, not out of its renunciation. In that moment she was free from the curse of the ring. Having rebelled against Wotan's will and being cut off from him forever, her will is now her own. In the context of Wagner's scheme of the *Ring*, these two qualities give her the potential to redeem the world.

Siegfried, like Brünnhilde, is free of Wotan's will, and free from the curse of the ring. Thus he is "free from pain," not in the literal, human-level, everyday sense of the word, but, like Brünnhilde, free from the pain of the curse. Wagner's long-held idea that man and woman together constituted the complete human being had its nascent expression in Siegmund and Sieglinde and found its full flowering in Siegfried and Brünnhilde. It is they, together, who have the potential to recognize injustice, root it out, and establish a just world in its place. Wagner had said to Röckel in the January 25–26, 1854, letter:

> Not even Siegfried alone (man alone) is the complete "human being": he is merely the half, only with *Brünnhilde* does he become the redeemer; *one* man alone cannot do everything; many are needed, and a suffering, self-immolating woman finally becomes the true, conscious redeemer: for it is love which is really "the eternal feminine" itself.[12]

Siegfried is born with all the attributes needed for redemption except one: compassion. He is strong, youthful, honest, brave, and unmotivated by greed for power or control over others. But injustice cannot be rooted out and replaced without the ability to go outside of one's self and feel the suffering of others. Siegfried is self personified. He is not evil. He does not wish harm on others. But as far as he is concerned, the world is there for his taking, not because he is excessively greedy, but because he knows nothing else. Having had no true teacher, he has learned from animals in the forest. Their instinct, based on survival, is to take from their environment what they need. Siegfried is not born with compassion; if he is to accomplish the act of redemption, it is something he will have to learn.

Zen Master Dogen wrote in his *Rules for Meditation*, "If your first step is false, you will immediately stumble."[13] Unfortunately, in spite of all his great potential, Siegfried's first step is false.

The first act for which Siegfried is known is the reforging of Notung. At the end of Siegmund's fight with Hunding, Notung lay in pieces. On one level of symbolism, Notung represented Wotan's will. The breaking of Notung was the breaking of that will. As we have just seen, from the end of *Die Walküre* onward Wotan no longer takes part in the events of the world. He no longer uses his will to influence the outcome of these events. After his argument with Fricka and the ensuing death of Siegmund, his will lay broken. Symbolically speaking, the reforging of Notung is the reforging of Wotan's will.

This by itself is not a negative action. There is nothing wrong with Wotan's will in and of itself. What matters is how that will is used. There is nothing wrong with reforging the sword. What matters is what is done with that sword once it is reforged.

The sword can be a symbol of life as well as of death. In old mythology, the sword symbolized the giving of new life, for the cutting of one object resulted in the creation of two new objects. In Buddhism, the Bodhisattva of Wisdom, Manjusri, holds in his right hand a sword representing the mind of the trainee cutting through the clouds of delusion and realizing the Light of Truth. Siegfried could have used Notung to give life. Instead he uses it for death. From that moment on he has blood on his hands.

The killing of Mime has always left audiences feeling uneasy. Even though it can be rationalized that Mime was trying to kill Siegfried and had forfeited his head in the contest of questions with the Wanderer, the act still doesn't sit right. Part of the reason is that in *Das Rheingold* Mime is a somewhat sympathetic character. He seems to be on the side of Wotan and Loge against Alberich, and the semicomical nature of his character engenders audience sympathy. His abrupt killing by Siegfried seems to us to be heartless and cruel, even if our intellects can find justification for it.

Another part of the reason is that we all have an intuitive knowledge of our own Buddha-nature. When it speaks to us, it urges us to have sympathy for those like Mime and Alberich, beings who have had unfortunate births and for whom life is suffering. The part of us that feels compassion for others wants to help Alberich and Mime, not kill them. Cosima recorded on March 2, 1878: "Comparison between Alberich and Klingsor; R. tells me that he once felt every sympathy for Alberich, who represents the ugly person's longing for beauty."[14] We wish that Siegfried had found some other solution to the problem of Mime besides killing him.

The killing of Mime, however, is not the only blood Siegfried has on his hands, nor is it the first. The act that brings Siegfried his greatest fame is the killing of the dragon Fafner. We saw earlier in this chapter what Wagner considered the most basic mythological symbolism of the hero killing the dragon. In chapter 4 we saw that the killing of the dragon can represent the releasing of the waters of fertility onto the world; the overcoming of fear of the unknown on the part of the spiritual seeker; the freeing of the True Self held prisoner by the dragon of delusion; the overcoming of fear of the feminine on the part of the young man coming of age; and, in a Christian context, the victory of Christ over Satan. There are those who argue that in *Siegfried* the killing of Fafner represents the killing of the fearful aspect of the feminine, because Siegfried goes from the dragon's cave to the rock, where he awakens Brünnhilde. The problem with this is that Siegfried, in killing Fafner, has *not* overcome the fear of the feminine, for as soon as he discovers that Brünnhilde is a woman and not a man he feels fear, feeling it for the first time in his life. So this interpretation cannot be used for *Siegfried*. Neither can the Christian interpretation be used, for the *Ring* is not Christian. Wagner had said to Cosima on April 7, 1879, "I like the Nibelungs, they are so heathen; not a spark of Christianity anywhere."[15] Here Wagner was talking about all the characters in his drama, not just the dwarfs. The interpretation of the freeing of the True Self from the dragon of delusion is very fitting when the story concerns a maiden chained to a rock, and the hero kills the monster arising from the sea, the maiden representing the True Self. But Fafner is not a dragon or monster that kills victims. He is a hoarding dragon, and he is guarding a treasure. What is important here is the nature of the treasure and the nature of the dragon.

The fertility symbol of Indra killing Vritra and releasing the waters on the world is related to our discussion here. Vritra was also a hoarding dragon. The treasure he guarded was the water of life, on both the agricultural level and the spiritual level. The hero Indra releases the waters of life for the whole world, thus benefiting everything in it. The killing of the dragon in this context is an act of compassion for the world and of world salvation.

On a subtle level, the interpretation of overcoming the fear of the unknown also applies to Siegfried, for the inner recesses of spiritual knowledge are always guarded by monsters and fearsome creatures in order to bar the way of anyone not yet worthy to enter. If Siegfried is to become the redeemer, he must be able to conquer all fear and penetrate to the innermost experiences of enlightenment.

There is, however, one further aspect to the dragon guarding the treasure, and this is the symbolism most important and relevant to the thesis of this book, for it is the symbolism used in Buddhism. The dragon, in Buddhism, represents the Defender of the Faith. The treasure is enlightenment. The dragon guards the treasure of enlightenment, not to hoard it or withhold it, but in order to give it freely to all those who, through great spiritual training, are worthy to receive it. The treasure house is open to all; it is we who must open our spiritual eyes and realize this.

Many Chinese paintings contain images of a dragon holding in one of its claws a jewel. This is the Mani Jewel, the jewel of enlightenment. These paintings represent the idea of the dragon holding in its protection the Treasure House of enlightenment. Dogen concludes his *Rules for Meditation* with the following:

> O sincere trainees, do not doubt the true dragon, do not spend so much time in rubbing only a part of the elephant; look *inwards* and advance directly along the road that leads to the Mind, respect those who have reached the goal of goallessness, become one with the wisdom of the Buddhas, *Transmit* the wisdom of the Ancestors. If you do these things for some time you will become as herein described and then the Treasure House will open naturally and you will enjoy it fully.[16]

In the context of this view, Siegfried's killing of Fafner is the killing of an aspect of the Eternal, and his taking the ring and the Tarnhelm from the cave is an act of stealing from the Treasure House. Obviously the Eternal, or the Truth, cannot really be killed or harmed; but what this act symbolizes is the raping of the Buddha-nature, an act that directly mirrors Wotan's act of conquering and forcing Erda, as well as the original acts of violence and theft against nature, the breaking of the branch and the stealing of the gold. Thus, without evil intent, but rather out of ignorance, Siegfried perpetuates the same karma that he and his generation inherited from Wotan and Alberich. As Dogen says, the Treasure House will open naturally. There is no need for violence and theft. Killing and theft are direct acts against the Precepts. As such they can never be, from the Buddhist point of view, acts of redemption, either of the individual or of the world. Buddhist symbolism never shows a hero killing a dragon. By killing Fafner and stealing the ring, Siegfried has perpetuated the Old Way. He has not instituted the New Way of recognizing and rooting out injustice. He has merely fallen prey to that same injustice, and in doing so he has forfeited his right and ability to be the redeemer. At this point in the *Ring*, if redemption is still possible, it lies with Brünnhilde.

Before Siegfried can ascend the rock and awaken the sleeping maiden, he must encounter Wotan's will, rearing up to its full height one last time.

Wagner begins Act III of *Siegfried* with Wotan as the Wanderer waking Erda from her sleep and asking for her wisdom. But Erda no longer has wisdom:

> Deeds of men
> have beclouded all my thoughts;
> my wisdom itself
> once felt a conqueror's force.

Speaking symbolically in the context of our discussion, this is the result of raping the Buddha-nature. One's own inner spiritual understanding has been clouded and obscured by non-preceptual actions to such an extent that our natural spiritual wisdom seems to be unavailable to us, hidden and cut off. It isn't, really. But the layers of karma can be so thick that the light of our own inner nature cannot shine through, and we feel that we have lost access to the fountain of wisdom and understanding that we yearn for. Wotan says to Erda, "you can advise me / if the swift-turning wheel can be stopped." This question has two answers. Karma already set in motion cannot be undone. But the non-preceptual actions themselves, the turning of the Wheel of Karma, *can* be stopped as soon as we take hold of our wills strongly enough and determine to turn our actions in the direction of the Precepts. New actions may interact with karma already set in motion. This is very important. We can turn our lives in the direction of spiritual training at any time. There is nothing stopping us. We have complete and total free will.

Erda tells Wotan that he can learn what he wants from their child. Wotan tells Erda that while she slept, Brünnhilde rebelled against his will, and he punished her pride by putting her to sleep upon a rock. Erda then reveals to him the real truth that he needs to know and understand:

How can pride's teacher
punish pride?
he who urged the doing,
punish the deed?
he who rules by right,
to whom truth is sacred,
scorn what is right,
rule by falsehood?
I'll return to the dark,
seal in slumber my wisdom!

Wotan doesn't need to know what will happen in the future. He needs to know the truth of what he has already done, and this Erda tells him. As long as we are unwilling to accept the consequences of our actions and try only to find a way out for ourselves, our inner wisdom will return to the dark and seal itself in slumber. Wotan tries to command Erda to stay and tell him what he wants to know: "How a god can master his care?" Erda answers:

You are not
what you declare!
Why come here, stubborn and wild one,
to trouble the Wala's sleep?

Wotan then tells her what he has willed and what he shall now bring to pass:

That the gods may die soon
gives me no anguish;
I have willed that end! . . .
today to the Wälsung
I have bequeathed my realm. . . .
She whom you once bore,
Brünnhild,
wakes to that hero's kiss.

Then your wisdom's
child will achieve
that deed that will free our world.
So back to your dreams;
dream on in darkness;
dream of the gods' destruction.
Whatever may happen,
the god will gladly
yield his rule to the young!
Return then, Erda!
Mother of dread!
World-sorrow!
Return! Return
to endless sleep!

Wotan's will has returned, and he speaks to Erda of what he wills and what shall be brought to pass because of that willing. Wotan is not yet fully contrite. This is part of the reason he is not yet ready for the salvation that would result in his rebirth as Titurel. Wotan has not yet fully renounced his will, nor the pride that comes with it. It remains for Siegfried to break that will one final time.

In chapter 4 I spoke of the tradition of sacred kingship and observed that the scene between Wotan and Siegfried retains elements of that tradition. Certainly we see Siegfried defeating Wotan in a fight of weapons, and a transference of power from one to the other based on that confrontation. We see the old king retaining power until a new, younger king takes that power from him. And we see the old king guarding a particular location until someone can come along and defeat him, thus replacing him. When Siegfried's insolence and lack of respect rouse Wotan's anger, Wotan bars his way, and Siegfried asks him who he is to bar his path. The old will of Wotan rises up and answers him:

I am the rock's defender!
And mine the spell

that enfolds the slumbering maid.
He who can wake her,
he who can win her,
makes me powerless forever!

This is a classic example of one aspect of sacred kingship. However, what is important in the context of our discussion is not the outward form or forms of the old tradition, but the nature of the transference of power from Wotan to Siegfried. This will illuminate the events that take place after the confrontation on the mountain.

A generation that inherits the karma from a previous generation has the choice either to continue in the same direction as the earlier generation or to take a new direction, hopefully averting the errors made previously and, in Wagner's words, replacing injustice with justice. This was the great hope for Siegfried. But Siegfried never fulfills that hope. Instead, he follows in the path of Wotan and Alberich. This is true even to the extent that he almost kills his own grandfather, and he would have if Wotan had not disappeared so quickly. The *Hildebrandslied* was not the only inspiration for this scene. On a subtle level Wagner clearly had Oedipus in mind as well.

Siegfried is so self-absorbed that he is blind to many of the realities of the world. Wotan perceives this very clearly and says to him:

I see, my son,
one thing you know—
to get your way as you want it.
Yet be careful,
for with eyes quite as blind
as that eye I've lost, you are gazing
on the eye that is left me for sight.

Siegfried does not understand this warning. He is used to taking anything he wants, even if it means killing for it. He sees nothing wrong with killing whatever is in his way. He tells Wotan to get out of his way or he'll end up like Mime. Even though Siegfried does not plot dishonestly in order to gratify his desires, and even though he does not wish the world harm, he still has no concept of preceptual action. He has no regard for the feelings or situation of others. He is concerned only with himself, and with the world as he sees it through his own eyes. He hardly gives anything else a thought.

There is a marvelous passage in Ephesians 6:12:

> For we wrestle not against flesh and blood, but against principalities, against powers, against the rulers of the darkness of this world, against spiritual wickedness in high places.

The key word here is "principalities." In the context of Christianity and this passage, the word "principalities" refers both to specific regions in heaven and to certain "powers." I am using the word in relation to powers and forces that lie behind what we see in the outside world. Thus, it is not just certain individual people, the "flesh and blood," who are the problem. It is the principalities that produce these people and which lie underneath and behind these human individuals. For example, we can look at certain men in history who have caused great harm and say, "Let's get rid of these people and things will improve." But this is an illusion. If we don't do something about the principalities, nothing will change. Hitler died, but genocide continues even today. Any number of rulers have been replaced over the years, yet atrocities against human beings continue. It is the principalities that must be converted and cleansed, not just individual people. In Buddhism this is often referred to as a "mountain of karma." Each person has his or her own mountain of karma to convert and cleanse, as does the world as a whole. If the karma itself is not cleansed, the "mountain" will remain, no matter how many individuals may "pop up" from it, coming and going throughout the years and ages. This is true for both an individual karmic stream and the world situation as a whole. If the karma in a particular stream is not cleansed, an untold number of lives will be born from it. The course of those lives will not change radically until something is done about the karma itself. The same is true for the world situation. If the same non-preceptual acts are perpetuated generation after generation, the world will not change.

This is what happens with Wotan and Siegfried. Contrary to Wagner's hope for him, Siegfried does not replace injustice with justice. Perpetuating the old karma of non-preceptual action, he uses his weapon for death. Thus the transference of power that takes place on the mountain does not help the world, for even though a new "king" has emerged, the old principality is still in place. It simply has a new head, a new face. Nothing has been redeemed.

When Wotan bars Siegfried's way with his spear, Siegfried with one blow of Notung shatters Wotan's spear in two. Wotan picks up the pieces and stands back, saying, "Pass on! I cannot prevent you!" Wotan then disappears into darkness, and the transfer of power is complete. The shattering of Wotan's spear by Notung is the reverse of the original shattering of Notung by that very spear, but the symbol is the same: Wotan's will has been broken. Notung, now belonging to Siegfried, is the new symbol of power in the world.

Like all the mythological symbols we have been discussing, the awakening of the sleeping maiden has multiple interpretations. On the simplest level of the old fertility rites, the pricking of the maiden's finger with the thorn and her subsequent falling into sleep represents the coming of winter, when nature "sleeps." The witch, a symbol of death, pricks the finger of the maiden with a thorn, a symbol of winter, and when she falls asleep the whole of nature sleeps with her. When the prince awakens her the flowers bloom, the trees put out green leaves, and her awakening becomes the symbol of spring and the awakening of nature after the passing of winter. This is a very simple and very basic interpretation.

The awakening of the maiden also represents the final stage in the rite of passage for the young man. The youth coming of age must undergo various trials as he grows to manhood, and marriage lies at the end of the successful traversing of that road. This also is very simple and very basic.

A third interpretation is the one that most concerns us here, and that is the maiden as True Self, or enlightened mind. We saw this with the monster coming out of the sea, and the same is true here. The maiden is put to sleep by the witch, who in this case represents delusion and the attachment to desire and impermanence that wants to keep us from our true state, the state of enlightenment. Thus the witch is portrayed as evil, and the hero, who represents the True Seeker, must overcome the magic spell the witch has put on the maid. The spell symbolizes the cloud of delusion that keeps us from experiencing our true state. When the hero breaks the spell with a kiss, the maiden wakes. This becomes the symbol of the awakening of the True Self, the awakening to enlightenment.

Certainly there is a rite of passage in Siegfried's finding and awakening Brünnhilde. This adheres to one of the symbols in the old sagas on which Wagner based this scene. The father has surrounded his daughter with a ring of fire, and only one brave enough to pass through the fire is worthy to claim the daughter as his bride. The ring of fire represents the challenge issued to the young suitor to prove that he is worthy.

Another aspect of the sagas that Wagner followed was the punishment of Brünnhilde for disobedience. She was put to sleep and made vulnerable to any man waking her, but at the same time was protected by a ring of fire so that only a great hero would be the one to win her. This aspect of the story combined with the idea of sleeping maiden as Enlightened Mind will form the basis for our current interpretation.

The world created by Wotan and Alberich is a world of male domination, in which women are chattel, objects to be won, claimed, traded, or conquered. This is part of the inheritance of the two initial acts of violence against nature and the primordial world. The separation of man and woman is an aspect of the separation of the Spear and Grail. And the reuniting of man and woman, so that both are returned to their pure state, is an aspect of the reuniting of the Spear and Grail.

Wotan had an intuitive knowledge of this when he created Siegmund and Sieglinde. It is very important that he did not, like Alberich, create only a son. He created twins, brother and sister, man and woman. The purity of the love between these two produced not only Siegfried, but also the inspiration for Brünnhilde's rebellion. Both Siegfried and Brünnhilde have, as part of their inheritance, the union of man and woman in their true state, the union of Spear and Grail.

The separated state of the world is symbolized by Wotan putting Brünnhilde to sleep on the rock and surrounding her with fire. Male domination, intoxicated with its own power, has put the feminine to sleep, surrounding her with a ring of fire so that none may awaken her except one who is unafraid of that fire. The true nature of that one becomes all-important.

If this one great hero is true to the path of reuniting the Spear and Grail, then the feminine will be awakened and restored to her true state. This would have happened had Siegmund prevailed, for he never considered Sieglinde as anything other than his complete equal. He even renounced Valhalla because she could not go with him. But Siegmund could not be the true redeemer because he was not completely free of the will of Wotan. Only Siegfried had the potential to accomplish that task. If, however, the hero is not true to the path of reuniting the Spear and Grail, the feminine will not be restored to her true state. This is what happened with Siegfried.

We have seen how Siegfried is, in spite of his great potential, merely the successor to the rule of Wotan, and the principality that Wotan and Alberich created. He has perpetuated their deeds instead of redeeming them. It is very revealing to place the relationship of Siegfried and Brünnhilde side by side with that of Siegmund and Sieglinde. Siegfried does indeed learn fear from Brünnhilde, which is certainly natural and to be expected when a young man first encounters the possibility of love with a woman. Brünnhilde also encounters a stage of fear when she sees Grane, her horse, and her old armor now cut away from her. She feels

defenseless and becomes very aware of her new vulnerability, at
one point even asking Siegfried to leave her alone on the rock
and allow their love to remain ideal but not consummated:

> O Siegfried,
> Glorious hero! . . .
> leave me in peace!
> Do not come near me
> with passionate frenzy;
> do not pursue me
> with masterful might,
> or else you'll destroy all our love! . . .
> O Siegfried!
> Laughing youth!
> Love yourself,
> and leave me in peace;
> destroy not this maid who is yours!

Sieglinde never talked to Siegmund like this. Of course, Brünnhilde's awakening is not only a waking from sleep, but also a sexual
and romantic awakening that she has never experienced before.
It is natural, in this context, for her to be afraid at this point. But
there is more than just adolescent sexual fear in these lines. She
knows, at least intuitively if not completely consciously yet, that
in the world to which she has just awakened, men and women are
not equal. As a Valkyrie, armed with weapons and the power to
choose life and death, she held power over men. But as a human
woman, stripped of her arms and armor, as well as her godhead,
she is defenseless, left on the rock to be claimed by the first man
who comes upon her. And to this man she must submit. Siegfried
declares his love for her so passionately that they both overcome
their fear and share a glorious time together. Brünnhilde renounces Valhalla and the race of gods one final and triumphant time:

> Farewell, Walhall's
> bright glittering world!

Your glorious halls
now may fall to dust!

And the two of them end with "Light of our loving, / laughter
in death!" But witness what Brünnhilde says to Siegfried during
the Prelude to *Götterdämmerung*:

What gods have given me,
I've given to you:
all that they taught me,
all is yours;
all of this maiden's
wisdom and strength
given to the man
who is now my master.

Sieglinde never called Siegmund her master. And Siegmund
never treated her like property or a prize. Siegmund cherished
Sieglinde so deeply that he would never leave her even for Valhalla, much less any place on earth. But the first thing Siegfried
does when the sexual honeymoon is over is to bound off into the
world to seek new glory while Brünnhilde is left behind. We have
the perfect image of the housewife left at home while the husband
goes off wherever he wants. Siegmund and Sieglinde could not
be separated except by death. Siegfried and Brünnhilde separate
almost immediately, of their own free will. It is Brünnhilde who
says at the start of the scene in *Götterdämmerung*:

To deeds of glory,
brave beloved!
My love for you
bids you be gone.

Even though the two of them are genuinely in love on a romantic level, it is not the pure, unselfish love of Siegmund and
Sieglinde. It is a selfish love, based on youthful passion and sexu-

al desire. It is not a spiritual love, based on suffering. Brünnhilde could not give or teach to Siegfried what he needed most: compassion and the ability to feel the suffering of others. Siegmund and Sieglinde understood compassion and suffering, but in the context of Wagner's scheme, they did not have complete free will. Siegfried and Brünnhilde have complete free will, but it is one of the great messages of the *Ring* that free will alone cannot redeem. It is only free will turned in the direction of compassion and fellow suffering that can redeem both the individual and the world. And this does not happen until *Parsifal*.

Cosima recorded on July 20, 1878:

> When I was looking through some papers with him yesterday, I came upon the original theme for "*Sangst du nicht, dein Wissen*"; I tell R. that the present one (meant at first for Buddha) pleases me far more. "Yes," he says, "I couldn't do it then, though I felt it; at the time it had to be completed for Weimar, and I found working repugnant."[17]

The full quotation is as follows:

Sangst du mir nicht	You said
dein Wissen sei	that all your wisdom came
das Leuchten der Liebe	by the light of your love
zu mir?	for me.[18]

Siegfried sings this to Brünnhilde during the scene in *Siegfried* when she is in the midst of her rising fear. The melody, or leitmotif, to which these words are sung is known as either "Siegfried's love" or the "world inheritance" theme. According to Carl Friedrich Glasenapp, Wagner's close friend and biographer, Wagner first conceived this theme in 1856 in connection with *Die Sieger*, where it was, as Cosima noted, "meant at first for Buddha." We may recall that in *Die Sieger* Prakriti finds her love for Ananda in the enlightenment of Buddhist training, not in romantic attachment. The term "world inheritance" is very interesting here, for that is precisely what we have been talking about. Siegfried and Brünnhilde have inherited the world from Wotan, Alberich, and Erda and have the chance to lead the world either on the path to enlightenment or on the path of continued karmic pursuit and attachment. The great tragedy of Siegfried and Brünnhilde is that they choose, albeit out of ignorance and not evil, the latter. And thus they fail in their task of redemption.

People have often wondered why Siegfried is duped so easily in the Gibichung hall. The truth is, he is not. He does not have to be, because he is already part of the male-dominant principality and the state of spiritual ignorance caused by the separation of the Spear and Grail. All that the drink given to him by Gutrune really does is symbolize and compress in time a process that would have happened anyway: Siegfried entering society, forgetting about Brünnhilde, and eventually becoming attracted to another woman. We need to remember that Wagner uses the idea of a potion only as a symbol of a particular state of mind. This is true in *Tristan und Isolde*, and it is true in *Götterdämmerung*. We must not think that Siegfried does what he does simply because he has been poisoned by Hagen and Gutrune. The poison is not in the drink; it is in his own mind. The poison is his unenlightened state of mind, his inability to feel compassion, his acts of violence and theft against nature and the Eternal, and his failure to see Brünnhilde in her true light as the embodiment of spiritual love and wisdom. Warren Darcy has posed an interesting question: "Those who persist in the belief that Siegfried is an innocent victim completely controlled by outside forces should ask themselves: is it possible to conceive of a potion that could make Siegmund forget Sieglinde?"[19]

Upon forgetting Brünnhilde, Siegfried is immediately attracted to Gutrune and desires her. And sure enough, as soon as Siegfried realizes he wants Gutrune, he offers to trade what he possesses, Brünnhilde, for what Gunther possesses, Gutrune. He swears a male blood-brotherhood oath with a man he has barely met and goes off to fetch his chattel.

The "rape" of Brünnhilde by Siegfried in the guise of Gunther mirrors the rape of Erda by Wotan and the rape of the Rhinemaidens by Alberich. I put the word "rape" in quotes because Siegfried does not sexually rape Brünnhilde. In fact, he places Notung between them when they sleep together in the cave, honoring his pledge to Gunther. His action is, however, certainly a conquest of Brünnhilde, and it is tantamount to rape. Brünnhilde tries to defend herself with the ring, but it is powerless in her hands because she has not renounced love. Siegfried says to her, "You shall be conquered by Gunther; / and that ring makes you his wife!" He then violently tears the ring from her finger, just as Wotan had torn it from Alberich's finger, and just as Alberich had torn the gold from the Rhine. And just as Wotan had forced himself on Erda, so does Siegfried, grandson of Wotan, force himself on Brünnhilde, daughter of Wotan and Erda. We have another example of Siegfried perpetuating the acts of a previous generation. When the two of them spend the night in the cave, Notung separates them. Notung, the new symbol of power in the world, divides male and female, Spear and Grail. The chaste maiden, symbol of the enlightened mind, lies raped and plundered. Just as Siegfried symbolically raped the Buddha-nature and stole from the Treasure House when he killed Fafner and took the ring and Tarnhelm, so did he again rape the Buddha-nature and steal from the Treasure House when he forced Brünnhilde and stole the ring from her finger.

In the scene just prior to this one, when Waltraute rides to Brünnhilde's rock to ask her to give the ring back to the Rhine, Brünnhilde refuses, saying that Siegfried's love means more to her than all the gods' loveless delights and glories:

My love shall last while I live,
my ring in life shall not leave me!
Fall first in ruins
Walhall's glorious pride!

It is sadly ironic that just as soon as she says this, the ring does leave her. Brünnhilde in this scene makes the same mistake that

Wotan made in Scene 4 of *Das Rheingold*: Too bothered and ob-
sessed by his own problems to listen when Loge suggested that he
give the ring back to the Rhinemaidens, Wotan never considered
that helping someone else might in fact help him. Brünnhilde,
in refusing Waltraute, makes the same mistake. She thinks only
of herself and her own love for Siegfried. She never thinks of the
Rhinemaidens, or the rest of the world. And she never considers
that helping the world might help her. The karmic consequence
of her selfish act is immediate. She refuses to give up the ring,
and so it is taken from her, and the suffering that results is far
greater than what she would have experienced had she followed
Waltraute's advice. Brünnhilde cannot teach Siegfried compassion because she does not have it herself. And she, like Siegfried,
has committed the same "sins" as the father.

There are two further ironies working side by side here. The
first is that Brünnhilde had an initial awakening to compassion
when she witnessed the love that Siegmund had for Sieglinde.
This was when she was still a Valkyrie, but now that she is human
herself and in love, that compassion deserts her. Her free will is
directed selfishly. This leads directly to the second irony. "Fall
first in ruins Walhall's glorious pride," she tells Waltraute. But
what falls first in ruins is her own pride when she is conquered
by Siegfried, the very one for whom she kept the ring.

The separation of Siegfried and Brünnhilde is partly a reflection of the world's state, where the Spear is separated from the
Grail, and partly a result of their failure as redeemers. Neither
was yet ready to perform this office, either individually or with
the other, in spite of the great promise they held at the beginning. Unenlightened, they come down off the mountain into the
world of men, a world of greed and corruption, symbolized by
the hall and family of the Gibichungs. Naive as they are, without
the spiritual strength of enlightenment they are easily sucked
into the world of greed and power and quickly become a part of
it. The trauma of the events on the rock and those that follow in
the Gibichung hall, especially for Brünnhilde, leaves deep emotional and spiritual wounds, and the karmic impregnations, that

is, the lasting karmic impressions, of these wounds will carry over into the next life for both of them, rising up in full force and fury in Act II of *Parsifal*.

When Brünnhilde is brought into the Gibichung hall as part of Gunther's wedding procession, she sees Siegfried and is stunned: "Siegfried . . . here . . . ! Gutrune . . . ?" Siegfried answers her, "Gunther's gentle sister, / won by me, / as, by Gunther, you." Brünnhilde says fiercely, "I . . . Gunther . . . ? . . . You lie!" She starts to faint, and Siegfried catches her. She looks up at Siegfried and realizes that he does not know her. "Siegfried—knows me not?" When she sees the ring on his finger, she realizes that it was he who came to the rock and tricked her, and she accuses him of falsehood and betrayal. He swears his innocence, remembering only that he got the ring from Fafner. Brünnhilde then calls on the gods:

Teach me a vengeance
more cruel than my grief!
Stir me to rage
still more keen than my shame!
Ah, though Brünnhilde's
heart may be broken;
bring her betrayer
soon to his death!

At no point does she try to understand why this might have happened to Siegfried, or what may have caused it. She thinks only of her own hurt and how to avenge it. Later, when she perceives Gutrune's part in the deception, she says:

Gutrune, she's the enchantress;
by her spells she stole his love.
My curse on her!

She curses Gutrune and still calls for Siegfried's death. In this way she has reverted to her Valkyrie self, rather than moving forward to her True Self. She wants blood and death, and will not be satisfied until she gets it. Like Siegfried, she shows a complete inability to feel compassion for others, or to see the world from any point of view other than her own. She too has become a cog in the wheel of delusion, the Wheel of Karma, and she turns this wheel with all her fury and might. She then commits the primary act that will cause her rebirth as Kundry. She directly participates in Siegfried's death. When Hagen steps forward and says that he can avenge her, she scornfully sneers at him, telling him that one flash from Siegfried's eyes would cause the bravest foe to cringe with terror. Hagen then asks her if Siegfried has any vulnerability, and she tells him that she protected Siegfried with her magic arts everywhere except in the back, because she knew he would never flee an opponent. Hagen now knows where to strike. In making this pact with Hagen, Brünnhilde forms a karmic bond that will cause her to be reborn in conditions where this karmic debt is still active. The activation of this karmic debt comes in the form of Klingsor's power over Kundry, his ability to wake her from sleep and force her to carry out his bidding. That Kundry also has the meritorious karmic connection to the Temple of the Grail is due to Brünnhilde's eventual perception of the truth about Siegfried's betrayal and her forgiveness of him, as well as her willingness to make the final renunciation and sacrifice.

Siegfried's unreadiness to be the redeemer is shown in his scene with the Rhinemaidens. There is an interesting parallel to Parzival at the beginning of this scene. As we saw in the last chapter, when Parzival first visited the Grail Castle and viewed the Grail procession, he was more concerned with proper behavior and his place in society as a knight than he was with Anfortas's suffering. He had a chance to redeem that suffering and the suffering of the whole community, but he chose to obey society's propriety rather than the call of the Eternal, and so he asked no question. Siegfried does the same thing in the scene with the Rhinemaidens. He tells them that he has had no luck in hunting and has nothing to give them. They then ask for the ring, and he says, "But then if I waste my wealth, / I'm sure that my wife will scold." This may seem like frivolous banter, which Siegfried thinks it is. But underneath there is a grave seriousness. Siegfried, like Parzival, is presented with an opportunity he does not recognize. He is already thinking of his place in society as a husband, completely oblivious to the larger ramifications of his actions and to the world situation. When he finally offers the Rhinemaidens the ring, not wanting their scorn, they want him to understand the full import of what he is doing and what the ring means. They tell him of the dire consequences of retaining the ring, and he immediately reacts by defending his honor and reputation, telling them that his sword has shattered a spear and killed a dragon. He tells them that they will never get the ring from him by threats and scheming. This is, of course, not at all what they are trying to do, but Siegfried is by now taking himself so seriously as a "hero" that he is deaf to the voice of the Eternal, which is speaking at this point through the Rhinemaidens. Wotan had at least listened to Erda when she warned him to give up the ring. Siegfried is more deaf and blind than Wotan, and his refusal to give up the ring to the Rhinemaidens mirrors Brünnhilde's refusal to listen to Waltraute. Both had a chance for truly selfless action, and both failed to recognize it. The Rhinemaidens swim away telling Siegfried that today he will die.

As Siegfried lies dying from Hagen's spear thrust, he has a revelation of Brünnhilde in her true form, that of *Heilige Braut*, Holiest Bride:

Brünnhilde!
Holiest bride!
Now wake! Wake from your slumber!
Who has forced you
back to your sleep?
Who bound you in slumber again?
Your bridegroom came,
to kiss you awake;
he frees you, again,

breaking your fetters.
He lives in Brünnhilde's love!

Siegfried had awakened her from her slumber but then had, symbolically speaking, put her back to sleep again by the way he treated her and behaved in the world. That is, he had put the enlightened mind to sleep by his actions. Now he is waking her again, breaking her fetters, for this time he is waking not a mortal woman but the spiritual mind itself. The music that begins this scene is Brünnhilde's awakening music from *Siegfried*, and here it reflects not only Brünnhilde's original wakening, but also Siegfried's spiritual awakening.

Ah! See those eyes,
open forever!
Ah! feel her breathing,
loving and tender!
Joyful surrender!
Sweet are these terrors!
Brünnhild waits for me here!

On one level, Siegfried is recalling his initial falling in love with Brünnhilde. But on another level he is experiencing the opening of his spiritual eyes and mind, symbolized by the object of his love, Brünnhilde. Because he is dying from a mortal wound, this spiritual awakening cannot be fulfilled in what is left of this lifetime. But the merit of this experience has entered his karmic stream, and because the last thing Siegfried sees with both his eyes and his mind before he dies is this vision of Brünnhilde in her true state, the power of this experience will carry over into his next life and will be the prime force and influence behind the conditioning of that new life. Buddhism speaks of a "proximate thought" or "death-proximate karma" with which a dying person is presented at the moment of death. This last image and thought process in the mind are a large part of what conditions a new birth. What one has done throughout one's life also influences this new birth, as does the karma of the whole karmic stream in general—no one thing alone is responsible for the new birth. However, the dying person's last image and thought process, though not exclusive, are still considered to be the most significant and powerful influence in the process of rebirth.

Hagen's spear thrust was the karmic consequence Siegfried had to experience for his killing of Fafner and Mime and his mistreatment of Brünnhilde. This blow paid, if you will, the karmic debt Siegfried had incurred for his delusive action. The spear thrust also had the effect of cutting through Siegfried's delusion, opening the way for his spiritual vision, his own awakening. Siegfried himself, throughout his life, had been spiritually asleep, unaware of the spiritual nature of the world and of the spiritual potential he carried within himself. On the rock he and Brünnhilde had awakened each other to romance and sex, but not to wisdom and compassion. Though Brünnhilde gave to Siegfried "all her wisdom," that wisdom did not include what was necessary to reunite the Spear and Grail. Brünnhilde herself did not have that to give. The two of them thus failed to accomplish the act of redemption in this life, but they learned and experienced enough in this life to be born again as Kundry and Parsifal, and in that next life salvation will be found.

Siegfried's death-proximate karma is his vision of Brünnhilde. Her thought processes and karmic images at the time of her death are an understanding of Siegfried's immersion in the curse of the ring and her consequent forgiveness, the igniting of the funeral pyre, and a vision in the midst of the flames of Siegfried as true hero and lover. This last vision, her karmic debt for the killing of Siegfried, and the merit of her final self-sacrifice and immolation all combine to condition her rebirth as Kundry, who is born with both a karmic attachment to Klingsor that must be severed and with the inherent spiritual wisdom ready for final enlightenment and Parinirvana. On the rock Siegfried awoke the human maiden Brünnhilde. On the mount of salvation Parsifal will awaken the True Maiden, the mind of enlightenment, the inherent spiritual wisdom that will redeem Kundry, Amfortas, himself, and the world.

When the hunting party returns to the Gibichung hall with the dead body of Siegfried, the curse of the ring immediately takes effect. Remember, this is not the curse Alberich thinks he put on the ring, but simply the natural karmic consequence of non-preceptual action aimed at the attainment of wealth and power. The half brothers Gunther and Hagen fight for the ring still on Siegfried's hand, and Hagen kills Gunther, reflecting the original killing of Fasolt by his brother Fafner. Hagen tries to claim the ring, but Siegfried's hand rises threateningly, and Hagen jumps back in fear. Brünnhilde steps forward and takes the ring from Siegfried's hand. From this point on she dominates the action. While the hunting party was away, Brünnhilde had walked along the shore of the Rhine and communed with the Rhinemaidens. Gutrune had seen this in her dream just before the party returned, and Brünnhilde confirms it during the Immolation Scene when she addresses the Rhinemaidens:

> I shall obey your advice.
> What you desire
> I'll give to you:
> and from my ashes
> gather your treasure!
> This fire, burning my frame,
> cleanses the curse from the ring!

Brünnhilde now knows all that has happened, and she is ready for the final act of self-sacrifice. She calls to the gods to look down and hear her, and she calls to Wotan and says to him of Siegfried:

> By his most valiant deed
> he fulfilled your desire,
> but he was forced
> to share in your curse—
> that curse which has doomed your downfall.
> He, truest of all men,

betrayed me,

that I in grief might grow wise!

Through her suffering Brünnhilde has gained the wisdom she lacked on the rock, and through this wisdom she gains the ability to feel compassion. When one fully comprehends the extent of the suffering caused by selfish and non-preceptual action, one no longer wants to further that kind of action. At this point one is ready for spiritual training. The path of that training is still very long and hard, but the first step has been taken. The karmic conditions of the world of the *Ring* have reached such a stage that all Brünnhilde can do is "cast the flame at Walhall's glorious height." She takes a firebrand from one of the Gibichung vassals and lights Siegfried's funeral pyre. In this final conflagration the ring is returned to the Rhine, and enough of the karma is burned to allow the possibility of a regenerated world, as well as the specific rebirths of the four main characters into the world of *Parsifal*. Whenever the slate is wiped clean, whether on the world level or on the personal, individual level, we must at all times follow the Precepts. Otherwise we will simply create another version of the old world. This will go on and on and on, over and over again, until we learn what it takes to stop the creation of suffering. In *Parsifal*, three of the four characters attain this understanding and subsequent salvation. The fourth, Klingsor, remains unwilling to give up self. As we saw in chapter 2, he clings to his old karmic tendencies, giving energy to the delusion of separate existence. Thus he will have to be reborn again, waiting until some future lifetime to experience the redemption that the other characters find in the land of Monsalvat.

Parsifal

We saw before that according to Buddhism, when a new person is born, he or she inherits the karma of the previous person. The new person is neither the same as the previous one nor entirely different. He or she is a new individual, but, having inherited

karma from the past, the new person may have many of the karmic tendencies of the previous person (or persons, for the karmic
stream goes back a very long way). And because not all karma
is negative, the new person will inherit the merit of beneficent
actions from previous lives as well as the non-merit of harmful actions. The merit of Wotan's renunciation carries over to
Amfortas, the merit of Brünnhilde's self-sacrifice carries over to
Kundry, and the merit of Siegfried's spiritual awakening carries
over to Parsifal. With Alberich and Klingsor the case is somewhat different, for Alberich did not do any discernible meritorious deed. What is it, then, that Klingsor inherits from Alberich
that allows him to be reborn in the vicinity of Monsalvat?

Part of the complexity of the workings of karma concerns the
karmic bonds or connections that beings create when they interact with each other, in either harmful or beneficent ways. Not all
these connections carry over into future lives, but the strongest
and most influential ones do. Karmic bonds can be created that
bind two or more beings together for many lives. Romantic connections, for example, can be so strong that two people marry
each other in the course of multiple lifetimes. Conversely, harmful acts can also bind people together, creating a form of karmic debt which will tend to cause them to be reborn together in
future lives. These karmic bonds and debts stay active until the
karma that originally caused them is cleansed, either by specific
actions, such as forgiveness or selfless deeds that heal the age-old
wounds, or through great suffering. If the full effects of harmful
actions are experienced, and from this experience of suffering a
person learns enough not to perpetuate the harmful deeds, then
the suffering itself can be a way to cleanse the karma. In most
cases the karma is cleansed through both suffering and acts of
forgiveness and healing.

The karmic bonds Alberich, Wotan, Siegfried, and Brünnhilde created among themselves were so strong that their karmic
streams were inextricably woven together. At the time of their
deaths, the karma of each of these four that most urgently needed cleansing involved the other three. Thus they are all reborn

together in a circumstance that will give all four the potential to cleanse that karma and attain enlightenment. That Klingsor fails where the other three succeed is due largely to the lack of merit in the karmic stream he inherits from Alberich. Because Alberich did not perform any act of contrition or healing, the karma that Klingsor inherits is very heavy and will be very difficult to handle in his present life. However, because Alberich, like the others, went through the final events and suffered accordingly, some of the karma in his stream was cleansed, and his suffering paid part of the karmic debt. This is all part of the reason that Klingsor is reborn with an opportunity to enter the service of the Grail.

Another and very important part of the reason is that within the workings of karma lies an inherent compassion. Rebirth is taken in whatever form best allows the karma to be worked out and resolved. Even when a particular rebirth is taken in circumstances of suffering, compassion is still present, for it is through this suffering that the karma has a chance to be cleansed. In the case of a human being, whether or not the karma and the personal koan are resolved in a specific lifetime depends on the actions of the person concerned. Alberich had been a crucial part of the separation of the Spear and Grail, and thus he is given a chance to amend that act in his rebirth as Klingsor—a chance to serve the Grail where once he had committed an act of violence against it. Thus he has an opportunity to make atonement.

Klingsor makes an honest effort to take advantage of this opportunity by asking for admittance into the Grail Brotherhood, but spiritual training at that level is too much for him. He is not yet ready, specifically in regard to the requirement of celibacy, and thus he fails in his attempt to enter the Grail community. Klingsor settles in a lonely valley in the midst of heathen lands, intending to do penance and perform holy actions. But he cannot control his sexual desire, and in a desperate attempt to stifle what he believes to be the sin keeping him from the Grail, he castrates himself, thinking that in this fashion he can be celibate and win admittance. But Titurel, horrified by this, bans Klingsor

from the Grail Brotherhood forever. In rage and rejection Klingsor retaliates by using his castration to acquire magic powers,
and from then on he tries to win the Grail by force. He steals
the Spear from Amfortas, aiming next for the Grail itself. Spear
and Grail are again separated. Rejected in his lust, Klingsor renounces love and commits an act of violence against the Temple
of the Grail, attempting through this act to win power over the
world. Because the merit in his karmic stream is not sufficient to
sustain the level of spiritual training he aspires to, he falls back
into the karmic tendencies he inherited from Alberich and ends
up repeating Alberich's errors rather than redeeming them.

Klingsor at this point has also fallen victim to pride. He could
have accepted that he was not yet ready for inclusion in the Grail
Brotherhood, which in essence is the level of monastic training,
and he could have found a less assiduous form of training of
which he would have been capable at that time. Not everyone
is ready to be a monk, but that does not mean that one cannot
participate in training. One does as much as one can at any one
time. More is not required. Klingsor could have trained as a lay-
man, waiting for the time when monastic life would have been
possible. But instead he falls prey to ambition and reacts to his
rejection with anger and vengeance. In repeating the errors of his
previous life, he compounds the negative karma to such an extent that he is not, in the lifetime and person of Klingsor, capable
of salvation. Thus he is destroyed along with his castle in Act II.
His redemption will have to wait for a future lifetime, whenever
and wherever that may be. According to Buddhism, all beings
will eventually cleanse and purify their karmic streams, and in
this regard all beings will come to enlightenment. Thus Klingsor
will, in a future lifetime, attain emancipation.

Wotan is reborn from the flames of Valhalla into the Temple
of the Grail as Amfortas, son of the Grail King Titurel. Two symbols are resurrected here: the Spear itself, refashioned from the
shattered spear of Wotan; and the original union of the Spear and
Grail. The Spear and Grail are together once again in the Temple,
placed under Titurel's care. But because the karma of the *Ring* is

not yet fully cleansed, these are outward symbols only, not yet inner realities. They are symbols of opportunity: a physical spear is housed with a physical vessel, but because the karma has not yet been cleansed, the Spear and Grail have not yet been truly reunited. The proof of this is that as soon as Amfortas comes of age and inherits the title and authority of Grail Guardian from his father, he promptly acts on his pride and ambition and loses the Spear. Thus, in reality, the Spear and Grail are still separated at the start of *Parsifal*.

This idea of outward symbol as opposed to inner reality also applies to the world at the end of the *Ring*. The world is destroyed, and a cleansing of fire and water certainly takes place, but the destruction of the outward form of the world does not constitute the salvation of the inner reality of the world. This is why Wotan's renunciation is not, by itself, enough for salvation, and why Brünnhilde is not fully redeemed by her sacrifice and immolation. This is the same as the death and rebirth of an individual person. The death, and thus destruction, of the outward form of one human being does not constitute the cleansing of the "mountain of karma" lying unseen behind that person. The karmic force is still there. A great deal of karma can be cleansed at the time of death and in the death process, but if there is reproductive karma left over that is still active, a new being will be born. The outward world of the *Ring* was destroyed, but not all of the karma was cleansed. Thus the outward world of *Parsifal* is born, just as a new human being is born. On both the world level and the individual level there is a freshness at the start, where everything is in place to begin with, just as a baby seems new and pure when it is first born and not yet divided from its environment. Thus, the Spear and Grail are outwardly together in Titurel's castle. However, because the karma Amfortas inherits from Wotan is still not completely cleansed, pride and ambition lead the young Amfortas to act in error, causing the Spear and Grail to be separated again. The world, as it was in the *Ring*, is in need of redemption.

The wound of Amfortas is the wound of karmic action. We saw earlier that Wagner did not place the wound specifically in

the genitals, as it is in the traditional legends. Wagner places the
wound in the side, the area of the body where Christ was pierced
with this same spear. Symbolically speaking, however, Amfortas
is castrated, for not only has he fallen prey to the temptation
of lust, he also finds himself unable to serve his office properly,
and eventually he cannot do it at all. His office as Grail King is
to perform the regenerative ceremony of the Grail. It is the life-
giving power of the Grail on which the community of Monsalvat
depends, including its aged founder, Titurel. In being unable to
perform this ceremony, Amfortas is, in effect, castrated. Without
the performance of the ceremony, the Brotherhood is rendered
sterile, unable to perform its duty in and for the world.

The loss of regenerative powers is not, however, the only aspect of Amfortas's wound. As we saw in chapters 2 and 3, it is
the wound of hubris, the excessive pride that leads to error in
judgment and error in action. It is also the result of compounded
karma. This why it is so intense and hard to cure. Remember
that Wagner had said that it was Tristan's wound inconceivably
intensified. Buddhism teaches that the karmic consequence for
wrong action is much more painful for those who have heard
the teaching than it is for those who have not. In other words, it
is more painful for those who "know better," but who commit a
wrong act anyway. This same is true for Tristan and Amfortas.

Tristan's wound was also the wound of karmic action, but
Tristan never had anywhere near the position and responsibility
of Wotan, nor had he ever had any opportunity like that of hearing the wisdom of Erda. Additionally, Wotan had come to see
the profound error of his actions and had as a result renounced
those actions and willed the end of the world as a way of washing
it clean. When Amfortas was born he inherited the merit of this
great contrition, and yet he went out and committed the exact
same error again, albeit with the best of intentions. He took the
Holy Spear into the world for conquest, even though in this case
he considered his foe to be an evil that had to be destroyed. He
fell prey to both pride and lust and as a result lost the Spear, the
very same spear that as Wotan he had torn from the World Ash-

tree. This time the consequences are so painful, both for himself and for those around him, that the true nature of suffering
caused by wrong action is indelibly impressed upon the karmic
stream. The many years of unimaginably intense pain and torment, both spiritual and physical, are what is needed to cleanse
this karma, and once it is redeemed, there will be no temptation
to return to the former error.

In the course of the preceding chapters I have mentioned the
dual nature of Kundry. In *Parsifal* she is the Loathly Damsel, the
woman who manifests the many aspects of the Eternal. Like the
Hindu goddess Kali, she is both preserver and destroyer, both
the giver of life and the taker of life, able to see both past and
future, exhibiting both a wrathful, horrid countenance and a
benevolent, beauteous visage. To those who turn away from the
Truth she appears as a great demon; to those who turn toward
the Truth she appears as the Divine Mother. She represents the
dual nature of all outward appearance, the two-sided nature of
maya, illusion, that which arises and passes away, but in truth
never is.

This is the spiritual and mythological symbolism of the Loathly Damsel. As usual, Wagner uses her entirely in his own way. He
retains her dual nature and adapts it to his scheme of *Parsifal*.
There are two main aspects to Kundry's dual nature in *Parsifal*:
she is both humble spiritual aspirant and archetypal Temptress;
and she serves both the Brotherhood of the Grail and its enemy
Klingsor.

Just as Siegmund was an agent of Wotan's will, Hagen was an
instrument of Alberich's will. When Brünnhilde made her pact
with Hagen to kill Siegfried, she created a bond with the entire
karmic force first created by Alberich and later extended through
Hagen. When Alberich is reborn as Klingsor, Brünnhilde as
Kundry is born with an inescapable connection to the power of
Klingsor. Thus Klingsor can summon her from her sleep, a cruel
mirror of Wotan summoning Erda after he conquered her, as
well as a mirror of Siegfried awakening Brünnhilde on the rock.
Brünnhilde, who once had protected Siegfried with her magic

powers, later renounced Siegfried and took refuge in Hagen. And now she is awakened from her sleep by the sorcery of Klingsor.

Brünnhilde also had a very strong karmic connection to Wotan, being both his favorite daughter and a resident of Valhalla. She shared in his renunciation, herself casting the torch that lit the grand funeral pyre. Thus Kundry also serves the Grail, and the spiritual wisdom that Brünnhilde gained at the end of the *Ring* is part of the merit that propels Kundry in the direction of the Grail Temple, and the desire for enlightenment.

I have said before that when we first meet Parsifal he seems to be Siegfried exactly. But Parsifal is not Siegfried anymore. There is now within him a great spiritual seed that needs only to be awakened. That awakening comes from Gurnemanz and the killing of the swan.

The shooting of the swan with an arrow comes from a story of the Buddha. In the forest the young Prince Siddhartha came upon a swan that a hunter had wounded with his arrow. Prince Siddhartha drew out the arrow and nursed the swan. Sometime later a group of his cousins appeared, armed with their bows. One of them saw the swan and said, "I claim this swan because I shot it." Prince Siddhartha said, "I claim this swan because I saved its life."

In Sanskrit the word *hansa* means swan. We can see this word in the monastic name Paramahansa Yogananda. *Parama* means "highest." Yogananda says in his *Autobiography of a Yogi*, "The white swan is mythologically represented as the vehicle or mount of Brahma the Creator. The sacred *hansa*, said to have the power of extracting only milk from a mixture of milk and water, is thus a symbol of spiritual discrimination."[20] In killing the swan in the sacred forest of Monsalvat, Parsifal has committed the same act against nature and the Precepts that Siegfried committed when he killed the dragon Fafner. The swan here can be seen as a symbol of spiritual training and harmony, just as the dragon in Buddhism represents the Defender of the Faith. Both dragon and swan are thus symbols of the path to enlightenment and of one's personal journey on that path. Both have been "killed" by non-preceptual action. In other words, the spiritual journey has been seriously hindered and harmed by the non-preceptual act of killing. Siegfried boasted of his deed, and his fame rested largely on its perceived greatness. Not so with Parsifal.

When Gurnemanz points out to Parsifal the truth of what he has done, Parsifal is deeply contrite, and he breaks his bow and flings away his arrows. As we saw before, this is a reversal of Siegfried's other great deed, the reforging of Notung. This is the beginning of Parsifal's great renunciation—of the quest for power in the world, for domination, for individual glory. It is the renunciation of greed, of selfishness, of the desire to impose one's own will on others. It is the directing of the will to greatness away from the self and into spiritual quest. Gurnemanz has awakened in Parsifal compassion for all living things. This awakening certainly has much farther to go, and Parsifal must still face many trials, but there is an all-important difference between Parsifal's renunciation and Wotan's. Wotan simply renounced further pursuit of wrongful action. After roaming the world primarily as an observer, he then spent his last days sitting in his great hall waiting for the end. He did not do anything specific to heal the wounds he had created. Parsifal does much more than just renounce wrongful action. After he witnesses the Grail ceremony and hears Amfortas's cry of agony, he clutches at his own heart, feeling Amfortas's suffering in his own body. He then leaves the Grail Temple, thrown out by Gurnemanz, and begins the journey that will eventually lead to his finding the cause of suffering and the means of its eventual cessation. Parsifal not only renounces what is wrong, he goes in search of what is right. He is not an observer but an active participant, the pathfinder in the search for redemption.

Wagner made it very plain that he did not intend the character of Parsifal to represent Jesus. Cosima recorded, for example, on October 20, 1878: "R. and I go out, calling on Wolzogen, whose article, 'The Stage Dedication Play,' pleases R. very much, though he remarks to me that W. [Wolzogen] goes too far in calling Parsifal a reflection of the Redeemer. 'I didn't give the Redeemer a thought when I wrote it.'"[21]

Keeping in mind that in his music dramas Wagner is concerned with the presentation in symbolic form of religious and
spiritual truths, we can still see in the development of the character Parsifal a profound parallel to the story of the Buddha. As I
draw these parallels over the coming pages, I am not saying that
Parsifal represents the Buddha, for this would be just as untrue
as saying that he represents Jesus. It is true, however, that an understanding of the parallel with the Buddha can be very helpful
in understanding what is happening in this last great work and
what the symbolism means.

Like Perceval and Parsifal, Prince Siddhartha Gautama was
brought up secluded from society, protected from the outside
world by a parent, in this case his father, King Suddhodana, his
mother having died seven days after his birth. King Suddhodana attempted to protect his son from the sorrows of the world
because he feared that if his son were to see the true suffering of
life, he would leave the palace and seek to become a monk. At
the Buddha-to-be's birth, eight learned Brahmins had examined
the child. Seven of them had held up two fingers, signifying that
the child would grow up to be either a great Universal Monarch
or a Buddha. The last, named Kondanna, had held up one finger,
signifying that the child would become a Buddha.

The Prince came of age and at sixteen he married the princess Yasodhara. Thirteen years later Yasodhara gave birth to a
son. Just before this the Prince went outside the palace walls for
the first time and saw the Four Signs: an old man, a sick man,
a dead man, and a wandering ascetic. The Prince saw firsthand
the suffering and impermanence of human life, represented by
old age, disease, and death. He then saw the holy man, representing the way of salvation from the suffering of existence. He
returned to the palace and found that he now had a son, but
he still made the decision to renounce the world and seek the
way of salvation. It was not his own suffering that prompted
his vow, but the suffering of others. He himself had been living
a care-free, luxurious life, with every need and desire attended
to. But he was so moved by what he saw in the outside world

that he vowed to find the cause of suffering, and from there the way to its cessation.

The Prince left the palace at midnight and entered the forest, where he shaved his head and beard and donned the garb of a monk. Known now as the monk Gautama, he lived for six years in the forest, until one morning, after assiduous meditation throughout the night under the Bodhi Tree, the Tree of Enlightenment, he saw the rising of the morning star, and at that moment he experienced complete emancipation and became the Buddha. He then reentered the world to teach, and spent the next forty-five years teaching both laypeople and monks, of both genders, until, at the age of eighty, he entered Parinirvana under the twin Sala trees in the hamlet of Kushinagara.

We have seen previously how in the life of Perceval/Parzival there were two awakenings to purpose: the first when the young Parzival sees the knights of King Arthur, which awakens him to his social purpose; and the second when the Loathly Damsel comes to King Arthur's court and publicly humiliates and chastises the young knight for his failure at the Grail Castle, thus awakening him to his spiritual purpose. In the Buddha's case there was only the second awakening, for the Prince was already awakened to his social position. He needed but the spiritual awakening, and this came with his seeing the Four Signs. The spiritual awakening to purpose of Wagner's Parsifal comes with the death of the swan and Parsifal's witnessing of the Grail ceremony, where he feels the suffering of Amfortas on his own body.

Parsifal then leaves the Grail Castle, just as Prince Siddhartha left the palace, and wanders in the forest searching for the cause of suffering. It was not his own pain that made him clutch his heart, but the pain of Amfortas's wound, the wound of karma. Parsifal's search is to find the source of the karmic stream, to see what started the Wheel of Karma turning, to find the source of human suffering. His wanderings lead him inevitably to Klingsor's magic garden and castle, the heart of the world of illusion. It is here that he will stage his battle with Mara's army, and it is here that he will find the cause of suffering.

Mara in Buddhism is the Tempter, though is he not Satan in every Christian respect. However, just as Satan tempted Jesus in the desert, so did Mara tempt the monk Gautama under the Bodhi Tree. Mara represents that aspect of ourselves which shows us all the choices, tempting us to choose the easy path of desire gratification rather than the difficult path of enlightenment. Mara is not an external or substantial entity. Rather, he, along with all his army, is a manifestation of our own mind, our own desires and delusions. During the night under the Bodhi Tree Gautama was very close to his enlightenment, and Mara, being desperate, called out all his forces, who attacked Gautama with spears, swords, and arrows. These were the spears, swords, and arrows of delusion, and Gautama, the Buddha-to-be, perceived that they were in fact only projections of his own thoughts and desires, and in themselves had no substantial reality. Thus he did not resist them, and because he did not resist them they had no power over him, and all the arrows and spears launched at him turned to flowers that fell at his feet. Eventually the army faded and disappeared, and there was nothing before his eyes but the morning star.

I talked in chapter 3 about Parsifal renouncing violence. He begins this renunciation by breaking his bow, and he will never again carry a weapon of his own making into the world for conquest. When he enters Klingsor's castle, his way is barred by the knights. Parsifal disarms Sir Ferris and uses this sword to defend himself against his attackers. He does not kill any of them, wounding them only enough to keep himself from harm. This is not yet a full renunciation of violence, but Parsifal has taken his first steps along the path that he will eventually master.

His encountering of the Flower Maidens is his encountering of the sense desires. This is one aspect of Mara, though by no means the only one. The maidens say to him:

> Now be our sweetheart true,
> begrudge not the flowers their due!
> Sweetly must you love us and cherish,
> or else we will wither and perish.[22]

This is a very good description of desire and of how we continue to keep our desires fresh and "ever-blooming." By constantly pursuing our desires and satisfying them, we constantly renew them and keep them alive. If we do not seek to satisfy our sense desires, they will, over time, "wither and perish." Here the maidens are asking Parsifal to pursue and gratify them so that they may ever flourish. Buddhism distinguishes between natural desires and the sense desires. Natural desires are those of food, clothing, and shelter. Our bodies need these things in order to survive. Buddhism does *not* tell us to deny our bodies what we need to remain alive and well. It tells us not to indulge ourselves in this regard, but it also tells us to take care of ourselves and respect the needs of the body on a natural level.

The sense desires are different. We do not need to gratify these desires in order to survive, and thus it *is* possible to control them by not rushing to gratify them every time they arise. This is part of spiritual training. We have the choice not to gratify a desire when it arises, and over time it is possible to reach a place in training where these desires do not control us the way they did at an earlier time in our lives. Thus, the Flower Maidens know that they will "wither and perish" if Parsifal does not pursue them.

There is a parallel here between Klingsor's castle and the Grail Castle. Remember that the Castle of Maidens is a worldly reflection of the spiritual Castle of the Grail. The Flower Maidens will "wither and perish" if they are not pursued and satisfied. The same is true with spiritual training. The "flowers" or fruit of training will "wither and perish" if training is not constantly renewed. This is one of the symbols of the Grail ceremony. The Grail is a symbol of regeneration. If we turn the Wheel of Karma, it is desire that will be regenerated. But if we choose not to pursue the objects of desire, then desire, like the mirage of Klingsor's castle in the desert, will be revealed as unsubstantial. If we then pursue instead the virtues of enlightenment, we will turn the Wheel of the Dharma. Thus Parsifal in this scene is being confronted with the great choice: to pursue the regeneration of desire or that of spiritual truth.

Parsifal plays with the maidens a bit but is not drawn in by them, and both Kundry and Klingsor know that they are frivolous and do not have the power to tempt him seriously. In a great moment both musically and dramatically, Kundry sings, "Parsifal!" Parsifal is immediately entranced, hearing "the name my mother once called me while dreaming."[23] Kundry then dismisses the Flower Maidens, knowing exactly where Parsifal's weakness lies. Like Siegfried, Parsifal yearns for his mother, and Kundry knows that the real temptation is love's yearning, both in a sensual way and an emotional and spiritual way. Kundry very cleverly tells Parsifal of his mother's love for him, how she raised him free from the evil of the world, how she watched over him as he grew, and how she died of grief when he left her. Kundry makes Parsifal feel as though he is to blame for his mother's death and then offers her own love as both consolation and atonement.

PARSIFAL: Sorrow! Sorrow! My misdeed? Where was I?
   Mother! Sweetest, dearest Mother!
   Your son it was, your son that slew you!
   Oh fool! Blind and blundering fool!
   Forgetful of you! Wandering wildly!
   Forgetful, blindly forgetful!
   Sweetest, dearest of Mothers!
KUNDRY: Had you not harbored pain,
   sweet consolation
   could not visit your heart.
   The woe that rends your soul
   shall now give place to a joy
   that springs from my love.
PARSIFAL: My mother, my mother! Could I forget her?
   Ha! Why is it I always forget?
   Why don't I remember at all?
   Just stupid folly lives in me!
KUNDRY: Confession
   makes guilt for errors vanish.
   Admission

to self will folly banish.
Just learn to love in fashion
that Gamuret once loved,
when Heart of Sorrow's passion
his passion hotly moved.
And she who gave you
body and senses
must keep both death and folly far.
She sends by me
her final blessing and farewell:
she gives you love's—first kiss![24]

This is the crucial moment not only in the single music drama *Parsifal*, but also in the entire five-opera work of the *Ring* and *Parsifal* together, for here the redeemer is fully awakened to the true nature of suffering. We have seen how Siegfried failed as the redeemer because he was incapable of feeling the suffering of others to even a small extent. Here Parsifal awakens to the suffering of the whole world. This awakening begins with his full understanding of Amfortas's pain, and then progresses further into an understanding of the nature of suffering itself. By feeling this pain fully in his own body and spirit, Parsifal perceives the source of suffering and the way to its cessation through the holy blood of the Grail. Lionel Salter translates the stage directions after the kiss as follows:

(Parsifal suddenly starts up with a gesture of the utmost terror: his demeanor expresses some fearful change; he presses his hands hard against his heart as if to master an agonizing pain.)
PARSIFAL: Amfortas!—
    The wound! The wound!
    It burns within my heart!
    O sorrow, sorrow!
    Fearful sorrow!
    From the depths of my heart it cries aloud.
    Oh! Oh!

Most wretched! Most pitiable!
I saw the wound bleeding:
now it bleeds in me!
Here—here!
No, no! It is not the wound.
Flow in streams, my blood, from it!
Here! Here in my heart is the flame!
The longing, the terrible longing
which seizes and grips all my senses!
O torment of love!
How everything trembles, quakes and quivers
in sinful desire!
(As Kundry stares at Parsifal in fear and astonishment, he falls
into a complete trance.)
My dull gaze is fixed on the sacred vessel;
the holy blood flows;—
the bliss of redemption, divinely mild,
trembles within every soul around:
only here, in my heart, will the pangs not be stilled.[25]

At first Parsifal feels Amfortas's suffering and understands
what he witnessed in the Grail Castle. He feels the wound bleeding in him. But then he goes beyond this, for he perceives that
it is not just Amfortas's wound bleeding in him, but his own
wound, bleeding in his own heart. This is the start of the final
assault of Mara's army, which will continue throughout the rest
of the scene and culminate in Klingsor's hurling the Spear at Parsifal. Right now Parsifal is feeling the torment of love in all its
aspects, not just romantic or sexual love. This is love's yearning,
which ultimately is the yearning for the Eternal itself, and it is
the arising of our own karmic desires that separates us from this
reunion. All of Parsifal's senses are quivering with desire, and he
recognizes this as the source of suffering. This is the recognition
of the Second Noble Truth, that the origin of suffering is *tanha*,
or craving. Parsifal then does exactly what the Buddha did during Mara's assault: he keeps his mind focused one-pointedly in

meditation. He fixes his gaze on the blood of the Grail, recognizing the redemptive power of this vessel. Parsifal perceives the innate enlightenment of all things, feeling that only in his own being is the turbulence of craving unquieted. All the karma is coming up to be cleansed. This is experienced as both a tempest of passions and an attack by an actual army. At this point it is absolutely vital for Parsifal that he keep his mind fixed on the Eternal, here symbolized by the Grail. It is here that his greatest weapon against the army of Mara is the "sacred *hansa*," that is, the ability to separate what is real from the unreal. This will apply to Kundry in an all-important way. From this point onward, through the end of Act II, Parsifal and Kundry will be reenacting the awakening scene on the rock between Siegfried and Brünnhilde, as well as the scene in *Götterdämmerung* where Siegfried tears the ring from Brünnhilde's finger, though on an indescribably higher level. Because Kundry has a karmic attachment to Klingsor, she is still bound to the web of delusion that Parsifal is beginning to cut through. The karma is coming up for both of them, but it is Parsifal who can now see the spiritual reality of the Grail in the midst of the maya of Klingsor's garden, and thus it is up to him to pull both of them through this critical trial. Both Kundry and Parsifal are on the verge of enlightenment, but one false step can plunge both of them back into the sea of Samsara for an unknown period of time. Parsifal must be able to perceive the dual nature of Kundry with absolute clarity: what in her is the Buddha-nature and what is the illusion; what in her is the karma talking and what in her is poised on the precipice of enlightenment.

The last lines of *Parsifal* are, in Stewart Robb's translation, "Highest healing's wonder! / Salvation to the Saviour!" Lionel Salter translates these same lines as, "Miracle of supreme salvation! / Our Redeemer redeemed!" Cosima recorded on January 5, 1982:

> When I tell him I have just been thinking of *Parsifal* and am
> pleased that this last work of his is also his masterpiece, he re-

plies, or, rather, interrupts me very excitedly, "No, no, I was telling myself today that it is quite remarkable that I held this work
back for my fullest maturity; I know what I know and what is
in it; and the new school, Wolz. [Wolzogen] and the others, can
take their lead from it." He then hints at, rather than expresses,
the content of this work, "salvation to the savior."[26]

What does "salvation to the savior" or "the redeemer redeemed" really mean? Why does the redeemer need to be redeemed? The answer lies in Parsifal's next lines. After he sings,
"Only here, in my heart, will the pangs not be stilled," he continues:

> The Saviour's lament I hear there,
> the lament, ah! the lamentation
> from His profaned sanctuary:
> "Redeem Me, rescue Me
> from hands defiled by sin!"
> Thus rang the divine lament
> in terrible clarity in my soul.
> And I—fool, coward,
> fled hither to wild childish deeds!
> (He flings himself in despair on his knees.)
> Redeemer! Saviour! Lord of Grace!
> How can I, a sinner, purge my guilt?[27]

The "profaned sanctuary" has multiple meanings. The most
obvious is the sanctuary of the Grail Temple, where the Spear
and Grail have been separated. This sanctuary is also the looted
sanctuary of nature, from which the branch of the World Ash-
tree and the Rhinegold were originally stolen. The idea of a
profaned sanctuary also carries various sexual connotations.
Amfortas lost the Spear because he succumbed to sexual temptation. The sanctuary of the Grail was polluted by "hands defiled by sin," the hands of both Amfortas and Klingsor. Klingsor,
with the sin of his self-castration on his hands, stole the Spear.

Amfortas lost the Spear, thus defiling the Temple, through his sins of pride and lust. The idea of the profaned sanctuary also refers to Kundry in her role as Temptress. It was through her temptation that Amfortas lost the Spear. Kundry, as part of her dual nature, represents woman in both her archetypal aspects: Divine Mother and Temptress. This particular aspect of the dual nature mirrors that of the Grail Castle and the Castle of Maidens. This is the idea of turning the Wheel of the Dharma or the Wheel of Karma. We all have a choice as to how we want to use our human bodies. We can use our bodies, as well as our minds and spirits, to cleanse karma or to make more of it. Kundry, in tempting Amfortas and the other knights, has used her body to create karma rather than to cleanse it, and thus has profaned the sanctuary of the Divine Mother. Kundry's embodiment of both karmic action and the way to salvation will continue to play a vital role as the scene continues.

There is a still higher level of symbolism to the idea of a profaned sanctuary. We all have within us a spiritual center, which is often referred to as a spiritual seat, or "lion's throne." In Buddhist scriptures the Buddha is often said to be sitting on his lion's throne when he preaches to the multitudes of gods and men. This is the spiritual seat that the Buddha took and from which he did not move during his battle with Mara's army. It is the seat of our own meditation, our own spiritual sanctuary. The Grail Castle is simply the outward symbol of this inner reality. By turning away from the Truth, thus turning the Wheel of Karma rather than the Wheel of the Dharma, we profane our own sanctuary. The thief of karmic desire steals into this sanctuary and loots it, leaving it in need of cleansing and purifying. The voice that calls from this profaned sanctuary is the voice of our own Buddha-nature, calling us back to our seat of meditation, where we can render our spiritual center sacred again.

There is another aspect to the savior calling for redemption: "Redeem Me, rescue Me." Here we must understand the true nature of the Me. Before his conversion, Saul of Tarsus was a cruel persecutor of the early Christians. On his way to Damascus there suddenly shone around him a great light from heaven: "And he fell to the earth, and heard a voice saying unto him, Saul, Saul, why persecutest thou me? And he said, Who art thou, Lord? And the Lord said, I am Jesus whom thou persecutest."[28]

Here the "me" refers not only to Jesus the man and teacher, but also to the whole Christian community, all the believers together, who are all part of the body of Christ. It also refers to the teachings of Christ. This all-encompassing "me" is the same as the Me in Parsifal's narration. Thus it is not an external savior who needs redemption, but the savior within, our own spiritual training. The voice of our True Nature calls to us at all times so that we may return to our own lion's throne and restore the defiled sanctuary. This restoration is our willingness to make the effort in our everyday training to turn the Wheel of the Dharma and not the Wheel of Karma.

During the whole of Parsifal's narration, Kundry has watched him in astonishment and admiration, and now she hesitantly approaches him:

Honored hero! Throw off this spell!
Look up and greet your fair one's coming![29]

Or, alternatively:

O valiant knight! Cast off this spell!
Look up! And love the one who loves![30]

Kundry at this time is still bound in Klingsor's power, that is, she is still enmeshed in the old karma. Thus love to her is romantic and sexual, not spiritual. At the beginning of Act II Klingsor had said to her, "He who spurns you sets you free."[31] What Parsifal rejects in Kundry is not her Buddha-nature, but her attachment to karmic desire. It is this attachment that must be severed if they are both to be saved. When Siegfried and Brünnhilde were on the rock, they reveled in the satisfaction of karmic desire. We have just finished reviewing what that led to. This is the reality that Parsifal is now perceiving more and more clearly. Thus he knows that to return in any way or to any extent to that previous error will lose salvation for both of them. Parsifal hears her voice and her words and recognizes the temptation Amfortas faced:

> Yes! This was the voice with which she called him;—
> and this her look, truly I recognize it—
> and this, smiling at him so disquietingly;
> the lips—yes—thus they quivered for him,
> thus she bent her neck—
> thus boldly rose her head;
> thus laughingly fluttered her hair—
> thus her arms were twined around his neck—
> thus tenderly fawned her features!
> In league with the pangs of every torment,
> her lips kissed away
> his soul's salvation!
> *(He has gradually risen.)*
> Ah, this kiss!
> *(He thrusts Kundry from him.)*
> Corrupter! Get away from me!
> Forever, forever away from me!

Kundry is unable to understand why she is being rejected, for she is offering Parsifal the love that she thinks will bring them both redemption. She also recognizes in him the quality of the redeemer, but because she is still bound in attachment to the karma and its illusion, she does not understand the truth of what Klingsor had said to her—that the one who defies her will be the one who frees her. Wagner had a marvelous insight into human nature concerning both Wotan and Kundry. Cosima recorded on June 4, 1878, "R. sees a resemblance between Wotan and Kundry: both long for salvation and both rebel against it, Kundry in the scene with P. [Parsifal], Wotan with Siegfried."[32] This is exactly how people often behave. We long for salvation but at the same time are afraid to let go of the karmic attachments

that hinder our experiencing that salvation. We cling to what we
know and think we can trust, even when our spiritual intuition
and instinct tell us that what we are clinging to is unstable. Because we all have the Buddha-nature, we all long for the Eternal
and for union with it. But by definition, union with the Eternal,
with God, necessarily means the dissolution of the finite self, at
least as we know it now. Thus the Infinite appears to us as both
salvation and negation. We long for the salvation and fear the
negation. This is precisely Kundry's predicament. Wotan, faced
with the potential redeemer Siegfried, was unable to let go of self
and ended up trying to fight Siegfried; only his physical defeat
made Wotan retreat. The same occurs with Kundry. Because she
cannot voluntarily give up her attachment to the old karma, it
must be rent from her. This is, on a transformed level, a reen-
actment of the scene on the rock in *Götterdämmerung* where
Siegfried, disguised by the Tarnhelm as Gunther, tore the ring
from Brünnhilde's finger. The disguise of the Tarnhelm represents Siegfried's entanglement in the delusion of the greed and
corruption of the world, his own true self hidden behind the veil
of maya. In this guise he forcibly takes from Brünnhilde the ring,
a token of her love for the true Siegfried. Because she had not
been willing to give it up voluntarily, to the Rhinemaidens, it had
to be torn from her. Now Parsifal, having shed the "Tarnhelm"
of delusion, is appearing before Kundry in his true guise, that of
redeemer. He is asking for the "ring"—in other words, all karmic
attachment—but because Kundry will not let go by herself, it
has to be taken from her by force. This is terribly painful, as we
will see in the course of the scene, but it is the only way Parsifal
can help her. His acts and words of seeming cruelty to her are
actually the greatest acts of compassion. Thus, when he calls her
"Corrupter!" and pushes her away, he is accomplishing the work
of salvation. Kundry, however, sees and feels only the rejection:

> Cruel one!
> If you feel in your heart
> only others' sorrows,

then feel mine too!
If you are a redeemer,
what maliciously stops you
from uniting with me for my salvation?

Here again Kundry can conceive of salvation only through romantic and sexual union. She is asking Parsifal for salvation, but she wants it on her terms, in the only way she can envision it. Parsifal knows that it can never come that way.

Kundry sees in Parsifal the quality of redemption and recognizes in him the savior she once, in a past life, mocked and reviled:

Through eternities I have waited for you,
the saviour so late in coming,
whom once I dared revile.
Oh!
If you knew the curse
which afflicts me, asleep and awake,
in death and life,
pain and laughter,
newly steeled to new affliction,
endlessly through this existence!
I saw Him—Him—
and mocked . . . !

Parsifal does know the curse, for he has felt it in the wound of Amfortas. This is the wound and the curse of karmic action. It is the compounded consequence of non-preceptual deeds committed throughout innumerable lifetimes. What Kundry is feeling at this point is the full weight of this karma and the suffering it entails. Because the karma is coming up all at once to be cleansed completely and finally, there is nothing to mitigate the pain, nothing to distract her from the full force of its momentum. Kundry is having past-life remembrances, and the part of her that is dedicated to the Grail and spiritual training perceives what she will call the "ever-renewed nightmare from which, though repentant, I scarcely wake." She is perceiving the consequences of actions over many lifetimes, yet she is still afraid to let go of the final attachment keeping her from realizing what Parsifal has seen and understood. Just as Wagner considered Amfortas to be Tristan greatly intensified, so did he consider Kundry to be greatly intensified over Isolde. Cosima recorded on September 14, 1882, after the first performances of *Parsifal* at Bayreuth, "When there is mention on the train of the Wagnerites' preference for *T. und I.* even over *Parsifal*, R. says: 'Oh, what do they know? One might say that Kundry already experienced Isolde's *Liebestod* a hundred times in her various reincarnations.'"[33]

It is the full force of these countless lives that Kundry is experiencing as she faces Parsifal and the mounting terror of what it means to let go of everything.

I saw Him—Him—
and mocked . . . !
His gaze fell upon me!—
Now I seek him from world to world
to meet him once again.
In darkest hour
I feel His eyes turn on me
and His gaze rest upon me.
The accursed laughter assails me once again:
a sinner sinks into my arms!
Then I laugh—laugh—
I cannot weep,
can only shout, rage,
storm, rave
in an ever-renewed nightmare
from which, though repentant, I scarcely wake.
One for whom I yearned in deathly longing,
whom I recognized though despised and rejected,
let me weep upon his breast,

for one hour only be united to you
and, though God and the world disown me,
in you be cleansed of sin and redeemed!

At this point Parsifal has perceived everything clearly, and he
sings the most crucial lines to Kundry:

For evermore
would you be damned with me
if for one hour,
unmindful of my mission,
I yielded to your embrace!
For your salvation too I am sent,
if you will turn aside from your desires.
The solace to end your sorrows
comes not from the source from which they flow:
grace shall never be bestowed on you
until that source is sealed to you.

One of the greatest aspects of this scene is that Kundry, on one
level, is part of Mara's army attacking Parsifal and challenging
his own salvation, while at the same time Parsifal is consciously
concerned not only with his own redemption and that of Amfortas, but with Kundry's as well. This is the true mind of enlightenment, the discerning wisdom that cuts through all illusion and
is able to see the Buddha-nature in all things. Thus Parsifal is
not treating Kundry as a "demon" who must be defeated and cut
off, but as a sentient being who also has the Buddha-nature and
who is in desperate need of saving. This is the highest compassion, to embrace and convert that which is attacking you rather
than treating it as an enemy and rejecting it. Parsifal is aware
of Kundry's temptation, which is all the more powerful because
she is not, at this point, consciously trying to tempt him for his
own downfall. She is desperately seeking salvation, but does not
know how to achieve it. She is seeking redemption in the old
karma because that is all she knows, and it is up to Parsifal to

be the one not to give in to her temptation, but to seek redemption in the letting go and cleansing of that karma. This is why he tells her that they would both be damned if he were to yield to her embrace. He must embrace her not as man and woman embrace, but as the Buddha embraced the whole world during his meditation under the Bodhi Tree. The solace to end her sorrows can never come from the same source from which those sorrows flow. Grace can never come to Kundry until the source of the old karma is sealed to her, and the only way for Parsifal to seal that source is to reject not Kundry's Buddha-nature, but her attachment to karmic desire. His refusal must be adamant and absolute. Parsifal cannot yield to her desire even for one second, much less for one hour. This is why what might seem like cruelty to her from one point of view is actually the greatest, and most necessary, compassion. The attachment to the old karma must be severed for all time, and if Kundry herself is not able to let go of it, Parsifal must rend it from her, as painful as that might be. This is what happens as the scene continues:

> . . . grace shall never be bestowed on you
> until that source is sealed to you.
> Another grace—ah, a different one,
> for which, pitying, I saw the brotherhood
> pining in dire distress,
> scourging and mortifying their flesh.
> But who can know aright and clear
> the only true source of salvation?
> O misery that banishes all deliverance!
> O blackness of earthly error,
> that while feverishly pursuing supreme salvation
> yet thirsts for the fount of perdition!

Parsifal is recognizing not only Kundry's distress, but also that of the whole world. He is recognizing the predicament of karmic attachment, where people desire salvation and yet give in to their worldly desires. When the desires are too strong,

people end up following the "fount of perdition," thus sacrific-
ing their own salvation. And this helpless floundering in the
sea of Samsara will continue lifetime after lifetime, age after
age, until people cease pursuing the objects of their desires and
pursue instead the path to God. Part of the attack of Mara's
army is that Parsifal too is feeling the torment of karmic desire.
The difference between his reaction to it and Kundry's reaction
is that Parsifal can discern what is real and what is not, and this
allows him to remain steadfast in his quest of the Grail amidst
the torrential storm of passions that are assailing him. Kundry
cannot remain rooted on her lion's throne because she has not
found it yet. Thus she is buffeted mercilessly in the winds of
this storm, helpless to find the stillness at its center. Her only
hope is Parsifal, and she clings desperately to him in the only
way she knows:

> (in wild ecstasy) Was it my kiss
> which thus revealed the world to you?
> The full embrace of my love
> then would raise you to godhead.
> Redeem the world, if this is your destiny:
> make yourself a god for an hour,
> and for that let me be damned forever,
> my wound never healed.

Kundry is now feeling the wound of Amfortas, for it is the
same wound. One very ironic aspect of Kundry's words here is
her offer to raise Parsifal to godhead through her love. Brünnhilde had found her love of Siegfried through her *loss* of godhead, and now, as Kundry, she is offering that same godhead to
Parsifal. This is also part of her temptation, and the temptation
of Mara. Parsifal is being tempted, just as Jesus was, to be possessor of the whole world. But like both Jesus and Buddha, Parsifal is beyond succumbing to worldly temptation, for he has
perceived, through experience, that which is permanent and
that which is impermanent. When this happens to the extent

that it did with Jesus and Buddha, there is no longer any desire for the world of impermanence, and any temptation will fail. Parsifal's mind is now fully focused on the Grail. He says to Kundry:

> I offer redemption to you in your sin.
> KUNDRY: Let me love you, godlike as you are,
>   and you would then give me redemption.
> PARSIFAL: Love and redemption shall be yours
>   if you show me
>   the way to Amfortas.
> KUNDRY: *(breaking out in fury)*
>   Never shall you find him!
>   Let the fallen one perish,
>   that woeful
>   seeker after shame
>   whom I derided, at whom I laughed!
>   Ha ha! He fell by his own spear!
> PARSIFAL: Who dared to wound him with the holy weapon?
> KUNDRY: He—he—
>   who once punished my laughter:
>   his curse—ha!—gives me strength;
>   I will call the Spear against you yourself
>   if you accord that sinner mercy!
>   Ah, this is madness!—
>   *(beseechingly)* Pity! Pity on me!
>   Be mine for one hour!
>   Let me be yours for one hour,
>   and you shall be led
>   on your way!
> *(She tries to embrace him. He thrusts her aside violently.)*
> PARSIFAL: Away, evil woman!

Kundry's temptation has failed, and so has her attempt to gain salvation in the way that she wished it. At this point Kundry reverts to her past life, cursing any path Parsifal takes that leads away from her and calling on Klingsor to destroy Parsifal, just as Brünnhilde had made a pact with Hagen to kill Sieg-fried:

Help! Help! Hither!
Seize the miscreant! Hither!
Bar his path!
Bar his passage!
And though you flee from here and find
all the roads in the world,
that road you seek,
that path you shall not find,
for any path and passage
that leads you away from me
I curse for you.
Stray and be lost!
You whom I know so well,
I give him into your power!

Klingsor appears on the rampart with the Spear in his hand, crying to Parsifal, "Halt! I have the right weapon to fell you! / The fool shall fall to me through his master's Spear!" Just as Ha-gen, through the urging of Alberich, aimed a spear at Siegfried, now Klingsor aims the Spear at Parsifal, but this time it is to no avail. The appearance of Klingsor is the last assault of Mara's army, and just as the arrows and spears of Mara were powerless against the Buddha, so is the Spear powerless to harm Parsifal, for he now serves the Grail with every ounce of his being. Thus the Spear stops above his head, just as the arrows and spears of Mara's army turned into flowers and fell at the feet of the Buddha. Parsifal grasps the Spear in his hand and makes the sign of the cross:

With this sign I rout your enchantment.
As the Spear closes the wound
which you dealt him with it,

may it crush your lying splendour
into mourning and ruin!

Parsifal's enlightenment is complete. The destruction of
Klingsor's castle and magic garden symbolizes the final piercing
of the cloud of delusion. The mist of maya has been dispersed
completely; the mirage created by karmic desire and attachment has been penetrated, leaving, as Wagner's directions say,
only withered flowers strewn on the ground. This enlightenment must still be tested, which it is over the ensuing years
of Parsifal's wandering, before he is fully ready to heal Amfortas and become the new Grail Guardian. But his successful
weathering of the temptations of Kundry and Klingsor has led
to his development of true spiritual sight, and the way to final
redemption is open.

As the castle is destroyed, Kundry "falls to the ground with a
scream. Parsifal pauses once more as he hastens away, and at the
top of the ruined wall turns back to Kundry."

You know where
you can find me again!
*(He hurries away. Kundry has raised herself a little and gazes after
him.)*

Kundry must experience the pain of the destruction of the
castle because she was not willing to let go of her own accord.
But Parsifal has not abandoned her. Because she had refused to
show him the way to Amfortas, he goes alone without her, but
he has not abandoned her salvation. Her attachment to Klingsor
and the whole karmic force that began with Alberich has now
been severed, and she is free to follow her desire for the land of
Monsalvat. She raises herself and gazes after him, and in longing
for him she finally directs her karmic stream one-pointedly in
the direction of the Grail. That she still must suffer ten years of
separation,[34] and the painful awakening in the forest by Gurnemanz is part of the consequence of her willful call to Klingsor

and her refusal to let go of desire on her own, but the path to salvation is now open to her too. This final salvation will come in Act III.

The Final Redemption

That Kundry's karma has finally been converted, and that she is ready for salvation and release is evidenced right at the start of Act III. It is the morning of Good Friday, and Gurnemanz, living in a small hermit's hut near a spring, hears very piteous groaning and goes to investigate.

> From yonder came the groaning.
> No beast cries so piteously,
> least of all today on this most holy morning.
> (*muffled groaning in Kundry's voice*)
> I seem to know that sound of lamenting.
> (*He walks firmly to a densely overgrown thorn thicket at the side,
> forces the undergrowth apart, then stops suddenly.*)
> Ha! She here again?
> The rough wintry thorn
> has been concealing her: for how long?—
> Up! Kundry! Up!
> Winter has fled, and Spring is here!

The old symbolism of the sleeping beauty is here again revived, thorns and all, as the sleep of winter awakes to spring. Brünnhilde/Kundry is again being awakened, but this time there is an all-important difference. Gurnemanz cries, "Up! Kundry! Up!" This is reminiscent of Klingsor calling to her "Come up! Come up!" as he too pulled her from her sleep. But the curse is gone, and it is not the old karma calling to Kundry to wake once again into the nightmare of Samsaric wandering, but rather the voice of impending salvation calling for her final spiritual awakening. Kundry herself shows a great transformation, both in her appearance and in her actions. Wagner's stage directions say, "Kundry is in the coarse robe of a penitent, similar to that in Act One, but her face is paler and the wildness has vanished from her looks and behaviour.—She gazes long at Gurnemanz. Then she rises, arranges her clothing and hair and at once sets to work like a serving-maid."

At first Gurnemanz thinks she is crazy, but as he watches her his opinion changes. Her first words to him are, "Let me serve . . . serve!" Gurnemanz observes her and says,

> How differently she moves from before!
> Has the holy day brought this about?
> O day of mercy beyond compare!
> In truth it was for her salvation
> that I was able to awake that poor soul
> today from the sleep of death.

That Kundry immediately desires to serve is a sign, along with her changed appearance and demeanor, that the karma has been cleansed. She is now whole-heartedly devoted to the Grail, and there is no longer any past karma holding her back from this service.

It is Kundry who first sees Parsifal coming. He is appareled in black armor with a visored helmet and carries a lowered spear. The scene here is the same as in the traditional legends: Gurnemanz tells Parsifal that this is a holy forest and that it is the morning of Good Friday. No one bears arms on such a day. When he asks Parsifal if he knows what day it is, Parsifal shakes his head, and Gurnemanz asks him to lay down his weapons. Parsifal immediately obeys, and plants the Spear in the ground, then kneels before it in prayer. This is the resurrection of the World Ash-tree. The spring outside Gurnemanz's hut is the spring of wisdom that ran dry when the branch was torn from the tree. The branch has now been returned. Tree and Spring are once again united and revitalized, and the dark winter of the Waste Land has given way to the dawning of spring. The waters once again flow, and nature is green with life.

When Parsifal takes off his helmet as he kneels before the Spear, Gurnemanz and Kundry both recognize him, and he them. Gurnemanz rejoices to have found him again, and Kundry "gazes fixedly, but calmly at Parsifal." When Gurnemanz asks him to whom was he seeking the way during his wandering, Parsifal answers,

> To him whose deep lamenting
> I once heard in foolish wonder,
> to bring him salvation
> I dare think myself ordained.
> But ah!
> An evil curse drove me about
> in trackless wandering,
> never to find the way to healing;
> numberless dangers,
> battles and conflicts
> forced me from my path
> even when I thought I knew it.
> Then I was forced to despair
> of holding unsullied the treasure
> to defend and guard which
> I earned wounds from every weapon;
> for I dared not wield this
> itself in conflict;
> unprofaned
> I have borne it beside me
> and now bring it home,
> gleaming clean and bright before you,
> the holy Spear of the Grail.

Parsifal has taken the final step in the renunciation of violence, taking upon himself the wounds of countless weapons without returning them, and refusing to wield the sacred Spear in battle or to use it for harm. By taking upon himself these wounds and not returning them, he has cleansed the karma from all the violence of his past lives, and specifically the past life of Siegfried. He has also cleansed the karma created by the misuse of the Spear itself, and thus brings it back "unsullied, gleaming clean and bright before you." In Christian terms the sin has been purged, and atonement made, for all of the wrongful actions perpetrated through the misuse and abuse of the Spear. It is a very important truth of Buddhism that "the old karma can always work on you." Buddhism believes that no one is ever "beyond" karma. Even the truly enlightened one is not beyond karma, but rather is one with it. Thus he or she makes no new karma. But even the enlightened ones are subject to the law of karma if they break the Precepts. In addition, even after final enlightenment, karma from the past can still come to one, as happened on a number of occasions with the Buddha himself. This is why Parsifal was forced to wander for ten years—not only because of Kundry's curse, but because he still had to experience the karmic consequences of certain past actions and thereby cleanse them. Once these consequences were fully experienced, the karma was cleansed, and Parsifal found his way to the Temple of the Grail. Because of the strength of the enlightenment he had experienced, even though he was outwardly wandering in the world of suffering, inwardly he never lost his way.

Gurnemanz, "breaking out in a transport of joy," cries, "O mercy! Bounteous grace! / O wonder! Holy, highest wonder!" (O Wunder! Heilig hehrstes Wunder!). This is virtually the exact exclamation made by Sieglinde to Brünnhilde when she heard that the child in her womb would be the great hero Siegfried. And now here stands Parsifal about to perform the healing of Amfortas. The redemption of the world, so long awaited, is at hand.

Gurnemanz then tells Parsifal that if it was a curse that drove him from the rightful path, its power is now broken, for this is the realm of the Grail. He relates how Amfortas has refused to perform the ceremony of the Grail, longing only to die; that the strength of the Grail Brotherhood has been drained; and that Titurel has died because he was unable to see the Grail. Parsifal, blaming himself for not healing Amfortas sooner, is about to fall into a faint when Gurnemanz and Kundry revive him with water from the holy spring. They remove the rest of his armor, and anoint his head and feet. Knowing that today he will be led to Amfortas, Parsifal scoops water from the spring and, bending over Kundry, who is kneeling before him, says, "My first office I thus perform: / Receive this baptism, / and believe in the Redeemer!"

For Wagner, baptism was a symbol of redemption, not merely a Church ritual. He had little use for the Church of his time; Cosima recorded on April 27, 1879, "He can think of nothing more unbearable than a priest, but that has nothing to do with the act of baptism or the symbol of redemption."[35] The baptism of Kundry is her long-awaited redemption, and it is not long now before she will enter Parinirvana. Cosima recorded on February 3, 1879:

> "I [Wagner] have come upstairs to tell you that the entry of the kettledrum in G is the finest thing I have ever done!" I accompany him downstairs and he plays to me the anointment of Parsifal by Gurnemanz, with its wonderful canon, and the baptism of Kundry with the annihilating sound of the kettledrum: "Obliteration of the whole being, of all earthly desire," says R.[36]

On January 6, 1881, Wagner and Cosima were discussing *Parsifal* and *Die Sieger*, and she recorded: "We talk of the fact that in both, *Parsifal* and *Sieger*, more or less the same theme (the redemption of a woman) is treated."[37]

All of Kundry's worldly karma has at last been cleansed, all her former sins expiated. As Gurnemanz relates the significance of Good Friday, saying that tears of repentant sinners form a holy dew over the meadows, Kundry slowly raises her head and looks up at Parsifal "with tearful eyes in calm and earnest entreaty." Parsifal says to her:

> I saw them that once mocked me wither:
> do they long for redemption today?—

Your tears too are a dew of blessing:
you weep—and see, the meadow smiles.
(He kisses her gently on the forehead. A peal of bells in the far distance.)

Both Parsifal and Kundry are completely beyond any sexual
connotation or desire. The kiss here is one of pure innocence, of
spiritual tenderness and recognition. In Act II such a kiss could
never have taken place, but now it happens naturally as a manifestation of spiritual love and acceptance. When Gurnemanz
hears the bells he says to Parsifal:

Midday:
the hour has come.
My lord, permit your servant to guide you!

The time has come for the final reunion of Spear and Grail.
The knights are begging Amfortas to perform the ceremony of
the Grail one last time, but he is unable to do it. Instead he begs
them for death:

No! No more! Ha!
Already I feel the darkness of death enshroud me,
and must I yet again return to life?

This last line echoes the plight of the old Kundry, awakened
over and over again from the sleep of death, only to return again
to the torment of life. This is, at least on one level, a symbolic
representation of karma and rebirth. I mentioned earlier in this
chapter that the destruction of the outward form of the world
or an individual does not constitute the cleansing of the unseen
karma existing behind that world or person. Thus death alone is
not salvation. This is the mistake Amfortas is making, and it is
why the knights will not kill him. It is the same situation as the
Flying Dutchman was in. Unable to end the curse by crashing
his ship on the rocks and dying, he had to wait for the redeemer,

in his case a woman faithful unto death. He could not be saved by the destruction of the outward form, only by the redemption of the inner spirit. Thus Kundry was brought back to life over and over, symbolizing the continual rebirths that a karmic stream will take until it is finally cleansed. Just as Kundry, in Act II, felt the wound of Amfortas, now Amfortas feels the wound of Kundry, for in essence there is no difference between the two:

> Madmen!
> Who would force me to live?
> Could you but grant me death!
> *(He tears open his garment.)*
> Here I am—here is the open wound!
> Here flows my blood, that poisons me.
> Draw your weapons! Plunge your swords
> in deep—deep, up to the hilt!
> Up, you heroes!
> Slay the sinner with his agony,
> then once more the Grail shall shine clear on you!

Redemption can never come through the breaking of the Precepts. The knights cannot illuminate the Grail by killing their king. They know this, and they all shrink back from Amfortas. Only Parsifal steps forward, holding the Spear and touching the side of Amfortas, thus healing him:

> But one weapon serves:
> only the Spear that smote you
> can heal your wound.

Just as Achilles, who had first wounded Telephus, "turned physician" and later healed him, so now must the Spear turn physician and heal Amfortas. Only the Spear, in the hands of the redeemer, can heal Amfortas's wound. What is really healing the wound is the return of the Spear to the Temple, the reunion of the Spear and Grail. It is this reunion that heals the wound of karmic action.

It is symbolic of final enlightenment, the cleansing of all past and present karma. With the karma cleansed, the wound is healed. As Amfortas's features "light up in holy ecstasy," Parsifal sings:

> Be whole, absolved and atoned!
> For now I will perform your task.
> O blessed be your suffering,
> that gave pity's mighty power
> and purest wisdom's might
> to the timorous fool!
> I bring back to you
> the holy Spear!
> O supreme joy of this miracle!
> This that could heal your wound
> I see pouring with holy blood
> yearning for that kindred fount
> which flows and wells within the Grail.
> No more shall it be hidden:
> uncover the Grail, open the shrine!

The opening of the shrine is symbolic of the opening of our own inner shrine of enlightenment, revealing the Buddha seated in meditation upon his lion's throne. In Japan this is called the *hara*. Literally, *hara* in Japanese means "belly," but in Buddhism the *hara* is not only the physical part of our bodies that we call our abdomen. More important, it is the center of our spiritual being, the seat of our own meditation. To experience enlightenment is to open the *hara* and reveal the Buddha within. This is often symbolized in the East by an actual altar with two doors meeting in the middle. When these two doors are opened, the altar reveals a small Buddha figure inside. By opening the shrine of the Grail, Parsifal is revealing the enlightenment within. The sanctuary is no longer profaned. It has been cleansed and purified, its light shining upon the whole world. This is the true regeneration, the true Emancipation.

As the chorus sings "Miracle of supreme salvation! / Our Redeemer redeemed!" Kundry "slowly sinks lifeless to the ground in front of Parsifal, her eyes uplifted to him." This is Kundry's entrance into Parinirvana. All of her karma has been cleansed, and there is no longer anything to bind her to earthly life. There is no need for her to remain. Parsifal is the designated redeemer of this time and place, and it is he who becomes the new Grail King, keeping the Grail alive in the world for the benefit of all beings. Kundry has accomplished what was necessary for her in this lifetime, and now her karmic stream has run its course. The drop has slipped into the sea. She leaves her body and enters the state of eternal meditation, forever at one with the great Dharmakaya, the great Body of Truth.

It is very important to understand that enlightenment is beyond the differentiation of sex. By ordaining women as full monks (bhikkhunis), the Buddha made it explicitly clear that there was no difference spiritually between men and women. Both have the Buddha-nature equally, and both have the ability to attain full enlightenment. Wagner also specified this, as Cosima recorded on June 27, 1880: "He then plays the first theme of Parsifal to himself and, returning, says that he gave the words to a chorus so that the effect would be neither masculine nor feminine, Christ must be entirely sexless, neither man nor woman."[38]

The Spear is pouring with holy blood, yearning for that kindred fount which flows and wells within the Grail. Male and female have become inextricably one, the blood flowing equally from both Spear and Grail. Spirit is flowing into spirit; the true communion has been found in the third position beyond the opposites. What Wagner originally conceived in Die Sieger has been actualized in Parsifal: salvation through the union of male and female not in a romantic context, but in a spiritual one. Parsifal and Kundry, one remaining and one departing, still at one forever in that eternal union beyond birth and death.

Epilogue

The *Ring* and *Parsifal* as one work is a great sermon, and certainly one of the very greatest works of art ever created. However, like any sermon, hearing it is not enough. A sermon is only useful and beneficial if we put its truths into practice. Listening to the *Ring* and *Parsifal* and then going about our business as though nothing has changed will not accomplish the work of our own redemption. The great tragedy of Wagner's personal life was that he too seldom practiced in his own everyday life the great truths and insights that he portrayed so grandly in his art. There is a humorous, but also very insightful, story that Cosima related on September 16, 1878. Wagner was taking one of his walks when he was greeted by a Protestant parson. The parson asked Wagner if he might talk with him, and Wagner,

> having first looked at him in the face and remarked that he did not care to be accosted in this way, invited him to walk with him. First of all the man asked him to defend the interests of the church, then he asked him not to write anything else offensive to morality. "What do you mean?" "Well, the mermaids, for instance." R.: "You are a very silly man; according to that, trees, birds, and the whole of Nature would be immoral." He: "You listen only to flatterers, you do not want to hear the truth." R. is good enough to give him a copy of *Parsifal* [the libretto]: "In this you will see that I am more Christian than you are." He: "That we shall know when we stand at God's right hand." R.: "Or at the Devil's left," and with these words he dismissed the importunate man.[1]

It is easy to see in this encounter what we might perceive as a very petty little man trying to bring a great man down to his own level. But there is another way to see this picture. The so-called great man, consumed by his own genius and importance, is confronted by the voice of a truth that he needs very much to hear, that of putting religious truth into practice in his own life. Wagner gives the parson a copy of his art, but the parson is not impressed, knowing that what matters most is not what we preach, but what we practice. Thus the parson is not intimidated by Wagner and stands right up to him when Wagner claims to be more Christian, saying, "That we shall know when we stand at God's right hand." Wagner swats him like a fly, which on the intellectual and artistic levels he is able to do easily. But Wagner does not listen when he is told, "You listen only to flatterers, you do not want to hear the truth."

This is what we all do, at least in some ways and to some extent. We hear what we want to hear, not what we really need to hear. A large part of spiritual training is to be willing to let go of self and hear the voice of the Eternal, no matter what form that voice may take. It is all too easy to react like Mime when confronted with the Wanderer. Mime lost his head, and so, in that lifetime, did Siegfried. Parsifal kept his head because when the voice of the Eternal spoke to him, he listened. He put down his weapons, his resistance and defenses, and listened with his heart. And the path to salvation opened up before him, a path which, in fact, had never been closed.

Notes

INTRODUCTION

1. Leon Stein, *The Racial Thinking of Richard Wagner* (New York: Philosophical Library, 1950), 93–94; Stein's italics.

CHAPTER 1

1. Arthur Schopenhauer, *The World as Will and Representation*, trans. E. F. J. Payne, 2 vols. (Indian Hills, Colo.: Falcon's Wing Press, 1958; reprinted New York: Dover, 1966), 2:623. Translation in brackets of Schopenhauer's Latin by the author.
2. Ibid., 1:196.
3. Narada Maha Thera, *The Buddha and His Teachings* (Kuala Lumpur, Malaysia: Buddhist Missionary Society, 1977), 506.
4. Schopenhauer, *World*, 2:508; Schopenhauer's italics.
5. Ibid., 1:383; Schopenhauer's italics.
6. Ibid., 1:411.
7. Narada, *Buddha*, 491–492.
8. Richard Wagner, *Selected Letters of Richard Wagner*, trans. and ed. Stewart Spencer and Barry Millington (New York: W. W. Norton, 1988), 357.
9. Trans. in Andrew Porter, "*Götterdämmerung*: Das Ende" (in program booklet for Richard Wagner, *Der Ring des Nibelungen*, San Francisco Opera Company production, 1990).
10. Ibid.
11. Ibid.
12. Trans. Porter-Jameson in Porter, "*Götterdämmerung*: Das Ende."
13. Trans. in Porter, "*Götterdämmerung*: Das Ende."
14. From Deryck Cooke, *I Saw the World End*, his translation. Quoted

in Porter, "*Götterdämmerung*: Das Ende."

15. Barry Millington, *Wagner* (London: J. M. Dent & Sons, 1984), 226.

16. Richard Wagner, *The Ring of the Nibelung*, trans. Andrew Porter (New York: W. W. Norton, 1977, 327–328. From here on, all quotations from the text of the *Ring* are from Porter's translation.

17. Trans. in Porter, "*Götterdämmerung*: Das Ende."

18. Wagner's stage directions, *Ring*, 328.

19. Geoffrey Skelton, trans., *Cosima Wagner's Diaries*, vol. 1 (New York: Harcourt Brace Jovanovich, 1978), 515.

20. Quoted from Warren Darcy, "The Pessimism of the *Ring*," *Opera Quarterly* 4, no. 2 (Summer 1986): 47 n. 44. Darcy says of his source: "Quoted by John Deathridge in 'Reviews,' *19th Century Music* 5 (Summer 1981): 85 (my translation). Deathridge cites as his source for the letter 'Catalogue 100, *Proszenium, Theater- und Film-Fachantiquariat*, Kemnath Stadt (Germany, n.d.).'"

21. Wagner, *Selected Letters*, 309. Wagner at this time was spelling Wotan "Wodan."

CHAPTER 2

1. Wagner, *Selected Letters*, 499. Wagner here spelled Parsifal as Parzifal.

2. Narada, *Buddha*, 468.

3. This meaning of the word *koan* is not to be confused with the meaning of the word when it is used to describe a particular question or story that cannot be understood intellectually, but must be understood and solved through meditation and training, as in Rinzai Zen's "Book of Koans."

4. Richard Wagner, *Parsifal*, libretto, trans. Lionel Salter, © Lionel Salter Library 2007.

5. Ibid.

6. Skelton, *Cosima Wagner's Diaries*, 1:952.

7. Recorded by Cosima on August 21, 1882. Geoffrey Skelton, trans., *Cosima Wagner's Diaries*, vol. 2 (New York: Harcourt Brace Jovanovich, 1980), 901.

CHAPTER 3

1. Bryan Magee, *Aspects of Wagner* (Oxford and New York: Oxford University Press, 1988), 5–6.

2. Matthew 26:39.

3. Wagner, *Parsifal*, libretto, trans. Salter.

4. Ibid.

5. Ibid.

6. Richard Wagner, *Parsifal*, libretto, trans. Stewart Robb (Chester, N.Y.: G. Schirmer, 1962), 11.

7. Ibid., 16.

8. Ibid., 17.

9. Ibid., 5.

10. Ibid.

11. Wagner, *Parsifal*, libretto, trans. Salter.

12. Ibid.

13. Ibid.

CHAPTER 4

1. Wagner, *Selected Letters*, 457. Wagner at this time was using Wolfram's spelling of Anfortas.

2. Ibid., 459.

3. Ibid., 457. In *Parzival*, Anfortas is wounded by the poisoned spear of his opponent, but this opponent is not Clinschor (Wagner's Klingsor), and the spear is not the Spear of the Grail.

4. Wolfram von Eschenbach, *Parzival*, trans. Helen M. Mustard and Charles E. Passage (New York: Vintage Books, Random House, 1961), Book IX, section 479, p. 256. "Your sweet uncle" refers to Anfortas as the uncle of Parzival.

5. James G. Frazer, *The Golden Bough* (1890; reprinted New York: Avenel Books, 1981), 228.

6. Jessie L. Weston, *From Ritual to Romance* (1920; reprinted Princeton, N.J.: Princeton University Press, 1993), 125–126. Manu, in Hinduism, is the counterpart of Noah, the one who survives the Flood, and in some cases is also a counterpart of Adam. The passage about Manu and Jhasa comes from Book III of the *Mahabharata*.

7. White Hill is possibly Tower Hill, or the place where St. Paul's now stands, according to Jeffrey Gantz, ed. and trans., *The Mabinogion* (New York: Dorset Press, 1976), 79.

8. Matthew 4:19.

9. For a more detailed discussion of these meditation heavens, as well as other planes of existence, see Narada, *Buddha*, 436–445.

10. Narada, *Buddha*, 441.

11. Ibid., 440.

12. Weston, *From Ritual to Romance*, 32.

13. Ibid., 14.

14. Joseph Campbell, *The Hero with a Thousand Faces* (Princeton, N.J.: Princeton University Press, 1972), 91.

15. Ibid., 91–92.

16. Weston, *From Ritual to Romance*, 140.

17. Samuel Angus, *The Mystery-Religions* (1928; reprinted New York: Dover, 1975), 14.

18. Weston, *From Ritual to Romance*, 146–147.

19. Ibid., 146–148. The passages in italics were quoted from Weston's own source: see Hepding, *Attis*, chapter 4.

20. Angus, *The Mystery-Religions*, 128–131.

21. Ibid., 124.

22. Joseph Campbell, *Creative Mythology*, Vol. 4 of *The Masks of God* (New York: Penguin Books, 1968), 459. At the end of this passage Campbell is referring to Wolfram's spelling of Anfortas in *Parzival*, and to the Grail as the Perfection of Paradise, one of the ways in which Wolfram refers to the spiritual meaning of the Grail.

23. Skelton, *Cosima Wagner's Diaries*, 1:547.

24. Roger Sherman Loomis, *The Grail: From Celtic Myth to Christian Symbol* (Princeton, N.J.: Princeton University Press, 1963 and 1991), 20–21.

25. Ibid., 21.

26. Weston, *From Ritual to Romance*, 175.

27. Ibid., 186.

28. Angus, *The Mystery-Religions*, 50.

29. Ibid., 114, 83, 312.

30. Weston, *From Ritual to Romance*, 149.

31. James George Frazer, *The Golden Bough* (1922; reprinted New York: Macmillan, 1951), 412.

32. *Elder Edda*, quoted in *Mythology*, by Edith Hamilton (Boston: Little, Brown & Company, 1942), 455.

33. Frazer, *The Golden Bough* (1922), 412.

34. *Mahabharata*, quoted in Joseph Campbell, *Oriental Mythology*, Vol. 2 of *The Masks of God* (New York: Penguin Books, 1962), 187.

35. Ibid., 187.

36. Campbell, *Oriental Mythology*, 188.

37. Sir Thomas Malory, *Le Morte d'Arthur*, ed. Janet Cowan, 2 vols. (Baltimore, Md.: Penguin Books, 1969), 1:Book II, 83.

38. Ibid.

39. Ibid., 1:Book II, 84.
40. Ibid. In Middle English, *tray* is a word for sorrow and *tene* a word for grief.
41. Loomis, *Grail*, 176.
42. Wolfram, *Parzival*, Book V, section 235, p. 129.

CHAPTER 5

1. Wagner, *Selected Letters*, 460.
2. Ibid., 458–459.
3. Wolfram, *Parzival*, Book XVI, section 1827, p. 430. Mustard and Passage state that the word *endehaft* may mean either "correctly" or "through to the end," meaning that Kyot told the story through to its end, rather than leaving it incomplete as Chrétien had done (p. 430 n. 11).
4. Chrétien de Troyes, *Perceval: The Story of the Grail*, trans. Burton Raffel (New Haven, Conn.: Yale University Press, 1999), ll. 436–437, p. 15.
5. Ibid., l. 630, p. 21.
6. Ibid., ll. 1654–1655, p. 53.
7. Loomis, trans. in *The Grail*, 32.
8. Loomis does not capitalize "grail" in this translation, "since for Chrétien and his readers the word *graal* was a common noun and did not denote the unique relic of the Last Supper." Ibid., 29 n. 3. Raffel does not capitalize the word either, and his translation reads, "A girl / Entered with them, holding / A grail-dish in both her hands." *Perceval*, ll. 3220–3222, p. 102.
9. Loomis, *The Grail*, 33.
10. Ibid.
11. Ibid., 34.
12. Ibid., 36.
13. Ibid., 36. Raffel translates the passage as: "A spear struck him right / Between the legs." Chrétien, *Perceval*, ll. 3513–3514, p. 111.
14. Loomis, *The Grail*, 37–38.
15. Ibid., 39.
16. Ibid., 40.
17. Ibid., 41.
18. Ibid., 44.
19. Chrétien, *Perceval*, ll. 6510–6519, pp. 205–206.
20. Wagner, *Selected Letters*, 459.

21. Wolfram, *Parzival*, Book V, section 245, p. 133.

22. Ibid., Book V, section 255, pp. 138–139.

23. Loomis, *The Grail*, 47.

24. Ibid., 47–48.

25. Ibid., 53.

26. Wolfram, *Parzival*, Book V, section 252, p. 137.

27. Ibid., Book V, section 254, p. 138.

28. Ibid., Book III, section 171, p. 94.

29. Ibid., Book IX, section 447, p. 241.

30. Ibid., Book IX, section 450, p. 242.

31. Ibid., Book IX, section 451, pp. 242–243.

32. Ibid., Book IX, section 452, p. 243.

33. Ibid., Book IX, section 452, p. 243

34. Ibid., Book IX, section 502, p. 268.

35. Of course, in *Lohengrin* Parsifal is the father of Lohengrin. But Wagner does not include this in *Parsifal*.

36. Wolfram, *Parzival*, Book IX, sections 501–502, pp. 267–268.

37. Ibid., Book IX, sections 493–494, pp. 263–264. We can see here the idea of Lohengrin answering Elsa's plea.

38. Ibid., Book IX, section 495, p. 264.

39. Ibid., Book IX, sections 472–473, p. 253.

40. Ibid., Book IX, sections 478–479, p. 256.

41. Ibid., Book IX, section 479, p. 256.

42. Ibid., Book IX, section 480, p. 257.

43. Ibid.

44. Ibid.

45. Ibid., Book IX, section 483, pp. 258–259.

46. Wagner, *Parsifal*, libretto, trans. Salter.

47. Ibid.

48. Wagner, *Parsifal*, libretto, trans. Robb, 22.

49. This is the point where, in *Perceval*, Gawain sets out to seek the Bleeding Spear.

50. Wolfram, *Parzival*, Book XI, section 560, p. 297.

51. Ibid., Book XI, section 562, p. 298.

52. Ibid., Book XII, section 601, p. 318.

53. Campbell, *Creative Mythology*, 455.

54. Ibid., 454.

55. Loomis, *The Grail*, 50. See p. 000 of this book for *Phantom's Frenzy*.

56. Wagner, *Selected Letters*, 500.

57. Wolfram, *Parzival*, Book VI, sections 313–314, p. 169.

58. Campbell, *Creative Mythology*, 485.

59. Wagner, *Parsifal*, libretto, trans. Salter.

60. Ibid.

61. Wagner, *Parsifal*, libretto, trans. Robb, 10.

62. Wolfram, *Parzival*, Book IX, section 453, p. 244.

63. Ibid., Book IX, sections 454–455, p. 244.

64. Wagner, *Parsifal*, libretto, trans. Robb, 4.

65. Wolfram, *Parzival*, Book XV, section 781, p. 406.

66. Ibid., Book IX, sections 470–471, p. 252.

67. Ibid., Book IX, section 483, pp. 258–259.

68. Wagner, *Parsifal*, libretto, trans. Salter.

69. Wolfram, *Parzival*, Book XVI, section 787, p. 410.

70. Ibid., Book XVI, section 788, p. 411.

71. Ibid., Book XVI, section 795, p. 414.

72. "Oeheim, waz wirret dir?" Ibid., Book XVI, section 795, p. 415.

73. Ibid., Book XVI, sections 795–796, p. 415.

74. Ibid., Book XVI, section 823, p. 428.

75. Wagner, *Parsifal*, libretto, trans. Robb, 22.

76. See p. 78.

77. Trans. in Millington, *Wagner*, 268.

78. Millington, *Wagner*, 268.

79. Matthew 26:26–28.

80. Wolfram, *Parzival*, Book III, section 145, p. 81.

81. Ibid., Book III, section 140, p. 78.

82. Ibid., Book III, section 140, p. 78 n. 8.

83. Campbell, *Creative Mythology*, 431–432.

84. Wolfram, *Parzival*, Book III, section 171, p. 94.

85. Ibid., Book IX, section 489, p. 261.

86. Ibid., Book XVI, section 827, pp. 430–431.

87. Ibid., Book XVI, section 797, pp. 415–416.

88. Matthew 3:16–17.

89. Wolfram, *Parzival*, Book IX, sections 469–470, p. 252.

90. Ibid., Book XVI, sections 824–825, p. 429.

91. Ibid., Book XVI, section 826, p. 430.

92. Ibid., Book XVI, sections 818–819, p. 426.

CHAPTER 6

1. Wotan as the Wanderer uses these terms for Alberich and Wotan in his scene with Mime in Act I, Scene 2 of *Siegfried*.

2. William Ashton Ellis originally translated this title as *The Wibelungs: World-History as Told in Saga*, dating it, incorrectly as we know now, to 1848. However, Wagner originally used the German word *Sage* (myth), not *Saga* (saga). His original German, *Die Wibelungen. Weltgeschichte aus der Sage*, is thus literally rendered *The Wibelungs: World-History from Myth*. I have taken the liberty of rendering it *World-History as Told Through Myth*.

3. William Morris, trans., *Volsunga Saga: The Story of the Volsungs and Nibelungs*, with selected songs from the *Elder Edda*, introd. Robert W. Gutman (New York: Collier Books, 1962), 51.

4. Skelton, *Cosima Wagner's Diaries*, 2:991–992.

5. Ibid., 2:29.

6. Ibid., 2:299.

7. See p. 170.

8. Pendragon is not part of Uther's name; it is his title. Arthur became Pendragon when he rose to power, though this term is not normally used to describe him in the romances. Arthur is the "Great Bear," born under the sign of Ursa Major.

9. From the *Elder Edda*, translated by William Morris and included in his *Volsunga Saga*, 242. Helgi had killed King Hunding, and was thus known as Helgi Hundings-bane. Morris has here retained the Norse spelling of Valkyrie as Valkyria. The word comes from *val*, slain, and *kyrja*, chooser. A Valkyrie was a chooser of the slain, and Valhalla was the hall of the slain.

10. Skelton, *Cosima Wagner's Diaries*, 2:52.

11. See p. 96.

12. Wagner, *Selected Letters*, 307.

13. Shasta Abbey, *The Monastic Office*, trans. Rev. Hubert Nearman, ed. Rev. Master P. T. N. H. Jiyu-Kennett (Mt. Shasta, Calif.: Shasta Abbey Press, 1993), 79.

14. Skelton, *Cosima Wagner's Diaries*, 2:33.

15. Ibid., 2:288.

16. Shasta Abbey, *The Monastic Office*, 79–80.

17. Skelton, *Cosima Wagner's Diaries*, 2:117–118.

18. Andrew Porter, translating for singing rather than exact word-for-word replication, does not put the English into the form of a question. The first line should read, "Did you not say" rather than "You said."

19. Warren Darcy, "The Pessimism of the *Ring*," *Opera Quarterly* 4, no. 2 (Summer 1986): 47 n. 41.

20. Paramahansa Yogananda, *Autobiography of a Yogi* (Los Angeles: Self-Realization Fellowship, 1959), 400n.

21. Skelton, *Cosima Wagner's Diaries*, 2:176–177. Hans von Wolzogen was a close friend of the Wagners and the editor of the *Bayreuther Blätter*.

22. Wagner, *Parsifal*, libretto, trans. Robb, 13.

23. Ibid., 13.

24. Ibid., 14–15. The name of Parsifal's mother, Herzeleide, can also be translated as "Heart's Sorrow" rather than "Heart of Sorrow."

25. Wagner, *Parsifal*, libretto, trans. Salter.

26. Skelton, *Cosima Wagner's Diaries*, 2:784.

27. Wagner, *Parsifal*, libretto, trans. Salter.

28. Acts 9:4–5.

29. Wagner, *Parsifal*, libretto, trans. Salter.

30. Wagner, *Parsifal*, libretto, trans. Robb, 15.

31. Wagner, *Parsifal*, libretto, trans. Salter. From here on all translations from the libretto of *Parsifal* will be from this source.

32. Skelton, *Cosima Wagner's Diaries*, 2:85.

33. Ibid., 2:910.

34. Cosima recorded on July 22, 1882: "We have rehearsals, Scaria appears as the aged Gurnemanz and is quite superb. R. had said 80 in the first act, 90 in the last." Ibid., 2:892.

35. Ibid., 2:297.

36. Ibid., 2:265.

37. Ibid., 2:592. The parenthetical phrase is Cosima's.

38. Ibid., 2:498–499.

EPILOGUE

1. Skelton, *Cosima Wagner's Diaries*, 2:150.

Bibliography

Aeschylus, Sophocles, Euripides, Aristophanes. Translated by G. M. Cookson, Sir Richard C. Jebb, Edward P. Coleridge, and Benjamin Bickley Rogers. Chicago: William Benton, 1952.

Aeschylus. *The Oresteian Trilogy.* Translated by Philip Vellacott. Rev. ed. Baltimore, Md.: Penguin, 1959.

Angus, Samuel. *The Mystery-Religions.* 1928. Reprinted New York: Dover, 1975.

Baigent, Michael, Richard Leigh, and Henry Lincoln. *Holy Blood, Holy Grail.* New York: Dell, 1982.

Baldry, H. C. *The Greek Tragic Theatre.* New York: W. W. Norton, 1971.

Bulgakov, Fr. Sergius. *The Holy Grail and The Eucharist.* Hudson, N.Y.: Lindisfarne Books, 1997.

Burbidge, Peter, and Richard Sutton, eds. *The Wagner Companion.* London and Boston: Faber & Faber, 1979.

Campbell, Joseph. *Creative Mythology.* Vol. 4, *The Masks of God.* New York: Penguin, 1968.

———. *The Hero with a Thousand Faces.* Princeton, N.J.: Princeton University Press, 1972.

———. *Occidental Mythology.* Vol. 3, *The Masks of God.* New York: Penguin, 1964.

———. *Oriental Mythology.* Vol. 2, *The Masks of God.* New York: Penguin, 1962.

———. *Primitive Mythology.* Vol. 1, *The Masks of God.* New York: Penguin, 1959.

Chrétien de Troyes. *Perceval: The Story of the Grail.* Translated by Burton Raffel. New Haven, Conn.: Yale University Press, 1999.

Dante Alighieri. *The Divine Comedy.* Translated by John Ciardi. New York: W. W. Norton, 1954.

Darcy, Warren. "The Pessimism of the *Ring.*" *Opera Quarterly* 4, no. 2 (Summer 1986): 24–48.

Davidson, H. R. Ellis. *Gods and Myths of the Viking Age.* New York: Bell, 1964.

DiGaetani, John L., ed. *Penetrating Wagner's Ring*. New York: Da Capo Press, 1978.

Durant, Will. *The Story of Philosophy*. New York: Garden City, 1926.

Eliade, Mircea. *Myth and Reality*. New York: Harper & Row, 1963.

Eliot, T. S. *The Waste Land and Other Poems*. New York: Harcourt, Brace, & World, 1930.

Encyclopedia of Classical Mythology. Englewood Cliffs, N.J.: Prentice-Hall, 1965.

Euripides. *Orestes and Other Plays*. Translated by Philip Vellacott. New York: Penguin Books, 1972.

Frazer, James G. *The Golden Bough*. 1890. Reprinted New York: Avenel Books, 1981.

Frazer, James George. *The Golden Bough*. 1922. Reprinted New York: Macmillan, 1951.

Gantz, Jeffrey, ed. and trans. *The Mabinogion*. New York: Dorset Press, 1976.

Gardner, Laurence. *Bloodline of the Holy Grail*. Gloucester, Mass.: Fair Winds Press, 2001.

Hall, Manly P. *Orders of the Quest: The Holy Grail*. Los Angeles, Calif.: Philosophical Research Society, 1996.

Hamilton, Edith. *Mythology*. Boston: Little, Brown, 1942.

Hieatt, Constance B., trans. *Beowulf and Other Old English Poems*. Toronto and New York: 1967.

Keizan Zenji. *The Denkoroku, or The Record of the Transmission of the Light*. Edited by Rev. Master P. T. N. H. Jiyu-Kennett. Translated by Rev. Hubert (Mark) Nearman. Mt. Shasta, Calif.: Shasta Abbey Press, 1993.

Kennett, Roshi P. T. N. H. Jiyu. *Zen Is Eternal Life*. Mt. Shasta, Calif.: Shasta Abbey Press, 1987.

Kennett, Roshi P. T. N. H. Jiyu, and Rev. Daizui MacPhillamy. *The Book of Life*. Mt. Shasta, Calif.: Shasta Abbey Press, 1979.

Loomis, Roger Sherman. *The Grail: From Celtic Myth to Christian Symbol*. University of Wales Press, 1963. Reprinted Princeton, N.J.: Princeton University Press, 1991.

The Lost Books of the Bible. Translated by William Hone, Jeremiah Jones, and William Wake. Cleveland, Ohio: World, 1926. Reprinted New York: Bell, 1979.

MacCana, Proinsias. *Celtic Mythology*. London and New York: Hamlyn Publishing Group, 1970.

Magee, Bryan. *Aspects of Wagner*, New York: Oxford University Press, 1988.

———. *The Philosophy of Schopenhauer*. Revised and enlarged ed. New York: Oxford University Press, 1997.

———. *The Tristan Chord: Wagner and Philosophy*. New York: Metropolitan Books, Henry Holt, 2000.

Malory, Thomas. *Le Morte d'Arthur*. 2 vols. Edited by Janet Cowen. Baltimore, Md.: Penguin, 1969.

Millington, Barry. *Wagner*. London: J. M. Dent & Sons, 1984.

Morris, William, trans. *Volsunga Saga: The Story of the Volsungs and Nibelungs*. With selected songs from the *Elder Edda*. Introduction by Robert W. Gutman. New York: Collier Books, Macmillan, 1962.

Mowatt, D. G., trans. *The Nibelungenlied*. London: J. M. Dent, 1962. Reprinted Mineola, N.Y.: Dover, 2001.

Narada Maha Thera. *The Buddha and His Teachings*. 1st ed. Kuala Lumpur, Malaysia: Buddhist Missionary Society, 1964.

———. *The Buddha and His Teachings*. 2nd ed. Kuala Lumpur, Malaysia: Buddhist Missionary Society, 1973.

———. *The Buddha and His Teachings*. 3rd ed. Kuala Lumpur, Malaysia: Buddhist Missionary Society, 1977.

Nietzsche, Friedrich. *The Birth of Tragedy*. Translated by Francis Golffing. Garden City, N.Y.: Doubleday, 1956.

Peckham, Morse. *Beyond the Tragic Vision*. New York: George Braziller, 1962.

Porter, Andrew. "*Götterdämmerung*: Das Ende." In program booklet for Richard Wagner, *Der Ring des Nibelungen*, San Francisco Opera Company production, 1990.

Schopenhauer, Arthur. *The World as Will and Representation*. Translated by E. F. J. Payne. 2 vols. Indian Hills, Colo.: Falcon's Wing Press, 1958. Reprinted New York: Dover, 1966.

Shasta Abbey. *The Monastic Office*. Translated from the *Sōtō-Shu Gyōji Kihan* (The Ceremonial Practices of the Sōtō Church) by Rev. Hubert Nearman. Edited by Rev. Master P. T. N. H. Jiyu-Kennett. Mt. Shasta, Calif.: Shasta Abbey Press, 1993.

Sigfusson, Saemund. *The Elder Eddas*. Translated by Benjamin Thorpe. London and New York: Norrœna Society, 1906.

Skelton, Geoffrey, trans. *Cosima Wagner's Diaries*. Vol. 1. New York: Harcourt Brace Jovanovich, 1978.

———, trans. *Cosima Wagner's Diaries*. Vol. 2. New York: Harcourt Brace Jovanovich, 1980.

Sogyal Rinpoche. *The Tibetan Book of Living and Dying*. San Francisco: HarperSanFrancisco, 1994.

Sophocles. *The Oedipus Plays of Sophocles: Oedipus the King, Oedipus at Colonus, Antigone*. Translated by Paul Roche. New York: New American Library, 1958.

Stearns, Monroe. *Richard Wagner*. New York: Franklin Watts, 1969.

Stein, Leon. *The Racial Thinking of Richard Wagner*. New York: Philosophical Library, 1950.

Sturleson, Snorre. *Younger Eddas*. Translated by I. A. Blackwell. London and New York: Norrœna Society, 1906.

Travers, P. L. *About the Sleeping Beauty*. New York: McGraw-Hill, 1975.

Wagner, Richard. *Parsifal*. Libretto. German text with English translation by Stewart Robb. Chester, N.Y.: G. Schirmer, 1962.

———. *Parsifal*. Libretto. German text with English translation by Lionel Salter. London: Lionel Salter Library, 2007.

———. *The Ring of the Nibelung*. Libretto. German text with English translation by Andrew Porter. New York: W. W. Norton, 1977.

———. *Selected Letters of Richard Wagner*. Translated and edited by Stewart Spencer and Barry Millington. New York: W. W. Norton, 1988.

———. Prose sketch for *Die Sieger*, in *Richard Wagner's Prose Works*, Vol. 8. Translated by William Ashton Ellis. London: Kegan Paul, Trench, Trübner and Co., 1899. http://home.c2i.net/montsalvat/sieger.htm (accessed August 11, 2001).

———. *The Wibelungs: World-History as Told Through Myth*, in *Richard Wagner's Prose Works*, Vol. 7. Translated by William Ashton Ellis. London: Kegan Paul, Trench, Trübner and Co., 1898; The Wagner Library, 2001. http://users.belgacom.net/wagnerlibrary/prose/wagwibel.htm (accessed April 13, 2002).

Weston, Jessie L. *From Ritual to Romance*. 1920. Princeton, N.J.: Princeton University Press, 1993.

Wink, Walter. *Violence and Nonviolence in South Africa: Jesus' Third Way*. Philadelphia: New Society, 1987.

Wolfram von Eschenbach. *Parzival*. Translated by Helen M. Mustard and Charles E. Passage. New York: Vintage Books, Random House, 1961.

Yogananda, Paramahansa. *Autobiography of a Yogi*. Los Angeles: Self-Realization Fellowship, 1959.

Index

Aeschylus, 48, 62, 199
Albigensian Crusade, 81, 122
Ananda (historical), 15
anatta, 37
Aristotle, 48
Arthur, King (historical period of),
   202–203
Athanasius, Bishop, Epistle of, 117
Attila, 192, 203

Bacchae, The, 57–58
Barbarossa, Friedrich, 128, 190,
   191–192, 195
Bhagavad-Gita, 102
bhikkhu, 15
bhikkhuni, 15–16, 237
Birth of Tragedy, The, 52
Buddha (Gautama, Prince
   Siddhartha, Shakyamuni), 8,
   10, 15–16, 37, 92, 94, 97, 122,
   166–168, 182–184, 189, 239, 256,
   258–260, 264, 267, 274–277,
   282, 287
Buddhism, 2, 6–13, 15, 18, 23, 35–38,
   57, 66–67, 74, 79, 94–97, 109–110,
   122, 181, 189, 196, 207, 221–222,
   225, 227, 233, 246, 249, 252, 254,
   256, 260–261, 282, 286

Chrétien de Troyes (died), 79
Christ (Jesus), 37, 41, 59, 64, 70,
   79, 92, 93, 98, 100, 109, 113–119,
   121–122, 135, 138, 172, 178–180,

184, 189, 226, 254, 257, 260, 268,
   275–276, 287
Christianity, 1–2, 10, 35, 51, 57, 65, 67,
   74, 78–79, 90, 92–93, 101, 112–113,
   116, 180, 189, 200, 204, 227, 233
Conte del Graal, Le (*Li Contes del
   Graal, Perceval*), 79, 127–128, 134,
   136–137, 160–163, 181

Dante, 47, 59, 74, 169
Devas, 95–97, 110, 219, 221
Didot Perceval, 80
Diû Crône, 80, 181
Divine Comedy, The, 47, 59–60, 125
dragon, symbolism of, 89, 92–93,
   105, 194, 226–228, 256

echtra, 110, 140
Elder Edda (*Poetic Edda*), 114,
   197–199, 204
Elysium, 110
Estoire del Saint Graal, 80
Eucharist, 79
Euripides, 48, 56

Feuerbach, Ludwig Andreas, 21–24
First Continuation, 79, 128, 136
Förster, Bernard, 2, 196
Four Noble Truths, the, 8
Four Signs, the, 258–259

Gerbert de Montreuil, 79, 102, 128,
   136

Golden Bough, The, 82–83, 102, 162–163
Grand Saint Graal, 80
Guiot de Provins, 128

Heine, Heinrich, 42
Heinrich von dem Türlin, 80, 181
Hildebrandslied, 199, 232
Hinduism, 7, 15, 57, 78, 95–97, 110
Hippolytus, 57–58
Holy Grail, origin of, 82
Huns, 198–199, 203

Irenaeus, Bishop, 116

Jesus (*see* Christ)
John the Baptist, 42, 116, 184
Joseph d'Arimathie, 79
Joseph of Arimathea, 79, 80, 98, 100,
    116–120, 173

Kant, Immanuel, 6–7
Karma (Kamma), Law of, 12, 155,
    211–212, 223–224, 282
Knights Templar, 180, 185
koan, 38, 40–41, 94, 251, 292n3
Kyot, 127–128, 138, 173, 295n3

Last Supper, 79–80, 100, 112, 116, 118,
    121, 172, 179, 296n8
Liszt, Franz, 126
Ludwig II, King, 23

Mabinogion, 81, 91
Macbeth, 170
Mahabharata, 78, 101–104, 115,
    294n6
Maha Maya, 97
Malory, Sir Thomas (died), 81
Manessier, 79, 102, 111, 137
Mara, 166–167, 259–260, 264–265,
    267, 273, 275, 277
Mary, mother of Jesus, 114
Mary Magdalene, 98, 121

Materna, Amalie, 43
Miller, Arthur, 48
Mort Artu, La, 80
Morte d'Arthur, Le, 65, 81, 116
Mystery religions, 50–51, 75, 78,
    82, 107–109, 112–113, 120–121,
    142–143, 163

Nemi, 82, 163
Nibelungenlied, 192, 198–200, 202–204
Nibelungen-myth, 193, 223
Nicodemus, 117–118
Nietzsche, Friedrich, 52, 196
Nirvana (Nibbana), 8–10, 12–13, 18,
    23, 57, 94–95

Oedipus Rex, 48–49, 55–56
Oresteia, 199
Otherworld, 111–112, 162

Parzival (composed), 81
Peredur Son of Evrawg, 128, 159, 164
Perlesvaus, le Haut Livre du Graal,
    80, 128, 164
Phantom's Frenzy, 140, 165
Philip, Count of Flanders, 128, 136
Pilate, Pontius, 117–118
Plato, 6
Prometheus Bound, 62, 199
Prose *Lancelot*, 80
Prose *Merlin*, 80

Queste del Saint Graal, 80–81, 102,
    128, 134, 151, 156, 158, 182–183

Ragnarök, 199
Religion and Art, 179
Rig Veda, 78, 102, 104
Robert de Boron, 79, 120
Röckel, August, 14, 30, 223–224

Samsara, 8, 92, 265, 275, 279
Satan, 62, 93, 226, 260

Schopenhauer, Arthur, 5–18, 20,
  22–25, 27, 30–34, 169, 196, 214
Second Continuation, 79, 137
Shakespeare, William, 49, 53, 153, 170
Sieger, Die, 5–7, 15–18, 22, 34, 36–37,
  77, 126, 165, 239, 283, 287
Siegfrieds Tod, 18–20, 77, 190
Sone de Nansai, 79, 119, 128
Sophocles, 48, 56
Suddhodana, King, 258
swan (also sacred *hansa*), 45, 69,
  70–71, 171, 184, 256, 259

Thidreks Saga af Bern, 199
Titurel, 77, 81

Valhalla, meaning of, 299n9
Valkyries, origin and meaning of,
  215–216, 299n9
Vedas, 102–103
Volsunga Saga, 192, 195, 198, 200–204
Voluspá, 199

Volvas (Valas, Wala), 170, 199–200
Vulgate Cycle, 80–81

Wagner, Cosima, 3, 30, 42, 109,
  196–197, 214, 226–227, 239, 257,
  265, 269, 272, 283, 287, 289,
  300n34
Wauchier de Denain, 79, 127, 137
Wesendonck, Mathilde, 13, 36–37,
  77–78, 80, 126, 139, 148, 165
*Wibelungs, The: World-History as
  Told Through Myth*, 2, 190–193,
  195
Wolfram von Eschenbach (born and
  died), 125
Wolzogen, Hans von, 257, 266,
  299n21
*World as Will and Representation,
  The*, 5–6, 15, 20, 214

Yasodhara, 258
Younger Edda (Prose Edda), 198

Grateful acknowledgment is made to the following for permission to use previously published and unpublished material:

G. Schirmer, Inc.: Excerpts from *Parsifal* by Richard Wagner, English translation by Stewart Robb. Copyright © 1962 (renewed) by G. Schirmer, Inc. (ASCAP). International copyright secured. All rights reserved. Reprinted by permission.

Harcourt, Inc.: Excerpts from *Cosima Wagner's Diaries Volume 1.* Copyright © 1976 by R. Piper & Co. Verlag. English translation copyright © 1978, 1977 by Geoffrey Skelton and Harcourt Inc. Reprinted by permission of Harcourt, Inc. Excerpts from *Cosima Wagner's Diaries Volume 2.* Copyright © 1977 by R. Piper & Co. Verlag München. English translation copyright © 1980 by Geoffrey Skelton and Harcourt, Inc. Reprinted by permission of Harcourt, Inc.

The Lionel Salter Library: Excerpts from *Parsifal* by Richard Wagner, English translation by Lionel Salter. Copyright © Lionel Salter Library 2007. Reprinted by permission.

Princeton University Press: Excerpts from *The Grail* by Roger Sherman Loomis. Copyright © 1991 Princeton University Press. Reprinted by permission of Princeton University Press.

Random House, Inc.: Excerpts from *Parzival* by Wolfram Von Eschenbach, translated by Helen Mustard and Charles E. Passage. Copyright © 1961 by Helen M. Mustard and Charles E. Passage. Used by permission of Random House, Inc. Excerpts from "Perceval, or the Story of the Grail." Copyright © 1957 by Random House, Inc., from *Medieval Romances* by Roger S. Loomis and Laura H. Loomis. Used by permission of Random House, Inc.

San Francisco Opera and Andrew Porter: Excerpts from "*Götterdämmerung*: Das Ende," article by Andrew Porter, published in San Francisco Opera Association's program for the 1990 *Ring* cycle. Used by permission of San Francisco Opera and Andrew Porter.

Shasta Abbey: Excerpts from *The Denkoroku* by Keizan Zenji, translated by Rev. Hubert (Mark) Nearman and edited by Rev. Master P. T. N. H. Jiyu-Kennett. Copyright © 1993 by Shasta Abbey. Used by permission of Shasta Abbey. Excerpts from *The Monastic Office*, translated by Rev. Hubert Nearman and edited by Rev. Master P. T. N. H. Jiyu-Kennett. Copyright © 1993 by Shasta Abbey. Used by permission of Shasta Abbey.

Viking Penguin and Joseph Campbell Foundation: Excerpts from *Masks of God: Creative Mythology* by Joseph Campbell. Copyright © 1968 by Joseph Campbell. Used by permission of Viking Penguin, a division of Penguin Group (USA) Inc. U.K. rights granted by the Joseph Campbell Foundation.

W. W. Norton & Company, Inc.: Excerpts from *Selected Letters of Richard Wagner* by Stewart Spencer and Barry Millington, editors and trans. Copyright © 1987 by Stewart Spencer and Barry Millington. Used by permission of W. W. Norton & Company, Inc. (U.S and Philippine Island rights). Published outside the U.S. and Philippine Islands by the Orion Publishing Group.

W. W. Norton & Company, Inc., and Faber Music Ltd.: Excerpts from *The Ring of the Nibelung* by Richard Wagner, translated by Andrew Porter. Copyright © 1976 by Andrew Porter. Used by permission of W. W. Norton & Company, Inc. (U.S. and Philippine Islands rights). Used by permission of Faber Music Ltd. (U.K., Canada, and other English-language rights).